"This class has been great for me. Since learning your material I have b able to go back into my pipeline and reach out to some investors currently created two deals with one specific investor who is buying a t family and we just got an accepted offer on a flip that we identified."

– HANS AUGUS'

"Gary, just wanted to let you know that I used the scripts you gav (including asking for an email recap) Tuesday and already have a investor!"

– KATE WE

(This was her 1st day in the program!)

"Gary, I started working with my first investor after just beginning program."

– DAN SURM

"How did you know I'm preparing my first big offer?!? Cash offer, $1.8n a development. Not a bad start!"

– MATTHEW LEDF(

"Gary Wilson has awesome real estate skills. The techniques he use innovative and unique in the business. I deal with real estate agents we and have never met anyone with his skills. I highly recommend giving (a call."

– TIM PHII

"I really learned a lot from your class. It is so different compared to the realtor class. I am making commissions with Investors. I am managing rentals for Investors. I bought my own investment property too! Thank you."

– GRACE WANG

"We just returned from San Francisco attending my mother's memorial. We scattered her ashes in the ocean. It was a difficult week, but I have great news. As of today I spent the last 24 hours negotiating and in a bidding war for my flip property. We are now under contract for $207,500 only $2,000 under asking and with a profit of $83K. We should receive a net check of $196K at closing. We are very excited. Our largest check:)"

– TERJE ROGNE

"Last night's investor meetup was a success! We had 9 RSVPs, some brought guests and a few past clients showed up for a grand total of 19 attendees… it's growing (even in 110+ degree weather!). Everyone had positive comments and participated in the discussion. All are veterans… One husband and wife are ready to fix and flip. Another is a mechanical engineer and wants to quit his job in the next year and do real estate investing full time… wholesaling? Fix and flip? A third wants to buy and hold, has a few single-family rentals now that he acquired when his mom died; he also had a few of his own where he's the financier (i.e. seller carry back). A fourth wants to wholesale, bird dog to pay down debt. Thank you so much for your help! I'm very excited!!"

– NATASHA TOMILISON

"I'm listing my first house tonight from my letter campaign! Got a call from the first round of letters I sent out last week and he wants me to come list his house tonight. I sent him the letter based on an eviction notice he filed on his tenant two weeks ago. Thanks for your help! The start of many more to come."

– HALL SMITH

"Just listed a new listing rental. The Investor Letter was the tool that got me this listing."

– ROGER NUBEL

"The Meetup yesterday went really well. I picked up 2 clients and Maureen, the lender helping co-host, picked up 2 clients. There is one guy in the group that has been investing for 35+ years and has done exceptionally well. He is open to sharing his knowledge too. Everyone got along well and stayed an extra 30 minutes just talking. They have already RSVP'd for next month. I would have to say it was a success."

– CHERYL CLEMENS

"We use the school report & LOVE the data!"

– DEIRDRE BRAMBERG

"I can't say too many times how much I appreciate your dedication and commitment to your students. Having taught and/or trained people for years, I know it takes a lot of energy! Thank you! God bless!"

– MAXINE D. JONES

"It's been a little while since we spoke. I hope you are well! Things have been going well for me overall and I have you to thank in part for my current success."

– DAVID EVANS

Real Estate With

Gary Wilson

THE MASSIVE PASSIVE
CASHFLOW METHOD

GUIDING YOU TO MASSIVE NEW WEALTH IN
REAL ESTATE IN 1 YEAR OR LESS GUARANTEED!

GARY WILSON

Real Estate with Gary Wilson
1740 H. Dell Range Blvd
Suite 281
Cheyenne, WY 82009

Ordering Information:

Quantity sales. Special discounts are available on quantity purchases by corporations, associations, and others. For details, contact the publisher at the address above.

ISBN: 978-1-949150-66-7

Printed in the United States of America

The Wizard Formula for Success:

W   Be willing to get out of your comfort zone.

I   Investigate your dream. In Real Estate, whether it's Flipping, Renting, Wholesaling, being an Investor/Agent, or all of the above – check it out first.

Z   Zero in on your plans. Start with one then add the others as you gain confidence and competence, leveraging your current activities.

A   Take action! Put one foot in front of the other and get a coach, just like those who make millions.

R   Ramp it up! Once you cash in on your first transaction take massive action to multiply your results.

D   Do it and don't do it alone. Many more have succeeded by getting the proper education, information, and guidance than have by attempting to do it on their own!

Table of Contents

NOTE: Gary Wilson is not an attorney. Readers, please repeat after me: "I know Gary Wilson is not an attorney. I am reading this book of my own free will and promise to make sure everything I do after reading this book, relative to real estate, will be in compliance with federal, state, and local laws."

Introduction

When I was in college, I was blessed to have a roommate named Socrates. Both his parents were Greek. His mother was born here in the States, but his father was born in Greece. So Mrs. Demet went to Greece to attend a high school graduation, and came home with Mr. Demet. They lived south of Richmond, Virginia.

They were a great family. They took me in and treated me like one of their own. Mr. Demet was a wonderful teacher, and fortunately for me, he was a generous teacher. He taught me right alongside Socrates. I could not have gotten a better education. As a matter of fact, the lessons I learned from him have been worth more to me than the education I got from college.

After I graduated I landed my first corporate nine-to-five job. Socrates and I again became roommates. Very good deal for me! We bought our first property together.

Now we had gone out to find a property, and being young college graduates living at the beach, we decided to buy a little townhome a few blocks from the ocean. It was great – of course it was going to be a chick magnet. We were going to live the life. But before the day was out Socrates' dad set us straight. We got out of that deal, thank goodness, because it would have been a real loser. He then took us by the hand and showed us what to do.

Instead we bought a nice little property in Virginia Beach – 478 Leslie Terrace – ten minutes from the beach, and two minutes from where I worked. Soc's dad cosigned the second mortgage and showed us how to do everything. He did not give us any money, though. Instead of giving us a meal of trout and salmon, he taught us how to fish.

At this point I started to dream! What if? What if I kept doing this and became a multi-millionaire, no… a billionaire!

I love the dreamers of the world, especially the ones who take action. They make things happen. We wouldn't be flying around in commercial jets today if it weren't for the Wright brothers. They believed they could create powered flight and they took action to make it happen. I love that story and I encourage you to get a book and read about it.

When I was a senior in college I interned at NASA in Langley, Virginia. I always wanted to be an astronaut. I was fortunate to see man take the first human step on the moon. I was six years, six months and 15 days old. The lunar module had landed on the moon the afternoon of July 20, 1969.

Later that evening I was outside in my pajamas with all the neighbor kids catching fireflies and playing hide and seek. Most of our dads were in Vietnam. Our moms were all inside Mrs. Hutchinson's house huddled around a black and white console television. They sat on the couch, arms interlocked and crying. I asked what the matter was (since in those days we were the first generation who watched war live on television and were used to "bad" news). My mom pointed to the television and I turned my head just in time to see Neil Armstrong drop down from the ladder and set foot on the moon. He then said, "One small step for man, one giant leap for mankind." At that point I knew I wanted to be an astronaut.

I didn't become an astronaut but I did intern for NASA and I've since been inside two space shuttles and visited the Johnson Space Center in Houston, Texas, and the Kennedy Space Center in Cape Canaveral, Florida.

When I was a kid I dreamed I could fly. Did you ever have that dream? Have your dreams come true? Well, they can. Real Estate helped me realize my dreams and they can help you realize yours, too. As an adult I dreamed of being free. I am now free in almost every way imaginable. When I graduated college though, I had to get a job. A J-O-B! Yikes!

MY FIRST EXPERIENCE WITH REAL ESTATE

My first day of work, I recall dreading "having to do this for the next forty years." I liked the people but hated the corporate nine-to-five gig – being stuck in an office with the beach so close and beautiful weather and gorgeous girls.

But I had to make money, right? I did and it allowed me to buy my first property with Socrates.

It was a four-bedroom, two-bathroom home. We bought it from a guy in the Navy. We assumed his first mortgage, refinanced his second, and gave him a note and a mortgage for the third – which was his equity portion of the property after the first and second mortgages.

Socrates and I lived there, and we rented the other rooms out. Essentially we were able to live for about $50 a month, because the other guys' rent covered our mortgage payment. I needed to invest only about $3,000 in the deal altogether.

We were on the water every day after work. Soc bought a used boat and a used van to tow it, and we went water skiing all the time. We pioneered pulling stuff behind boats besides skis. We tried surfboards and other crazy stuff we thought would work including just us on our backs.

I saved a good bit of change because I wanted to buy more property. I remember Soc's dad telling us, while we stood at the dock of one of his beach homes, "If you boys do what I show you, you will not have to work for anybody else past the age of thirty-five." And thankfully for me, he was a real life example of success, someone who was actually investing in real estate and making money doing it.

I learned something very profound during this time. I learned I was not built to be sitting behind a desk in a corporate job, Monday through Friday, nine to five, for forty years; I knew I had to do something about it.

But then guess what happened? I found the girl of my dreams, got married, and had children. At that point, Mr. Demet did not think it would be a good idea for Soc and I to try to hang onto the home together. Virginia real estate rules were complicated, and with me being married and him not, we decided Socrates would buy me out. I got $8,000 out of the deal. Remember I put $3,000 in, and got $8,000 out in about a two-year time frame. Not bad – a 266% return! I knew I would never be able to do that in the corporate world.

My new bride, Susan, and I bought our first house together. It was nice, new, just one mile from the ocean and only $85,000. Today that house is worth $350,000. Just like a lot of other smart people, I should have held onto it when we moved to Pittsburgh. But we needed the money. I know, you think I am crazy. Why would I move from the beach to Pittsburgh? Well, my wife was from Pittsburgh, and I felt like I needed a new beginning to pursue my dreams and make my way in the world.

I began focusing on my professional career – Computers in Banking. I worked so much at one point I actually had a cot in my cube. My daughter was not even three years old and Susan was pregnant with our son, Andrew. I got called into my boss's office and was told I had earned a $500 bonus for all my effort. What a slap in the face! That was just about half a week's pay and I had worked extra hours that much dozens of times over.

I learned a hard lesson. First of all, no one else was doing what I was doing, yet they were making the same amount of money. Second of all, I was just a number. Other than the people around me, no one who really mattered knew who I was or what I was doing. I was wasting my time.

I knew I had to do something else. Fortunately I had a valuable commodity... I had knowledge of a software system that allowed me to move to another bank in Pittsburgh. I had raised my salary by quite a bit from moving from Virginia Beach to Pittsburgh, and in short order, I increased it again by more than 50% in about an 18-month timeframe.

But I was not happy. My spirit was dying. I felt like I had lost my freedom, and I did not like being cooped up indoors all day. I am an outside person.

Suddenly I was thirty-five years old. It had been ten years since I had sold my portion of that property to Socrates. I remembered what his dad told me. I was now the age he had said when I would not need to work for anybody else.

I was maturing enough to realize I was living according to what the world expected of me – not what I wanted for myself. I never lost my desire to own investment real estate and since I was getting up at 5:00 in the morning to beat traffic and get a parking spot and be at work by 6:30, I got to see a lot of Carleton Sheets. I could almost recite his infomercial line by line.

I finally bit the bullet and bought his course. I studied it just like a school textbook. Then within six months I entered into a contract to buy my first two properties – a pair of fourplexes in a borough called Westview, just right on the city line. It was my first solo foray into real estate. I was back in the saddle and a new chapter of my life had begun.

The lessons I learned from Mr. Demet were beginning to bear fruit and this is what I want to share with you. I believe with undying faith in the American Dream. It is alive and well for people, including those who are from foreign lands like Mr. Demet. I further believe that investing in Real Estate is the best path to realizing the American Dream. He was a real life role model, showing me it absolutely could be done.

I know a lot of you reading this do not have that, but I hope you will use me as that example. Yet I don't just want you to be like me... I want you to be better than me.

I am going to show you everything I did to accumulate a portfolio of 250 units in about five years. I started off with a pair of fourplexes. I believe in real estate. I believe in the American dream. Yes, you can do it! In today's economy it is more possible than ever.

Prices are still relatively low, according to historical averages, and interest rates are as low as they have been in fifty years. What more could you possibly ask for?

My promise is to teach you what I have learned, and not just how, but why certain techniques work the way they do. This is something I found missing in a lot of courses I have taken and books I have read. I promise that if you follow the suggestions in this book that you will be investing in real estate – the right way!

GETTING STARTED

100 and 102 Center Avenue

100 and 102 Center were purchased side by side from a woman who was retiring and whose husband had Alzheimer's. I was pretty good at saving, so I had $50,000 tucked away. I think it was an $180,000 property. I was able to put a 20% down payment out of pocket – $36,000 for both properties, and finance the remaining $144,000.

I bought these two properties back in August 1998. I still have them today and they bring in a nice monthly income for me. The real estate value is appreciating, too. At first, I did most of the work and all of the management. I learned a lot by doing things that way. I don't regret it and would even recommend it to others as a way of learning the ropes.

My first challenge was a vacant unit as soon as I closed on the property. It was probably a good thing though. The previous tenant was behind on her rent. It gave me an opportunity to renovate the place and charge higher monthly rent. I raised it from $350 to $400 per month. That was one of the only times my wife helped at an apartment. The new tenants were pretty good about paying but they were a little rough on the place. They were young party animals.

I used the rest of my life's savings and bought another property with 20% down out of my own pocket and mortgaged the other 80%. This was a three-unit in Etna.

You are probably wondering, "Hey Gary, all these other guys are teaching to not use your own money." Well I know that they are, and I get it. But I am going to tell you right now, in today's economy, cash is king. As a matter of fact, cash is always king; and the man with the cash gets the best deals. I understand if you have to finance when you are first starting off though, just like I did.

I still have these properties, they cashflow like crazy, and the area is awesome. I basically did it by just using good old-fashioned common sense. When you use other techniques like no-money-down or owner financing, you do not really have rights of ownership. You put yourself at risk. When you are growing your portfolio it might feel okay, but you will be over-leveraged.

What nobody teaches you is what happens when life happens.

What happens to your highly leveraged portfolio when the economy tanks, people lose their jobs, or tenants get divorced? You know it happens. When you own a lot of properties, you are going to deal with these human nature phenomena. People get married, people die, kids are born, people get jobs, they transfer, they lose jobs, they get married, and they get divorced. All those things happen and they affect you because you are providing their housing.

Have you ever wondered why some people seem to make it really big in Real Estate while others struggle and give up or declare bankruptcy or go into foreclosure? It's not directly related to the techniques they're using. It's because they use those no-money-down techniques too much. Those techniques have their place but if you use them all the time and you're too highly leveraged, when the economy changes then you're in a small boat in big waves!

Some of the most well-known Real Estate authorities have lost properties to foreclosure and gone into bankruptcy. I'm not going to name them but I know some of them personally. You can look them up yourself. You'll be surprised.

The reality is they had to start over… and starting over is expensive. Loss is expensive. Can you see why it might be better to play offense than defense? Grow, but do it using sound practices that ensure you have equity and cashflow and can weather the storms in life. Those storms will come and when they do you don't want to have a bunch of dinghies (small equity and small cashflow positions) when the big waves hit. You want big equity and big cashflow. You want a boat that can weather the storm. Can I get an Amen?

My question to you is, do you want to be highly leveraged when bad times come along – because they will come – or do you want to have a safe, sound, solid portfolio based on solid principles, and solid common sense, where you can weather the storm, maintain your properties, and come out on the other side shining like gold? That is what I advocate.

49 Grant Avenue

49 Grant Avenue ended up being a real winner. It was almost a scary looking property, but it was a three-unit, and made a lot money.

It was September 1998. The lady I purchased the building from was a former real estate agent who did a lot of business in Etna. I gathered later that she was a real shyster. We had to delay the closing because she hadn't collected all her rent. I balked because I believed she should have done that already. We delayed but still she didn't collect all her rent. We closed anyway at 5:30 PM.

There were water bills to be paid on the property that she convinced the closing agent she had paid. She lied. The closing agent should have held funds in escrow to cover the bills but didn't. I had to fight with the closing company's attorney for six months to get these paid. It was their loss.

The next thing I had to do was have the third-floor tenant move because he was a crackhead. I convinced him without getting the authorities involved. Then I had to deal with the tenants on the first two floors. I could always collect rent from them but it was like pulling teeth. I eventually evicted them all and replaced them with great tenants.

Then business started getting better – as I got better at the business of real estate investing.

741 Florence

In October 1998, I bought 741 Florence Avenue from a lawyer who was moving to New Orleans. She offered owner financing and I wasn't going to pass up the chance. I only had to come up with $5,000 of my own money.

I was able to get her to give me the same interest rate banks would give me. I purchased it for $42,000, and she held the note for the other money.

At the closing table I realized a glaring mistake on the settlement sheet. I was not given credit for my $5,000 down payment, and the prorated interest was backwards. Had I not caught the mistakes I would have lost over $5,000. Another big lesson – scrutinize every detail. Mistakes do happen in this business and it always costs money.

The property was a duplex with the first-floor apartment rented to a wacky elderly woman who is still there today. She was eccentric, made enemies of all the neighbors, kept the temperature inside her apartment in the 50s in the winter while wearing a coat, hat, and gloves indoors, and had every square inch of space packed with stuff. But she paid her rent on time every month in full without fail.

I did try to raise her rent by $10 after I took ownership of the place, but she was "having none of that, young man. Now be on your way!" So I got out of there as fast as I could with my tail between my legs wondering how I let some little old lady get the best of me.

The second floor was empty. I believe this was the last time Susan helped me prepare an apartment for renting. It took a lot of time and energy but we managed to get the job done and rented it to a nice little alcoholic drug addict lady with two illegitimate boys (I didn't know that until later).

So far I was doing okay. I was making mistakes but still making money. One of the things I like about this business is that you can make mistakes yet still make money. I don't recommend it, but it's possible.

Several years later I sold it for $72,000; so I made $30,000 on the sale and the whole time I owned it, cash flowed. Cash flowed like crazy on that place.

Now I was getting to the point where I had exhausted my personal cash, so I looked around to determine where I could get more. I opened up a $25,000 personal line of credit – that is an unsecured line. It is based on your reputation as a good credible borrower. I actually went on and borrowed money against my own personal home using a home equity line for $40,000. That took me to 100% financing on my personal home. I know you may think it sounds risky, but it was a managed risk and one I was willing to take. And it was a risk that paid off.

205 South Ohio Street

In January of 1999, I closed on 205 South Ohio Street in Avalon. This was a three-unit building I bought from an elderly couple who simply couldn't care for the place anymore. There was an odd mix of tenants. The previous owner paid the gas bill. I had my work cut out for myself.

I went to do my inspection on a very pleasant fall day. I'm glad I was there on that day because I learned firsthand that I would need to add two more gas lines and separate the heat. As I was standing out front with the realtor, I noticed the second-floor windows were open while a window air-conditioning unit was blasting away.

When we walked into the first-floor unit, the heat was on high and the tenant was running around in his boxers. He controlled the thermostat. The heat – and money – was literally going out the windows. I learned a valuable lesson before I had to feel the negative effects of it. Do not pay for someone else's heat!

As soon as I closed on the deal I got the gas lines separated and the heat separated. I also kept the rents the same. That was part of my strategy for the place in order to make money.

I think I paid $32,000 for the property, and sold it for $62,000. Nearly doubled my money on the sale, plus I had cashflow over all those years. I think I owned it for greater than ten years. I always own my properties for about ten years, sometimes more, sometimes a little less.

206 and 208 Clay Street

I bought these properties from a church who had received it as a donation from an estate. It was a two-unit side by side – one brick and one vinyl. Old and small, each unit had two bedrooms and it cost only $35,000.

When the settlement company received the no-lien letter from the borough it stated the water meter may need to be replaced. Nobody thought anything of it. The settlement company didn't see that as a requirement for closing.

Shortly after closing the borough called to say that we definitely needed to replace the water meter. I met the technician at the property and discovered that the meter was fine. We did however discover that the electronic reading device had been disconnected. The technician reconnected it and synchronized it with the water meter. I was told that it was a catch-up reading and since the settlement agency had been instructed to replace the meter (which would have resulted in an accurate reading for closing), I received a water bill for over $500.

Of course I fought this. I agreed with the settlement company that no definitive mandate had been given to replace the meter. The lien letter had stated that the meter "may" need to be replaced, not "must" be replaced. The settlement company wouldn't back me up with a title claim because the word "may" is ambiguous. They were right. I eventually won my argument.

Lessons learned: First, even professionals make mistakes, and second, always be persistent – especially if you know you're right.

I purchased the property for $35,000, enjoyed a nice cashflow from the rentals, and sold it just a few years later for $50,000.

48 Cherry Street

I bought 48 Cherry Street, a three-unit in Etna, for $50,000 from a young couple who had intentions of living in one unit while upgrading it, and then doing the same thing with the other two units. When they listed the property, they were still in unit #1. The reality of being a landlord had kicked in and they didn't like it. They also didn't like all the money and time it took to get things done. They had rented the third floor to the wife's sister at a steep discount and the second floor was rented to a complete idiot at a ridiculously low rate.

So they decided to sell and I immediately saw the potential of quickly upgrading the units and charging higher rents. Plus, I didn't have to live there.

The first floor was already complete and rented to a nice little old Italian lady with dozens of kids and thousands of grandkids and great-grandkids. She was one of the best tenants I ever had. I love that lady and still keep in touch with her today. While we were working on the top two floors she used to feed us – A LOT! Needless to say her unit was one of the nicest in town.

We tore out a wall in the second-floor unit to open up the living room and let in more light. The rest was just basic painting and flooring. We also rented the garage in back. The old owners had been bringing in about $400 per month. When I was done renovating, the building brought in $1,250 per month. Now that's how you make money on investment property.

Lesson learned. Don't focus on a property as it is today – use your imagination to see how it could be tomorrow!

39 Walnut Street

I bought 39 Walnut Street for $62,000. It was a duplex with a three-bedroom unit downstairs, a three-bedroom upstairs, and a garage. It was in a pretty good neighborhood of mixed owner-occupied and rental properties. The mayor's daughter lived next door. It also had a nice covered front porch, nice covered rear porch and a fenced-in yard.

I spun the garage off and rented it separately. At the same time I got permission from the borough to create a two-car parking pad in the rear of the house, still leaving plenty of yard to enjoy. Initially the rents were both well below $500 per month. Over time I increased that to $600 each. The tenants I inherited paid their own water and stayed in place for a few years, which helped a lot. I didn't raise their rents until some improvements were made and then I didn't raise them to market level all at once.

Lesson learned: when buying three-bedroom apartments you will almost always be catering to families. Make sure the neighborhood is suitable for families.

When I sold that property years later, it was making almost $1,400 a month.

749 Florence Avenue

This property was a fully-rented duplex, just two doors down from 741 Florence. At that point I had a pretty good share of my real estate holdings in Avalon. I liked having two properties close together and others within a few blocks.

This property was distressed, and so were its owners. They were an elderly couple, and when the husband showed up at closing he needed an oxygen tank. I think they were asking $40,000 initially. I bought it for $32,000. Once again I put 20% down and took a mortgage for the remainder. By this time any money I put down was being generated from cashflow of my other real estate holdings, not my savings account.

The upstairs tenants are still there today. They are some of my best tenants. At that time their rent was really low – $250 per month. Understandably, they didn't want me to raise it to the market level of $450. I met them halfway. I performed only essential upgrades and raised their rent to $350. They would live with the old carpet, etc.

The lady downstairs was a single mom of three, all living in a one-bedroom apartment. She was a pig and behind on her rent. She told me some cockamamie story about giving her rent to a man who was posing as a property manager. I can't remember what she had been paying – or rather not paying – but after she left I turned her old apartment into a very nice unit and charged market rate of $400 per month.

I also installed two new furnaces and put on a new roof the next year. Years later I sold it for, I believe, $65,000.

Lesson learned: don't be afraid to take on a place that may look scary if there is a lot of upside potential in multiple areas such as rent increases and increased value due to improvements.

802 and 804 Taylor Avenue

This was the last property I bought in my first year of operation and it was the crowning jewel of my Real Estate Empire. It was one big four-unit building with a pair of one-bedroom units on the first floor and a pair of two-story, three-bedroom units above.

The one-bedroom units weren't in bad shape and were currently rented. The three-bedroom unit on the right was vacant and needed some improvements before renting. The other three-bedroom unit was being rented as a one-bedroom because the second floor needed to be improved before it would be rentable. The electricity on the right needed to be separated between the two units. Finally, the gas needed to be separated between the units on both sides.

Sounds like a lot of work but I bought the place for $80,000 and the upside potential on rent and equity was tremendous. After buying nine other properties in less than a year I needed to take a different route in order to purchase this one. I took out a commercial line of credit secured by the equity in my nine other properties from a small private lender named Larry Newman whose company is called Briar Cliff Financial. I used that money as the down payment, and again got a first mortgage for the remaining 80%.

I immediately separated the gas and electric and passed the responsibilities of paying those bills into the tenants' hands. At the same time, I got the vacant three-bedroom unit ready to rent. I was having a hard time renting it when finally, at the end of the summer a Section-8 tenant came along. It was my first Section-8 tenant and I was a little nervous, but also a little desperate. They wound up being some of my best tenants ever. The next step was to get the other three-bedroom unit ready and rented.

As it turned out, the tenants in one of the one-bedroom units wanted to move into a larger unit, while the tenant in the newly finished unit didn't need all that space. So they swapped – lucky me! I now had a fully rented building bringing in almost $2,000 per month.

I quickly paid off the commercial line. As a matter of fact I also paid off my home equity line of credit and personal line of credit all within the next year. I sold that building a few years later for $132,000, so I made over $50,000 on the sale; cash flowed like a maniac while I owned it.

25 South Sprague

25 South Sprague was owned by a woman who inherited it from her late father and was in the middle of a divorce from her husband. It was a three-unit property with the main house consisting of a one-bedroom unit downstairs and a two-bedroom unit upstairs. There was a separate building in the back that had a garage and was converted into a one-bedroom unit. All three units were rented at the time and are still rented to the same tenants today.

The buildings had recently been sided and didn't need much in the way of improvements. There is off-street parking for two, it's close to shopping, a hospital, and almost anything else a person might need in Bellevue. I would like to improve the unit in the back but I sort of treat the tenant there as my own personal charity case. She is supposed to pay me $325 per month but usually I get something odd like $140. I know I should be the good business person but she is elderly and has some mental issues. I conferred with my wife and she said I should do this so it must be okay.

819 Stanton Avenue

819 Stanton Avenue is a three-unit brick house in a nice section of Millvale – the same Millvale that makes national news for flooding every time it rains. President Bush stopped here after Hurricane Ivan and promised to personally see to it that the flooding problems would be resolved. Governor Ed Rendell had said the same thing. It has been a few years and it is worse now than before. The Democrats blame the Republicans and the Republicans blame the Democrats – and the poor residents and business owners continue to suffer. (By the way, water bills are twice as high in Millvale as they are in other areas. Part of this is to go to solving the flooding problem. I believe it has all been money well waisted. OK, off the soap box I go.)

819 Stanton really didn't need much work other than separating the heat between the first and second floors. I lost both of those tenants because I now required them to pay for their own heat while I kept the rent the same, which was low. The unit on the third floor had its own electric heat source. The electric was already separated on the building.

Now this was a profitable property. I also rented the garage separately for another $125 per month. I have always been able to get good tenants in this building. I still have it today and it makes a lot of money for me.

100 Logan Avenue

100 Logan is one of my favorites. It is a farm-style house situated down a long driveway in a country setting on the edge of Millvale. Whenever I advertise a vacancy here I use the words "Country in the city." I've never had a problem renting either unit. It is a two-unit: a two-bedroom downstairs and the top two floors make a three-bedroom. Both have separate entrances on different sides of the house. The upper unit is almost like living in a single-family home. I bring in $1,100 per month total on the house and my mortgage payment including taxes is $425. I paid only $44,000 for it. This place is a goldmine. The work I did to it was merely cosmetic.

There was one big problem a few years ago. I had to replace the water line from under the street to the house. It cost about $13,000 to do it. It turns out the local gas company had laid a new gas line under the street a few years before. The plumber had evidence that the crew doing the work had to re-lay the storm sewer line as a result of the new gas line. The crew placed this new line directly over my water line instead of the other way around. As a result of natural settling the new sewer line over time crushed my water line. I pursued the matter and was reimbursed $11,000. I was lucky! The crew who did the work was no longer in business and the insurance company who represented the gas company no longer represented them. It was a real stretch but along with my plumber we presented a pretty good case.

The house really doesn't fit the character of the area but because of its unique qualities it has been a winner. Lesson learned: sometimes these unique or even odd properties do a good job of attracting a certain number of people and no other property can compete due to their unique nature.

128 and 130 Goodwin Avenue

128-130 Goodwin was a four-unit and is now a five-unit property. For a while during my real estate investing career I was not impressed with Millvale. But after I purchased 100 Logan I began to see some of its potential. It had recently undergone some improvements along its main business corridor, into some of the residential areas and more importantly in its local government. It was out with the old and in with the new.

In recent years it had benefitted from the CRA (Community Reinvestment Act) designation. A lot of the old councilmen had been ousted and replaced with new (often younger) forward thinking individuals. Millvale had even gone as far as buying some of the run-down properties themselves and selling them to first-time home buyers with low interest loans. *The times they were a changin' and I was a benefittin'.*

Unfortunately, as I'm sure you remember from overrun news clips, Millvale suffered immensely from flooding from the remains of a pair of devastating hurricanes in the late summer and early fall of 2004. This was a major setback for the area. With the exception of a few recent flooding events, Millvale has been slowly recovering – in large part due to the resiliency and faith, hope, and love of its proud and patient citizens. I love and admire these people, and they and I will continue to benefit from their dedication and hard work.

I bought this little gem for a cool $51,900. The rents were low and the hot water was common among three of the units which means I had to pay that bill. As you might have guessed that didn't last long. I quickly separated the hot water and soon after raised all the rents to market level. I was making $1,450 a month already but I was not done yet. I saw potential for a fifth unit on the top floor of the building. If I could pull this off it would add $350 per month to the income. My monthly mortgage payment including taxes and insurance was $513 per month. I got the proper occupancy requirements satisfied and had the new unit completed in about two months. I was now making $1,800 per month gross and as you can see this property was transformed into the proverbial cash cow!

I still have this property today and won't be getting rid of it anytime soon. Lesson learned: never judge a book by its cover. Millvale is a great little town with a strong rental base. I have great neighbors and the property itself was easily improved from a great deal to an awesome deal.

416 North Home Avenue

416 North Home was one of the last properties I bought using my current methods. It is a five-unit building in Avalon. I paid $94,000 for it. It consists of two efficiency apartments, 2 one-bedroom apartments and a two-bedroom apartment. All utilities are completely separated. When I acquired the property the rents were a little low and the place needed some improving. I set about addressing both right away. All the units now have new furnaces, the dormers on the roof are new and all the units have new flooring. The main hallway was also updated.

I had to put up with some tenant issues for a while until I got the place under control, but now I am getting $325 per month for the efficiencies, $375 per month for the one-bedroom apartments and $500 per month for the two-bedroom apartments. My monthly mortgage payment including taxes and insurance is $944. Since the tenants pay all utilities including water, I am making over $850 a month positive cashflow on this property. This isn't a grand slam home run of a deal but it is a very good one and I would do this over again in a heartbeat.

Lesson learned: when it comes to larger properties, the really good deals don't come around as often as the smaller ones, so when one comes along that has room for improvement – take it. Even if you can't transform it to an awesome deal right away, given a little time and the larger number of units, it can increase your income and net worth substantially in due course.

R.E.R.

It was about this time that everything changed. I was doing okay by some peoples' standards but I still wasn't able to break ties with the corporate nine-to-five world and quit the rat race.

I was driving to work at 6:00 one morning in the freezing cold of the dead of winter in Pittsburgh, PA, and I heard these two guys – Jim Toner and Jeff Rubin – talking on the radio about a free seminar coming up in which they were going to talk about Real Estate Investing. They had started a company call Real Estate Riches which teaches individuals how to invest in real estate. Well, the subject matter was right up my alley and I could afford "free." So, I went to the seminar.

I was the nerd in the front row with my pad and paper taking notes. It was about two hours long and I had learned enough from my own investing experience that what they were presenting to me was a sound formula. This seminar was unlike any other I had been to – and I had been to a few (in that I couldn't buy anything there or even sign up).

R.E.R. requires its prospective students to have an interview first with Jim and/or Jeff. I called the next day to schedule my interview and spoke to Jeff who was a little reluctant to have me on board. He couldn't understand why I wanted to sign up if I already owned so much real estate. He may have also suspected that I had developed a few bad habits which might be hard to break. He may have been right but I managed to convince him to hear me out. I had my interview with Jim and I believe he saw that I was basically harmless – but more importantly that I was of the right frame of mind to be successful in real estate investing. R.E.R. agreed to take me on as a student and I borrowed money from a credit line to pay for the program.

At that time the class consisted of three Saturdays in a row. On the second class we actually visited a few prospective properties and analyzed them. At the third class Jim asked us students how many offers we had made. Now since I was a veteran and feeling pretty confident I knew I would be the star of the class. One student had four offers out – I had none. That was enough to light the fire under my butt. The rest as they say is real estate history. Read on.

26 High Street

When I bought 26 High Street I was completely out of money (temporarily). I didn't want to wait. I wanted to put what I'd learned to use ASAP. I had narrowed my search down to the final three and had Jim Toner out to look over my selections. We settled on 26 High Street. It was a duplex at the time but I wanted to turn it into a single-family dwelling, thinking it might be easier to manage. That was a mistake. I should have left it as a duplex.

That was the first of many mistakes I made, because as I later learned, I could have made more monthly income by keeping it as a duplex. I later turned it back into a duplex.

The second big mistake I made was my choice of contractors. I picked the guy with the cheapest bid and I paid dearly for that choice. This was a pretty sizable job and this guy worked all by himself. He took forever and he didn't do the best work. It took six months to finish this project when it shouldn't have taken more than one month. I had to have another guy and his brother come in to finish up. I finally finished though and went to the bank to get a new first mortgage on the place.

Even with all the mistakes, I still made money – enough to pay off all the debt on the place, plus the credit line I used to pay for the R.E.R. course. I never doubted that the formula would work but I was less than enthused at how hard it was to pull off. I must say though that all the mistakes were my own.

Lesson learned: don't be so afraid of making mistakes in real estate (of course you want to avoid them as much as possible because they cost you money) because it is forgiving and profitable enough to still make money.

1249 Benton Avenue

1249 Benton was the second property I bought using the R.E.R. program. I made the horrible decision to give the guy who botched 26 High Street a second chance. I hate it when I have to make a mistake multiple times before I learn my lesson. This asshole took forever. He almost cost me my tenant (she is still there, by the way). I had to fire him for good this time and I had to finish the project myself.

I did manage to meet my budget and I took cash out when I refinanced. I also had a pretty good cashflow on the property. I still have this property today. All the other houses around mine have improved to the point where now mine doesn't look so good. If and when the tenant leaves, I'll make some improvements to the front and put in new windows and then sell for profit. For now though I've got enough to keep me busy.

Lesson learned: DON'T DO WHAT I DID AND HAVE TO LEARN A PAINFUL LESSON MORE THAN ONCE!

1221 Woodland Avenue

1221 Woodland Avenue was the third property I bought using the R.E.R. program. This one I did according to plan with little or no mistakes. I bought it for $20,000 and had to put less than $5,000 into it. It appraised at $50,000. I took a $40,000 first mortgage out on it. So I pocketed $15,000. Plus I rented it for $675 per month which gave me about $200 per month positive cashflow after the mortgage payment plus taxes and insurance. It was at this point that I was well on my way.

This was about thirteen months after I became involved with R.E.R. In another five months I would leave my j-o-b at PNC and the corporate nine-to-five world.

I purchased fifty-two properties using the R.E.R. program – mostly single-family homes. They are relatively easy to find, fix, and rent or sell. I can always go by and look at my houses any time I want. I am in control of them and decide what to do with them. I like that.

There are a lot of ways to buy real estate. Two are the most basic. The first is what I call 'Turn Key'. Buy the building the same way you would buy your own home – make a down payment and finance the rest with a mortgage and note. The second way is to buy wholesale, remodel, and sell for profit or rent and refinance.

In a slow market buying turn key is the preferable way, especially if you are buying a multi-unit rental property. The banks prefer it this way also. They like the fact that the property doesn't have to, or hasn't had to go through, extensive remodeling. They like the fact that it is already in use and is generating income. You can also get more favorable rates and terms this way.

I know it's not very glamorous and it runs counter to what you've seen on late night television. Yes, you can buy real estate without using any of your own money but it is more expensive that way, it's harder to get a good cashflow, the banks certainly don't like it, and when they're offering loans at ridiculously low rates, why not take advantage? Plus, it's easier to have a positive cashflow when you buy the traditional way and don't have to make crappy offers on crappy properties.

Money: How to Deploy It

Every one of us, including you, wants to be financially independent. You think you know what you want but I can tell you that what you need is to be financially free.

This book will give you a powerful tool in your arsenal to achieve financial freedom and independence in less time. Let's get started.

I am a big fan of using cash to buy real estate. It gives you more advantages than any other method of acquiring property. I know all of the theorists who insist that you should never touch principal. If you put things into context, what they are referring to is using principal for non-investment purposes.

Deploying investment capital to build wealth and income is a good thing not a bad thing. Deploying investment capital to purchase doo-dads for personal use is foolish. For the purpose of our discussion I want to review the different ways to keep and use money in various forms of investments.

Savings

This is probably the least effective way to preserve capital. It is however one of the safest. Funds in a savings account are relatively liquid, which means you can access them without penalty. Some banks will allow you to withdraw funds one to three times per month. Savings accounts can be a good way to keep an emergency fund on hand. If you have funds in excess of emergency requirements, then you can safely access this for the purpose of buying investment real estate.

CDs

CDs may pay a little more interest than savings accounts, but not much. They do however usually have early withdrawal penalties. Sometimes you simply forfeit interest earned. CDs may have a place in some people's lives but not mine. Back in the day when I was a young banker, we had CDs that paid 15% and the terms were as long as ten years. You can bet your bottom dollar that I would gladly own some of those CDs now. Unfortunately, owning a CD now will likely cost you money instead of making it. If you have money held in CDs you may want to consider using it to purchase income producing real estate instead.

Mutual Funds

There are literally thousands of mutual funds, hundreds of mutual fund companies, and dozens of categories of fund types. I like no-load growth stock mutual funds to hold money long-term, over and above my real estate holdings. I like money market funds for short-term holdings and especially for storing money that I will use to buy more real estate. Bond funds are made up of short-term, medium-term, and long-term bond holdings. You have to know what you're doing relative to the interest rate environment to invest wisely in bond funds. Short-term bond funds are the least risky, but they still do have risks. I generally would not use even short-term bond funds to hold money that I will eventually use for purchasing real estate.

Stocks

Investing directly in stocks can truly be risky business. Even seasoned professionals get smoked when gambling in the stock market. This is not the place to keep money you intend to use later to buy real estate. If you are enamored by the idea of striking it rich in the stock market then God bless you and please get a lot of education and tread gingerly into those shark-infested waters. If you really want to be in stocks, why not consider a mutual fund that invests in stocks? Always look at the management of the fund and the manager's track record, not just the track record of the fund itself. Also, look at their performance in up and down markets. Good luck!

Bonds

The basic rule with bonds is that you buy when rates are high and sell when rates are low. This is because people will pay a premium for high-yielding bonds when rates are low. Plus, while you own the bond you can make a decent return. If you buy high-grade bonds then your risk is reduced along with your rate of return. The bottom line here is – how do you know when you are in a high-rate environment versus a low-rate environment? Even the pros have a hard time with market timing. I do not suggest that you use bond funds to hold money that you intend to use for purchasing real estate.

Real Estate

Ah, real estate. Finally! This is what I am writing this book for. I love real estate, not because I love the business of being a real estate investor but rather because of what owning a lot of real estate has allowed me to do. I used to love real estate for the investing as well, but over time it started losing its luster. I still own investment real estate – don't get me wrong. But what I did during my evolution as a business person was to start other businesses from the profits of owning investment real estate. I opened a real estate brokerage business, a real estate settlement business, a rental property management business, and even an appraisal business. I had plans to start a mortgage brokerage business when the Big Recession hit and all the rules changed… that would have put me at a horrible disadvantage. So, literally within hours of signing documents to launch the business I pulled the plug based on my intuition. It turns out my intuition was correct. I watched as about one-third of mortgage brokers evaporated almost overnight.

The point I want to get across to you is that while you can make money in real estate, owning real estate can make the dream of starting another business in an area of life that you enjoy much more realistic. I know people who started travel agencies, bought horse farms and stable horses, offer riding lessons, and basically pursue their passion for the equine life. I know people who moved closer to the water and started standup paddle board shops, surf shops, fishing shops, and charter businesses. The possibilities are endless. If you daydream of faraway places and fun activities, owning real estate can help make those dreams a reality. If you are in a W-2, nine-to-five job, it would be highly unlikely you could ever realize many of your dreams.

I love the dreamers of the world. If it weren't for dreamers like the Wright brothers we wouldn't travel by airplane, we wouldn't use a mouse to control a computer, we wouldn't talk on cell phones, we wouldn't drive cars, we wouldn't vacation in faraway places that would never have been discovered by courageous explorers, and we wouldn't have a country created so that all men could live freely as equals in their pursuit of wealth and happiness.

I say dream. Make it a daily practice to spend at least a half-hour dreaming – or what I call constructive daydreaming. The possibilities are endless.

I believe God wants us to be happy not sad, wealthy not poor, healthy not sick. I believe it is our duty to fulfill the purpose that He has intended for our lives, which is to bring others closer to Him. What better way to do this than to be our highest and best selves, living examples of how joyful life can be when we make the absolute most of the precious gift of life He has given us?

When you own investment real estate you are providing a good service to your fellow man. You are helping yourself by helping others first. And herein lies one of the greatest truths of success… and that is, if you help enough other people get what they want then you will get plenty of what you want. You can thank Zig Ziglar for that pearl of wisdom which is actually scriptural in its origin.

Now for one of the other pearls of wisdom, I am going to encourage you to not really *own* real estate. That's right. You will *control* it without actually owning it. It is far better to own companies than to own real estate. Read on.

Business Structure: LLC
Limited Liability Company

Note: I am not a lawyer. I recommend that you seek the advice of a competent lawyer when deciding on which entity to use when growing your real estate empire.

There are several legal entities used to form group investments.

General partnerships can be formed by as few as two people, with each person sharing equally in the management. As a general partner, each person can take part in day-to-day management of the properties owned by the partnership. This joint venture is ideal for a partnership between a lender and a developer formed to develop a particular piece of property.

As general partners, each partner is totally liable for all the debts of the partnership, regardless of the amount of money each partner invests in the partnership, known as Joint and Several Liability.

For example, assume that in a general partnership, one partner invests $500,000 in cash and the other partner invests only $5,000 cash. But as an additional contribution, the partner who invests only $5,000 agrees to oversee the construction of the project and build the property for cost. Each general partner would be totally liable for any and all judgments levied against the property if the project fails. Of course, insurance might be available to protect them against various losses, but on any uninsured loss, each partner would be fully liable.

In a general partnership, the title to the property is held by the partnership, not the individual partners. For example, A&B Partnership might consist of investors A and B, but the title is held by A&B Partnership. The partnership owns the real estate, while the individual partners have a personal property interest in the partnership.

This becomes an important consideration in certain situations, such as with death or divorce. The asset owned by the investor is really not real estate but an interest in the group. While the real estate has a marketable value, the interest in the group investment might not have the same value. It is possible that the estate of the deceased person or the divorced spouse might not be able sell the property to free up his or her ownership interest. This is another area in which the lack of liquidity in a group investment might be a disadvantage.

It is the partnership that must file a tax return at the end of the year, reporting the results of the property operations using federal income tax Form 1065. However, no tax is paid by the partnership.

The partnership will allocate to each partner his or her share of taxable income or loss depending on the formula contained in the partnership agreement. Most formulas call for a pro rata distribution of profits or losses among partners, but there are provisions in the tax code that allow for a *disproportionate allocation.* Such an allocation might give one partner all of the cashflow and the other partner all of the tax losses. A tax attorney or accountant would be needed to draft such disproportionate allocations.

The individual partners will receive a Schedule K-1 from the partnership reporting their allocation of taxable profit or loss for the year. The information from the Schedule K-1 is then reported on the individual partner's federal tax Form 1040 and might result in an increased or decreased tax liability for the individual partner.

Because of the allocation of income or loss to the individual partner and the resulting reporting of that allocation on the individual's tax return, a general partnership is called a **pass-through entity**.

Limited partnerships

A limited partnership must have two or more partners. One partner must be a general partner who manages the partnership and has the authority to bind the partnership. The general partner is willing to assume unlimited liability. The remaining partners are classified as limited partners.

By definition, a limited partner has limited involvement in the partnership, including limited involvement in property management, leaving all of the management to the general partner. To protect his or her status as a limited partner, the partner must not take any actions that would cause the partner to be reclassified as a general partner.

A limited partner is liable only for the money he has at risk. This means that if a limited partner has invested $5,000, he would lose only that amount in the investment. His liability is limited to his investment.

Some partnerships have provisions for additional investments over and above the original investment. This provision is sometimes called a *capital call* or an *assessment provision*. If a provision such as this were in the partnership agreement, limited partners would also be liable for that amount over and above the initial capital investment.

Even with a capital call or assessment provision, limited partners know at the outset the total extent of their liability.

To maintain the limited liability feature, limited partners must be limited in their involvement in management. They must be passive with regard to their management of the partnership's business. If investors begin to take part in management, they suddenly look like general partners to the IRS and face the potential of losing their protection of limited liability.

Ownership interests in limited partnerships are personal property and not real property, and there is seldom a market for limited partnership interests. Investors in limited partnerships must be prepared to stay in the investment groups until the property investment cycle is completed.

Just as in general partnerships, limited partnerships file an informational return with the IRS and distribute Schedule K-1s to individual limited partners, who then report their share of income or expense on their own tax returns. Limited partnerships are pass-through entities.

Limited partnerships have finite lives, meaning that the partnership agreements call for a date on which the partnerships will end. This is different from the lives of corporations, which are infinite.

Limited partners should be certain that the lives of the partnerships are long enough to allow the partnerships to hold the properties a sufficient time and to have sufficient life to allow the partnerships to sell the properties and carry back seller financing for a reasonable number of years.

In limited partnerships, as in general partnerships, titles to the properties are held by the partnerships, not the individual partners. The partnerships own the real estate, and the individual partners have a personal property interest in the partnerships.

Limited Liability Company (LLC)

An LLC may be formed by only one member. The owners are its members who can manage the entity directly or appoint managers to operate the entity or supervise officers hired to run the day-to-day activities of the entity. The key documents for an LLC are the articles of organization and the operating agreement.

An LLC created under the laws of one state might do business in other states by registering the LLC in each state in which it desires to do business.

In a limited liability company, investors are called members, not shareholders or partners. All members can have limited liability whether they are active or passive with regard to their role in management. This is a major difference between limited partnerships and limited liability companies and allows the members of an LLC to take an active role in the management of the business of the group.

An LLC is a pass-through entity. Income or losses from the operation of the business are passed directly through to the members of the group without being taxed at the organization level.

In limited partnerships and corporations, specifically S corporations, there are restrictions as to who can be a partner or a shareholder. Many of these restrictions are eliminated in LLCs. For example, LLCs have no restrictions against foreign investors being members of the group or against a corporation being a member of a group. In addition, there are no restrictions as to the number of members in a group or whether a lender to the group could also be a group member.

The possibility exists in LLCs for providing disproportionate allocations, as discussed in the General Partnership section, and there can be multiple classes of investors. One class of investors might be lenders, another class might be equity investors who want a preferred return, and another class might be equity investors who want the tax shelter and appreciation.

For example, a doctor with a small pension fund could invest the pension fund money in a group and take a secured position as a lender. She could then invest her own money and take a fixed portion of the cashflow as a return. She could also bring in other doctors to invest and give them the tax shelter and the remaining cashflow and appreciation.

The limited liability available to shareholders in a corporation might be lost if the corporation fails to hold regular meetings or keep an updated set of corporate books. When the corporate formalities are not adhered to, creditors are able to pierce the corporate veil of protection for the shareholders.

In LLCs, the lack of corporate formalities itself will not allow creditors to proceed directly against a group member, bypassing the protection of limited liability.

Many states allow the formation of an LLC with only one member, but each state has its own rules as to who the members of a group can be and whether there can be multiple classes of members in an LLC.

It is possible that groups such as limited partnerships, general partnerships, and sole proprietors who wish to convert their current entity structure to an LLC might be able to contribute their properties to an LLC on a tax-free basis. However, corporate conversion to an LLC is most likely a taxable event.

In a real estate venture, as well as in any other business venture, seldom is one of the investors willing to assume general liability for all obligations of the business as is required of the general partner in either a general partnership or limited partnership. Of these three pass-through entities, the LLC offers the best protection from liability for the operation of the business.

Corporations

This is the typical form of entity used by larger business organizations. A corporation is formed according to the laws of an individual state and might then be registered to do business in any other state.

The shareholders own the corporation. The shareholders elect the directors, who in turn hire the officers of the corporation. The officers run the business on a day-to-day basis.

Generally, the corporate entity is not favored for the ownership of real estate because of the double taxation that exists by virtue of the fact that the corporation must pay taxes on the taxable income generated by the property and the individual shareholder pays taxes on the cashflow distributed as dividends. This double taxation is avoided by the use of a pass-through entity, such as a partnership or an LLC.

In addition, the strict requirements of maintaining corporate formalities or being faced with the loss of limited liability make the corporate structure a difficult one in which to own and operate real estate group ownership.

Real Estate Investment Trusts (REIT)

This form of group ownership is favored on Wall Street and used in the largest capital formation transactions. It is a specialized area in which special legal and financial consultation must be sought out and obtained. A REIT is actually a corporation to which special rules are applied so that it can avoid taxation at the corporate level. Two of the special rules are that each year the corporation must distribute 95% of the cashflow to its shareholders and that there must be at least 100 investors in the REIT within one year of its date of formation.

What is the best way to hold Real Estate? I have purchased a lot of properties and most of them have been held in LLCs. I have had as many as twenty properties in my own name, too. I have clients who hold property in S corporations. I have clients who hold property in trusts. I have clients who hold property in partnerships – limited and general.

The two easiest ways to hold property are in your own name and in an LLC. Liability to you personally is limited because the underlying asset – your rental property – is held under a tax identification number that is separate and unique from your social security number. So, other people and entities including government entities, particularly the courts, see an LLC as another individual. It is taxed separately at the state level and any tax burden can be passed through to you personally at the federal level. Then you would include any income or loss of the separate LLC on your personal income tax statement.

Tax Benefits

One of the biggest benefits of investing in real estate is that the income derived from it is considered passive income. What that means is that it is the least taxed revenue. The income you receive from being an employee, sometimes referred to as W-2 income, is the most heavily taxed. If you are a W-2 employee, take out your last paystub and look very closely. You will see that the first to get paid out of "your" paycheck is the federal government. The second is the state government and the third is the local government. You may have other deductions for insurance and retirement. The last to be paid from your paycheck is YOU!

There is really good news though. Passive income, like your rent, is paid directly to you and nothing is deducted at that time. You get to deduct the cost of all the expenses associated with your rental property before you claim your net revenue as income on your tax return – and then and only then is it taxed for federal, state, and local taxes. And to sweeten the pot, you don't pay social security or any other tax on this income, just income tax.

One of the great benefits of using an entity such as an LLC to hold your rental property is that all profit and losses can be passed through the entity and on to you personally without the liability. This makes it easier to prepare and file tax returns. Not only that, you may have expenses of operating your LLC, and you can deduct those costs from your net operating income before claiming any income from your rental properties on your personal tax return. Some of these costs may be in the form of retirement savings, in a plan that you choose and design. You may even have your LLC pay yourself rent if you run your holding company out of one of your rental properties.

The bottom line is that you have much more control over when you pay taxes when you earn passive and pass-through income. This is at least some reprieve from a government that is now engaged in an all-out mission to take from the rich and give to the poor until the rich are rich no more.

AVOID PASSIVE LOSS LIMITATIONS

With the aforementioned non-cash componentizing deductions piling up, your properties are going to be throwing off paper tax losses which you want to fully deduct against your other income.

Except for $25,000 of losses, rental property losses are subject to passive loss limitations. This means real estate investors cannot deduct property tax losses against non-passive income such as salaries, business income, gains, IRA distributions, etc. If the investor's adjusted gross income (AGI) is above $150,000 they will not even be allowed the $25,000 exception for deducting such losses. Moreover, even if the investor is eligible for the above exception, but has over $25,000 in property losses, the excess over the $25,000 is still subject to the limitations. Being subject to these limitations means the investor cannot currently deduct the losses in the year incurred. The losses are "suspended" and must be carried forward until the property is sold at a gain. The savings from the losses are also delayed as well as the investment use of such savings.

To avoid being subject to these limitations, the investor must document at least 751 hours (or an average of about 14.5 hours a week) with the majority of their time in the real property business. A "real property trade or business" is defined as any real property development, redevelopment, construction, reconstruction, acquisition, conversion, rental, operation, management, leasing or brokerage trade or business. This includes real estate investors who do rentals, management, rehabbing, wholesaling, retailing, foreclosures, short sales, self-storage and other type of real estate activities. With the right planning and documentation even those with full time jobs can meet these requirements.

Do this and fully deduct your property tax losses without limit, save a ton of taxes, and increase your cashflow every year!

AVOID THE IRS

There are over thirty ways to audit-proof your tax return. Here are two powerful ways:

1. File an extension for your tax return. File as late as legally possible, typically October 15 following the tax year. Because of the IRS computer's "first come, first serve" system, returns filed early are more prone to audit. To file extensions, use IRS Forms 4868 for individuals and 7004 for entities such as LLCs and partnerships. Understand however, that filing an extension does not postpone the payment of any taxes you owe. This is not its purpose. The purpose is to reduce your chances of an audit, stop the April 15th mad rush, and numerous other advantages.

2. Attach written explanations to your return for items that you believe unusual or audit-prone. Include the appropriate tax law citations with these explanations. For example for high travel and entertainment deductions you can attach this audit-proofing statement: Auto, entertainment and travel deductions are necessary for my business and are done in strict accordance with the substantiation requirements of IRS regulation 1.274-5T(c), including maintaining written account books with date, place, persons, amounts, and business purpose. Also on file are related bills and receipts as well as notarized statements explaining and attesting to the business use and purpose of these items.

Sign and notarize the statement. This will help keep you out of the audit pile.

UNDERSTAND THAT SAVING TAXES ACCELERATES WEALTH

In my tax presentations, one of the first things I cover is why and how saving taxes can make you richer, faster. Well, here it is…

If you begin with just $1.00 and double it tax-free for only twenty days, it becomes $1,048,576 (over a million dollars). Take that same $1.00, taxed every year at 30%, and it will be worth only about $40,640 – A LOSS of a MILLION DOLLARS! Why is this so? Because with tax-free compounding, earnings accumulate not only on the principal amount of money but also on the tax-free earnings as well. Compounding money at high rates of tax-free return is a definite advantage of real estate, especially with a great tax plan.

The wealthy know that taxes are a primary factor in determining whether you get rich or stay poor. Let's say, for example, you're able to save just $2,000 annually on your tax bill. (With a good tax plan it will be much higher). You invest the $2,000 annually in an IRA which earns a tax-free annual return of 10%. After twenty years, you'll have over $114,000. If you can save $10,000 annually on your tax bill and invest it in a Simple IRA for twenty years, you'll end up with almost $573,000!

$5,000 in tax savings (which is found money) as a 10% down payment can allow you to buy an additional $50,000 in real estate! Assuming a 20% yearly return you would earn $10,000 which in five years would accumulate to $50,000!

You can use the tax savings to upgrade your rental properties for more monthly cashflow. One of my students, Richard, used $2,000 of tax savings (like found money) to employ the Mr. Landlord technique of adding optional upgrades to his facilities and increased his cashflow by $200 a month or a yearly total of $2400 which divided by $2000 = 120% return! But because the $2,000 in tax savings is found money, the return is really infinite!!

So does saving taxes make you wealthy? What would you say now?

SUBSTANTIALLY INCREASE DEPRECIATION DEDUCTIONS VIA COMPONENTIZING (COST SEGREGATION ANALYSIS)

Depreciation is your most valuable deduction because it does not require you to expend cash to get the deduction, yet it creates cashflow in your pocket from the deduction's tax savings.

For example, a $20,000 depreciation deduction reduces your ordinary income. In a 30% bracket this will save you $6,000 in taxes. This is like found money because you did not have to spend any additional cash to get the deduction. The $6,000 as a 10% down payment can allow you to buy an additional $60,000 worth of real estate, which at a 20% yearly return, would be $12,000 more income every year. Plus, like money in the bank, you get the deduction and tax savings every year (for the recovery period of the property). Yet when you sell, you can have no recapture and thus not have to pay any of these tax savings back by selling the property, tax free, via the powerful 1031 exchange (covered later). You still continue to pocket the tax savings from depreciation. Money makes money; but saving taxes (every year) makes a whole lot more money so you can get wealthier, quicker!

So how can you make this already valuable deduction save you even more? Componentize!

Componentizing (or Cost Segregation Analysis) is something I have been using for over twenty-five years to dramatically increase my cashflow (and wealth) via tax savings from much larger depreciation deductions. Many of my students also use it with the same money-saving results.

By componentizing, you break out components from the property cost that allow you to use shorter recovery periods with the result of much larger deductions and savings. An overview of these components and strategies follow:

5-Year personal property – Included in the cost of your property are many items of "hidden" personal property that can be written off over 5 years, using a faster accelerated method, instead of 27.5 or 39 years, using a slower straight-line method. Typically, the amount of personal property will be at least 10-20% of the cost of a rental property. Some examples include: kitchen cabinets, shelves, storage, carpeting, appliances, movable wall partitions, including non-weightbearing interior walls.

One of my students, Ron, installed $80,000 of non-weightbearing movable walls in his commercial property. Because the walls can be moved without adversely affecting the building structure, they are considered personal property and can be depreciated over 5 years (accelerated) instead of 39 years (slower) straight-line. This equates to a $16,000 a year deduction vs. $2,000. Tax savings of over $5,000 for five years! (Plus Ron expanded his rental market with the movable walls giving his tenants more options as to office space). There are many other items of such personal property fully supported by tax law citations.

15-year land improvements – Also included in the cost of your property are many items of land improvements that can be written off over 15 years, using an accelerated method, instead of not being depreciated at all if they were part of the land. Some examples are landscaping, paved surfaces, and parking lots.

Land improvements to the building – These are depreciated along with the building (27.5 or 39 years), instead of not being depreciated at all if they were part of the land. Some examples are outside lighting and utility connections to the building.

A low land value maximizes depreciation deductions – The land portion of the cost of the property is not eligible for depreciation deductions. The less of the property cost allocated toward non-depreciation land, the more toward the other depreciable components, the more non-cash deductions, the more savings. Don't be talked into using a high land value! You can justify a very low (or no) non-depreciable land value if you know the rules. Keep the following in mind – Allocations toward depreciable land improvements reduce the amount allocated to non-depreciable land. Special valuation factors have also worked to the taxpayer's advantage in lowering the value of land (such as housing shortages).

Fully deduct the remaining basis of components that are replaced (gut out). For example, in doing a rehab, if you replace existing property components with a remaining componentized cost basis of $30,000, you can claim the entire $30,000 as a full ordinary deduction. In a 30% bracket this puts $9,000 of savings in your pocket, yet you did not have to expend cash for the deduction!

So how much extra did you pay in taxes not using componentizing because your tax advisor did not know about this incredible legal strategy? Probably a lot!

GENERATE REPAIR DEDUCTIONS

There are three major tax-saving benefits of classifying expenditures as repairs rather than capital improvements. One of them is immediate tax savings. For example, the owner of a rental property is in a 31% tax bracket and pays $20,000 as a repair is an immediate deduction which is worth $6,200 in tax savings. But if the $20,000 is capital "punishment" it must be written off over 27.5 years = an annual deduction of about $720 year = tax savings of only about $200 in the first year. A difference in immediate tax savings of $6,000! These tax savings could be used as an immediate source of down payment monies for other income-producing real estate.

There are over 20 tax saving ideas to convert capital improvements into fully deductible repairs! Let me share some of them with you.

Componentize improvements – Just as a big forest is made of many smaller separate trees, so is an extensive plan of improvements made up of a series of smaller, separate repairs. That is, much work resulting in the "permanent improvement" to a property, in essence, consists of a series of "separate repairs." Such repairs could be immediately deductible if documented separately. Otherwise they will lose their nature as repairs if they are part of a general plan of improvement or reconditioning. You therefore need to componentize or fractionalize the large expenditures into a larger number of smaller repair categories. Do this with separate invoices for each repair job.

Bills & contracts should be worded as "repairs" – Use such words as: "repairs," "prevent damage," "patch," "temporary," "incidental," "minor," "fix," "piece meal," "annual," "less than a year," "decorating," "painting," "small," etc. Also, the prefix "re" is effective. For example, "repaint," "rematch," "repaper," "recoat," "resurface," "redo," etc. These have been in the taxpayer's favor in deciding that expenditures were repairs. Do the above and put more tax-saving dollars in your pocket!

BUY YOUR FIRST MULTI-FAMILY INVESTMENT PROPERTY & LIVE RENT FREE

Use an FHA loan to purchase a multifamily property that generates enough income to allow you to live for free while you occupy the property, and healthy cashflow when you eventually move out.

A recent example of executing this strategy is a duplex recently purchased in Manayunk, a small section of Philadelphia comprised largely of college students and young professionals. This investor purchased a duplex that had two identical units that each had two bedrooms, one bath and one parking space. I've rented several apartments on that street so I knew that a two-bedroom apartment with parking rented for $1100/month plus utilities.

The investor paid $250,000, which included a seller's assist that covered all of his closing costs and his monthly payment for principal; interest and PMI came to about $1,250/month. All in, his monthly total with taxes and insurance came to approximately $1,550/month. The investor was able to rent the first-floor apartment for $1,100/month plus utilities and then occupied the top floor apartment with a roommate who pays $550/month plus utilities.

So the investor is currently getting $1,650/month plus utilities in rent and spends only $1,550 per month for principal, interest, taxes and insurance. The additional $100/month surplus goes into a reserve account to cover repairs or future capital improvements and the investor currently has *virtually no monthly housing expense*!

When this investor inevitably moves out, he will generate $2,300/month plus utilities and will still have the same $1,550 per month payment for principal, interest, PMI, taxes and insurance. His monthly surplus will be $750 per month which will easily cover his operating expenses and still allow for a healthy cashflow.

So to recap, it's possible to use an FHA loan to purchase your first investment property for very little cash, allowing you to live virtually rent free while you occupy the property, and to make generous cashflows after you move out. This scenario is low risk because as long as the property is 50% occupied the majority of the debt and expenses are covered and the second unit is largely profit. The ROI on an investment like this can be quite good and there are significant tax deductions that the investor can take advantage of. Hopefully now you can see how using an FHA loan to purchase a multifamily property is a smart way to buy your first investment property with very little money down.

LEVERAGING YOUR MONEY IN TODAY'S MARKET

Buy properties already up and profiting on DAY 1! (And use the bank's 4.5% money for your first mortgage.)

Get your down payment from a 401K (borrow from yourself, not others).

Get your down payment from a whole life insurance policy (put its cash value to use instead of earning an embarrassingly low rate of return).

Get your down payment from a commercial line of credit against your other rentals (yes, banks want to lend money now).

Use cash for a down payment. (Did I say cash? Yes, I said cash. When coming out of a recession, prices will go up and rents will go up and interest rates will go up. Use cash. Trust me, you will get the best deal.)

AVOID INEPT CPAs

One of the biggest reasons why real estate investors (and others) pay too many taxes is bad advice from inept or overly conservative tax advisors. An article in *Money Magazine* revealed that 50 different tax preparers were given the same family's financial records. The result? Fifty different answers as to what the family's taxes should be. And we are talking about significant differences as high as 54%, plus the amount of taxes due varied by thousands of dollars. Most erred in favor of the IRS! *Money Magazine* also did an article titled, "Whose Side Is Your Tax Preparer On?" In many cases, it's not yours! Unlike doctors, accountants are not formally categorized into various specialties, such as a "Tax Specialist" or a "Real Estate Tax Specialist."

Here are some suggested questions to ask a prospective tax advisor:

How much is 2 + 2? If they say "4," don't hire them. However if they say, "What would you like it to be?"… then this may be the one to hire. That is, you do not want someone who is overly conservative. A conservative tax advisor is like a slow racehorse – worthless! On the other hand, you do not want the tax advisor to be reckless, blundering, or imprudent. Remember the overall objective is to both maximize tax savings and minimize IRS problems.

Tell me about a recent tax change about real estate that may interest me. This will tell you how sharp and updated the person is about taxes affecting real estate.

Will you help me plan my taxes to ensure the best possible outcome under different scenarios? You do not just want a "bean counter" or "glorified bookkeeper" to simply put numbers on a form. You want someone not only to prepare your return, but also to plan it. Expect to pay more for this. However, the additional investment could save you significantly.

What steps do you take to reduce the chances of my return being audited? This is an excellent test of their knowledge and willingness to be diligent and concerned about your tax situation.

Can you provide references from real estate investor clients as to your quality of service? When you are checking with the reference ask specifically, why they like the tax advisor. For example, did they come up with tax-saving ideas that others did not think of? Were they very thorough by explaining your tax situation? Did they call you during the year to make tax-reduction suggestions? Would you recommend them to your mother? If the reason why they like them is too general or more personal than business, this may not be a good referral source.

You want a tax advisor who can: (1) Assist you in rethinking your tax situation under current laws, especially those affecting real estate, (2) Apprise you of tax-reduction opportunities (old & new), (3) Alert you to IRS "tax traps," (4) Give you prompt, courteous service and (5) Be ethical. If you believe that your tax advisor basically has what it takes, have a candid discussion with them and see if you can help provide any missing links. If after your discussion, the tax advisor is not open to new ideas, then stop the bleeding and immediately get rid of them!

One thing is for sure, like a bad tenant… having NO tax advisor is a heavenly dream next to having a bad one.

Also, do not limit yourself to just someone "local." With today's technology we are closer to each other than ever before, despite being many miles way. Don't let physical distance get in the way of money-saving advice.

RENT INCOME IS NOT SUBJECT TO SOCIAL SECURITY TAXES

Rents for the use of property are not subject to self-employment (social security) taxes. IRC 1402 (a)(1). This is so, regardless of the number of rentals that are owned.

ALERT: CPAs often erroneously classify rent income for the use of property as self-employment (social security taxable) income – causing the investor to pay about another 15% of the income in taxes. Ouch! For seven years this happened to one of my students with their self-storage facilities. When they realized the CPA's blunder, they could only go back three years to amend the return to recoup the past paid taxes. It was too late for the prior four years of $10,000 in taxes!

ON NEXT PURCHASE, ALTER WHO PAYS FOR VARIOUS EXPENSES ON THE HUD-1 TO SAVE YOU TAX DOLLARS

While it is customary for the seller to pay for all real estate commissions out of the proceeds he or she receives, there is no reason why you can't alter the sales price so that the net proceeds to the seller is the same yet the buyer can take the expense of paying the commissions and therefore the tax benefit. The result is the same to the seller including the effect on their taxes. Furthermore, you can alter who pays the transfer tax and accomplish the same thing, which means the seller gets the same net proceeds and has no negative impact on the capital gains tax or income tax they pay and yet the buyer gets the full tax write-off.

Financing: Use Cash –
Just Say "No" To Debt

If you have ever read any of Carleton Sheets' material then you know that there are at least 30+ ways to buy real estate. Some are very good and some are not so good depending upon your circumstances.

The bottom line is that the more money you borrow to buy real estate, the more you will be at risk. The absolute best way to buy real estate is to use cash, pure cash, baby. The truth is that people die, people have babies, people get married, people get divorced. People get new jobs. People lose jobs. It happens. It's not a matter of "if" but "when." So ask yourself, what will happen to your highly leveraged empire if the economy turns sour?

What if there is a real estate bust like what happened in 2008-2010? What happens if the pool of decent renters is raided by lenders who need to loan money and so they relax their standards like they did beginning in the 1990s with the Clinton administration and continued until 2007? I'll tell you what happens. All of your good renters become homeowners and you get left with the dregs of society. That's what happens and that, more than anything else, will cripple your real estate empire. And if it doesn't, then it will certainly put you in a horrible position when the economy spins into a recession and your properties lose a lot of value. Then you're stuck with all these bad tenants wrecking your properties and not paying their rent. Then you can't get another loan to keep things afloat because the banks won't lend you money anymore. Get the picture?

Besides, I can show you mathematically how you can build a much stronger, less risky, and more profitable real estate empire by using all cash and only cash. If you graph it out it will look like it takes a while to get going and it will. However, when your mega cash cow starts to feed itself, look out. You will be a juggernaut that can't be stopped. You will absolutely make a lot of money. No one can stop you. You will owe no one. And better yet, the next time there is a recession you will be the one everyone is running to, to buy their properties. You will be King of the world!! GWARRRRRRRR!!! Who's Your Daddy Now ??? Go ahead. Take your best shot, you no-money-down gurus.

Now having said that, I know that because you can borrow money now at around 4%, a lot of you will do it. Go ahead. I did too. I can promise you though that in the end you will learn to regret it and you will see that it is taking you longer to build your massive money-producing monster. If you do borrow, promise me that you will put down at least 20%. I recommend 25% or more. This way you will get the best rates and terms. Remember, all you borrowers out there, to keep your ratios in check. Never owe cumulatively more than 2/3 of what you own and never have debt payments more than 1/3 of your gross rents. If you manage these ratios, the banks will always love you, and unless you are a complete moron you should always be making money.

Before borrowing from commercial banks to buy real estate, if you have a 401K you should check with your employer because you may be able to borrow against your 401k an amount up to 50% of its balance. It gets even better. You aren't borrowing from anyone else. You are borrowing from YOU, Inc.! And guess what? The interest you pay on what you borrow is paid to YOU, too! And guess what else? It isn't taxed either. You know, maybe our government isn't so bad after all. In fact I bet there is one good guy in our government who was an entrepreneur at one time and saw this amazing opportunity to do something really good for a lot of people. The cost of borrowing from a 401K is usually a small administration fee. No application fees. No appraisal fees. No junk fees of any kind.

If you are just starting out and don't have a lot of cash lying around, like us seasoned veterans, do take heart. You would be amazed at how easy it is to form a partnership with an individual who does have money lying around. Sometimes a veteran real estate investor will partner with one or more newbies to teach them the ropes – and more importantly to have one or more bird dogs out there doing the hunting.

When they find a suitable prey the investor puts up the money and he and his protégé split the profits. I have seen this work with doctors also. In fact it could work with anyone who has more time than money.

Another way to begin acquiring real estate when you are starting out and don't have a lot of cash is to borrow from a private investor. They usually charge more in interest and fees than a bank but they are also more open-minded and creative. They usually understand the real estate investing game pretty well and aren't interested in forming partnerships or teaching newbies. They will often finance up to 100%. They may also loan you money that you secure with other property you have.

They're really not that hard to find either. Some mortgage bankers and brokers keep private investors in their back pockets to keep a deal moving forward rather than watch it die an agonizing death where nobody gets paid. Private investors can be tough. I have used them. I do not recommend it although I know some of you will have to try because you just have to have that sweet deal. I get it. I really do. I ended up being okay, but it did cost me a lot of interest payments.

Still another way to acquire properties when you don't have cash is to use hard money lenders. They call them hard money lenders for a reason. It is a hard way to do business. They charge exorbitant interest rates and exorbitant fees to get the money. They usually have a very quick term, sometimes referred to as a balloon payment. In other words, you have three to six months' use of their money paying interest only, then at the end of the three- or six-month term you have to pay back all of the principal amount that you borrowed. If you can't pay it back they will take your property. And they will. Trust me. Sometimes people use this method to buy a rental property that needs work. They will borrow enough money from the hard money lender to buy the property and rehab it so that they can then rent it out. Then they go to a commercial bank to get a traditional mortgage on the property to pay back the hard money lender and even have excess cash from the traditional loan to line their pockets.

For years when money was easy, I would pay cash for a property and for the remodeling, then borrow from a bank in the form of a traditional first mortgage with easy terms and a low interest rate. This way I would continue to build my rental property empire while at the same time increase the amount of capital I had to work with. Keep in mind that it all has to be paid back and if you are a borrower you have to keep your ratios in check or you will stop growing and wind up borrowing from private investors or worse yet, hard money lenders.

In the end, Cash is King. If you use any other method to acquire real estate then you are putting yourself at risk – and sometimes grave risk. Life happens and when it does, remember the golden rule: "The man with the Gold makes the rules." If you don't owe the banks and other people, you get to make the rules. If you owe the banks and other people, *they* make the rules. And they aren't as nice as you. Don't be a sucker and fall for all that debt crap. Be a man and pay cash.

The Right Kind of Realtor:
The Investor-Agent

In the world of real estate investing, there is no other kind. If you are using your neighbor's son then you are a loser and you will pay a dreadful price. Every real estate agent on the planet will tell you that he or she is the right agent for you and they are the best at helping you. Make sure you ask them how much real estate they own. How many other investors are they working with? If they have so many other investors then how do they have the time to help you? Keep asking questions. Eventually, they will run out of crap to tell you.

I originally got my real estate license because I was sick and tired of realtors who didn't know what they were doing in the world of real estate investing. The rules of engagement are 180 degrees different than for the owner-occupied real estate business.

My neighbor was my first realtor. I had to fire her and it pissed off the whole neighborhood. She wouldn't, or couldn't, learn what she needed me to teach her. So I fired her and got my license. I eventually developed a system to teach other realtors how to work with investors. Trust me, it makes a huge difference. Having a traditional real estate agent try to help you with your real estate investing is like having a motorcycle mechanic work on your airplane.

If you invest in real estate the way I am teaching you, then you will one day own an airplane. Now imagine yourself getting ready to take your plane down to Florida to play golf when you just find out that your regular mechanic is off sick. The airport has a motorcycle mechanic, who happens to be the air traffic controller's nephew's neighbor, who just happens to be a recent graduate of the Acme school of motorcycle mechanics because he got laid off from his last job. How does that make you feel?

Well, remember a lot of real estate agents are real estate agents because they got laid off from their last job – and getting their real estate license took only sixty hours and cost only a few hundred bucks. Does it sound like they are highly qualified to help you invest your precious hard-earned money? I didn't think so. Don't be stupid. If you use one of these imbeciles you will end up losing your money and wishing you were going down in the plane that the bozo motorcycle mechanic worked on. By the way, I have no problem with motorcycle mechanics in general, only the ones who are foolish enough to work on an airplane.

There are a few things you can do to enhance your relationship with your real estate agent. One of them is to sign a Buyers Agency Agreement. I have taken and seen material from other real estate gurus who say you should have as many real estate agents working for you as possible. Trust me, they don't understand agency from a legal point of view, an ethical point of view, or a business point of view. In this business you need real players on your team. A good real estate agent who truly understands the rules of engagement when it comes to real estate investing is worth their weight in gold.

You wouldn't have multiple tax accountants prepare your taxes. You wouldn't have multiple lenders making you the same loan. You wouldn't have multiple closing companies working on the same file, so why would you have multiple real estate agents sending you properties from the same pool of properties? They all are pulling properties from the same database and they all have the same tools and access. Using multiple agents is only going to piss them off. They won't stick around and they certainly won't give you their best when they don't have an exclusive agreement with you. Get real. If you were working for commission and a client was using multiple real estate agents how much energy would you put into that effort with little to no assurance of getting paid?

More importantly, you don't want traditional real estate agents working for you anyway. You want an investor-agent who is an investor and/or has a proven track record of helping other investors profitably grow their portfolios using the rules of engagement I teach.

The other important factor in using a buyer's agency agreement is that it affords you certain rights and requires the real estate agent to assume certain responsibilities that would otherwise not be in place and in the end be to your disadvantage.

Another important piece of information is having Proof of Funds. This tells your real estate agent that you are qualified, and it also gives your real estate agent leverage and power when working with other agents. Proof of Funds can either be a bank statement showing that you have the available cash to make a purchase, or a lender pre-qualification, lender pre-approval for a loan, or a Line of Credit statement showing that you have the funds ready for you to borrow.

Think military. Think sports. Think family. Think friends. Think profitable business. A good real estate agent is a critical member of your team. I strongly encourage you to treat them that way.

Are you doing what is necessary, right now, for you to not just survive but to thrive? Are you ready to get started on your path to freedom? Success requires education, information, and action.

To find out more, visit:

RealEstateWithGaryWilson.com

For a limited time, get 1 month FREE membership
to our Silver community where you have access to
free tools, contracts, Real Estate Statistics, and
Expert Insider Information including personal interviews,
and other books for FREE!

The time to take action is now, so let's get started. Turn the page and get ready to change your life.

Rental Profits
Without the Pain

Locating, Targeting, & Analyzing Properties for Rentals

The following links will be a very useful guide if you are new to an area where you want to invest.

In the U.S.:

- banktracker.investigativereportingworkshop.org/banks/
- BRBPublications.com
- melissadata.com/lookups/cartzip.asp
- zip-codes.com/county/pa-allegheny.asp (replace the state and Allegheny with any other location)
- hudhomestore.com/Home/Index.aspx
- homesteps.com/index.html
- listings.vrmco.com/
- homepath.com/
- ReboGateway.com

In Canada:

- JLR.CA
- Canada Post www.canadapost.ca
- Statistics Canada http://www.statcan.gc.ca/eng/start
- All Property data from tax records: https://www.propertyline.ca/pages_english/products_services/multi_property_search.html
- Foreclosures: http://www.foreclosuresearch.ca/members/signup-m.php?price_group=-20&product_id=16
- Court records: https://www.canlii.org/en/on/
- Postal code targeting: https://www.canadapost.ca/tools/pg/8_Data_Targeting/TMpctguide-e.pdf

When you go out on your hunt for property you must keep things in perspective. First of all, you are not going to live there, your tenants are. What you perceive as being acceptable may or may not be acceptable to a prospective tenant or future buyer. As a result, if you find yourself saying, "I could never live here, let's go," then you are already in trouble.

What you see as substandard may be perfectly acceptable to someone else. Besides, who are you to judge or determine where or how someone else should live? Get over it, get off your soap box and get your head in the real estate investment game.

The sooner you come to grips with this, the sooner you can start making money. Now you can go out and identify good rental areas. They may or may not be in areas with strong home ownership.

A good rental area may not be an area where you would personally live, but it may have some of the same characteristics such as proximity to schools, shopping, bus service, parks, major highways, hospitals, police stations and firehouses. Generally speaking, it is good to be near schools and parks. It is also good to be close by shopping and transportation. While you don't want to be miles and miles away from hospitals, police, and fire protection, you also don't want to be only a block away either. You do not want to be too close to industrial sites, directly behind shopping centers, or storage facilities.

Once you have narrowed down the target areas based on the criteria we just discussed, you can start to look at the characteristics within the neighborhood. I suggest you focus on neighborhoods that have wide enough streets for parking on both sides and easy travel for cars in both directions.

Are the streets tree-lined? Are the neighbors taking at least basic care of their yards? You don't want to be in a neighborhood where neighbors leave all of their crap on the front porch and the driveway. You don't want to be in a neighborhood where neighbors aren't cutting their grass or trimming their bushes. You want the neighbors in your rental neighborhood to keep their yards free of clutter... including little Johnny's plastic forts, bicycles, skateboards, and Rover's stinking piles of crap.

The worst scenario is the boarded-up house. Don't buy in this neighborhood. Beyond the previous description is what is referred to as the 'war zone'. Stay out of the war zone. People get shot in the war zone. There is no such thing as a good house in a bad neighborhood. It sucks. Everyone near a big city knows of elderly people whose neighborhood has gone downhill after the many decades that they lived there. The elderly couple's house may still look cute but right next door, the local crack dealer is creating hell on earth.

It happens in every city. Have faith though. There are many examples of older neighborhoods that have been brought back to life. The technical term is 'gentrification'. It is a good thing. It is beautiful and wonderful to see. I have seen it and been part of it.

HOW TO FIND THE RIGHT NEIGHBORHOOD

Focus on where you will get the best Return on Investment (ROI).

By now, I'm sure you have questions and maybe even concerns. Fear not. Millions of others have walked your path before. Here is a brief explanation of the different socio-economic classes of neighborhoods. You may be surprised to know that there are rentals in all of these areas including luxury high-end.

High-end neighborhoods are not where you want to be in the rental business if you want a decent ROI. The reason is that you will pay top dollar for these properties, yet the rents you can command do not keep pace with the prices of these properties. In other words, while you can get $1,000 per month rent for a $100,000 house you should not expect to get $10,000 per month rent for a $1,000,000 house. In fact you may only get $5,000 per month for a million-dollar house.

You may think that you will get much better tenants for a million-dollar house but don't bet on it. There are people who don't pay their $5,000 rent just like there are people who don't pay their $1,000 or $500 rent. I know of cases personally where this has happened.

Middle-class homes may be tempting and they will provide a better ROI than high-end homes. There are some areas of the country where middle-class houses work well for rentals. These areas usually have a low median home price. You can make these work because the average rent for the area is high, relative to the average home price. If you are in one of these areas, middle-class homes may be your thing. Generally speaking, it will not be your thing, though. You can do better with a house that rides the fence between middle and lower-class. You can call it lower-middle-class or upper-lower-class. Sounds crazy, huh? Read on.

Low-income neighborhoods usually work well as rental neighborhoods. Notice I did not say 'bad neighborhoods,' I said 'low-income.' What I mean by that is lower on the socio-economic scale. The people living in these neighborhoods may not be as financially well off as you or me, but it doesn't mean they are bad people. There are plenty of economically poor folks who are good people – and there are plenty of wealthy people who are bad characters. Your job, through screening, is to determine who can afford to rent your property, then to determine whether they are good or bad – their character.

Within the broad range of lower-class neighborhoods there are at least three layers. I suggest staying in the upper layer. You can venture into the middle layer if you like, and when you become more experienced you can even place a bet that a middle layer is moving up to the upper layer and get in at the front end of an improving neighborhood.

Keep this in your back pocket for now, but a favorite strategy of mine is to turn a neighborhood on my own or with other investors. What you do is buy as much inventory as you can in a neighborhood and improve the houses enough to move the whole neighborhood into the next layer. You can even go as far as convincing the city to put a little money into the pot and put in new sidewalks and street lights. Ask and you shall receive! This is an advanced strategy with risks so you need to have some experience and connections first.

The upper low-end neighborhoods are where you will find the greatest ROI. You will have to be thorough in your screening and select the neighborhoods where people are taking care of the yards, children, and dogs. You may not want to live there but you are not going to live there. Your tenants will live there, because they want to. They will not however want to live in a war zone.

War zones are usually identified by your intuition telling you to RUN!! Trust your intuition. Trust your powers of observation, too. If you see cars up on blocks or homes up on blocks, run. If you see windows and doors boarded up, run. If it is a bright sunny day and you don't see a living soul around, run. If you hear pop, pop, pop… run. Do I need to say more?

Most of what has been described in the previous paragraphs may have sounded like it was directed at single-family homes. However, all of it applies to two-, three- and four-unit properties as well. It also applies to larger properties. At the end of the day you need to get to know your neighborhoods. You can change a house, but you can't change where it is located.

TARGETING PROPERTIES

Today we are in a very strange real estate environment. Markets across the country are in various stages of economic recovery. Some markets have almost no inventory while others still have too much inventory. Pittsburgh, Pennsylvania, has pretty much gone through even its bank-owned inventory. Five years ago I could find 3,000 properties in foreclosure in the Western Pennsylvania MLS system. Today I can find only maybe 300. In Hampton Roads, Virginia, arm's length inventory is a little tight but there are still a lot of REOs to churn through – and even more short sales. In Southern California and Phoenix, Arizona, properties are flying off the shelf and values are climbing into the double digits.

If you are a seasoned investor – or you are on your way to becoming one – you really don't care so much what the inventory is like as much as finding the best properties at the best prices relative to the market. Within that context, your rules of engagement don't change. You just may be hitting your target more frequently or less frequently depending on inventory.

Under no circumstances do you change your criteria or rules of engagement.

I have always done well with REO and estate properties. I have bought properties that were neither and have done well. At this point I should describe the pros and cons of the different types of properties.

REO

REO is the accounting term banks use to categorize properties that they have been taken back in foreclosure. Ten years ago you had your choice of REO properties, because there were so many. Banks would take almost any price because they simply had to get rid of inventory. Some banks have and still do try to sell REOs themselves through an internal department, but the vast majority of banks hire a real estate broker to list and sell their REO inventory. I was one of these brokers. Of course, I was an investor first but after I got my real estate license and eventually formed my own brokerage company, Win Realty Advisors, I was a good candidate for these banks to hire. I had 18 years of experience in banking so I spoke their language and I had more than two decades of experience investing in real estate – so I knew how to sell a lot of REO properties to a lot of people. I sold more properties in one year as an individual agent (no team, no support) than anybody else. I broke all kinds of records and I didn't miss time with my family, or even work on Sundays. I created a system to use that I actually used for myself as an investor. I simply applied it to the brokerage and it worked. In fact, I went on to teach a lot of real estate agents how to use this system. I made a lot of money for myself, other investors, other real estate agents, and banks in the world of buying and selling REOs. There were so many of them I literally got tired of all those REOs. So, as the market evolved and our moronic government tried to step in and save the day, short sales became the mainstay of a lot of investors and real estate agents.

Short Sale

A short sale is the laymen's term for properties that are technically in default but have not yet gone through foreclosure. As of this writing there are still a lot of short sale properties in inventory. More in some areas, less in others. When our government twisted the bankers' collective arms to not foreclose as much on so many homes, the answer was the short sale. If you were involved on the front end of the short sale business, then you know how frustrating and agonizing it was to do one of these deals. A large percentage of them took more than a year to close. In spite of the government's interference, banks thought up all kinds of road blocks to successful short sale transactions.

Banks were notorious for changing file handlers midstream in a transaction and everybody involved had to start all over again. This happened to almost every single transaction. On many it happened on more than one occasion during its lifecycle. It was extremely frustrating. Banks would also, at the last minute, force real estate agents to take less on their commission before the bank would cooperate on the sale – even when the agent had a contractual agreement with the owner of the house for a specific percentage.

In all of their unethical glory, the banks would go as far as to say that if the agent didn't cooperate they would blame the failed sale on the agent for being greedy. Many distressed homeowners gave up during the short sale process because it was easier to just walk away and allow the foreclosure to happen. After a few years of pain and agony the banks finally began to improve on their short sale processing. It's far from perfect but it is better. What is usually a little bit easier than short sales, but sometimes frustrating, is an estate sale.

Estate Sales

Estate sales come about usually as the result of the homeowner dying and leaving real property to their heirs. If there isn't a spouse still alive, then the ownership usually passes to sibling children. More often than not the sibling children at first see dollar signs and are hopeful for a windfall. The reality is that the home they inherited is usually old and in need of a variety of repairs, systems upgrades, and just downright remodeling. The siblings get discouraged because the house doesn't sell for their unrealistically high-priced expectations, and are now suffering through repeated price drops. They begin to argue and so no one wants to cooperate in forking over money to improve Mom and Dad's house and their childhood home. They were supposed to get a lot of money after all, not have to fork it over. So, here comes the investor dressed in shiny amour and galloping onto the scene on a handsome white horse. Yeah, right. The sons and daughters of the deceased parent have been forewarned about us. Trust me. Most realtors don't understand us (even though they say they do) and so they have painted a not-so-appealing picture of us to their clients. All this does is hinder progress. To an investor, this is a business transaction, nothing personal. The bottom line is that the current owners have a problem and the investor has the solution. If the projected return on investment isn't suitable to the investor, he/she will move on. He/she is taking on a lot of risk and requires a profit that compensates for time spent, energy and money on the project – and of course assuming the risks that go along with this type of sale. At the end of the day, if you as the investor can put up with a lot of emotional baggage from the grown children who are tasked with liquidating their parents' and their childhood home, then you can usually make a tidy profit on these properties. These people are "don't wanters" and we are helping them offload what they don't want. Another type of "don't wanter" is the retiring real estate investor.

Retiring Investors

At the end of every real estate investing career, successful or not, is a real estate investor who now wants to liquidate his or her properties. You can always tell the successful real estate investors because they have held their properties through thick and thin, usually ten or more years. An old advisor, Gerhard Flugfelder, once told me that every investor must live by the rule of seven. This doesn't mean that the investor must hold their property for seven years. What it means is that, on average, every investment property will hit a slump an average of every seven years. Please note I said average. Another successful investor told me that every investor has to get through their first three years without a disaster. If you read the earlier chapters, you know about the massive flooding in 2004. This happened in my sixth year. It was very trying and taxing but I didn't give up, partly because I'd had six years to build up my anxiety tolerance muscle. In any case, if an investor sells a property after just a few short years of ownership it is usually because they hit their bad year and didn't want to stick around for the better days ahead. Of course there are other circumstances, like death and divorce, where an investor is forced against their will to sell. I have experienced this myself. If this happens to you, in the case of divorce, you will find out who your friends and allies are very quickly. Sometimes other investors sell so that they can get the most capital possible for a larger purpose. No matter how you slice it, experienced investors will one day want to sell. They know what their properties are worth. They know what other investors look for. So, they generally price their properties so that they will look appealing to other investors. Investors who do sell their properties usually sell them "turn key."

Turn Key

Turn key properties are already rented out. They are in service so they are usually up to code, safe and reliable. They may not look very pretty but they are usually fundamentally in sound shape. I started making my fortune buying turn key properties. They had solid foundations, separate gas and electric (or they were easy to separate, in the case of multi-units), and the main systems – heating, hot water, electrical, roofing, siding and windows

– were in good enough shape and not in any immediate danger of needing to be replaced. However, these properties may be in need of cosmetic care. This is what we call 'lipstick and rouge', i.e. paint and carpet. I can find these properties in every town on the planet. I can usually strike a good deal with the owner because most consumers don't believe or agree that if they put a little money into the property that it would sell much more easily and for more money. They don't understand the psychology behind perception and value. When a traditional consumer walks into a house that needs a little TLC – something that may cost you or I as investors $1,000 – it will be perceived by the traditional consumer as costing $2,000. Worse yet, the consumer begins to look for (and see) other issues requiring more money – all of which results in them walking away or making unreasonably low offers. On the other hand, if you spend a little money and put a little TLC into a home for sale, essentially eliminating obstacles to a purchase, the traditional consumer will think more highly of the home and may perceive even more value than might really be present, resulting in a nice offer. The latter approach also results in a home being sold more quickly. The point is that I can use this psychology to my advantage when buying or selling a home whether for myself or representing another investor. I have become pretty comfortable at guestimating the cost of lipstick and rouge. I have also become comfortable at guestimating the cost of rehabbing a property. This becomes valuable when purchasing a property wholesale, well below the values in the surrounding area, with the intention of rehabbing and then refinancing (if I choose to do so) after I rent the property out.

Buy Low, Rehab, Rent, Refi

I don't necessarily advocate this approach for beginning investors. It requires the learning of an entirely new set of skills and disciplines, and new investors already have their hands full learning the skills and disciplines of running a real estate rental business. However, whether you are starting out and have watched the late night TV real estate gurus telling you that anybody can do this or you have been to the front lines a few times, you will eventually be tempted to buy low, rehab, rent, and refinance. I have done many dozens of these myself and I made a lot of money doing it. Remember though that I had at least fifteen turn key purchases under my belt before I moved up the next rung of the real estate investing ladder.

When you buy low with the intention of rehabbing before putting a property into service and renting it out, you have to master the skill of estimating the rehab project. Even the pro's don't always get this right. This takes practice and is usually best accomplished when accompanying a seasoned contractor in the process – at least for the first few. The good news is that there is a method to accomplishing this. You have to become the master of analyzing properties.

ANALYZING PROPERTIES

He who masters the discipline of proper property analysis will become the master of profit.

The first and more critical analysis to perform is the financial analysis. A good majority of this can be accomplished on your computer. It also all starts before you get in your car or set foot on a property.

There are certain formulas and ratios that you must learn and they are easy. The first ratio is that when you add the cost of purchasing a property to the cost of rehabbing a property, the total of these two costs must not exceed 70% of the After Repair Value (ARV) of the subject property. This is the minimum acceptable ratio. The less money you have in purchase and rehab costs relative to ARV the better.

You may think from time to time that you can fudge a little on this ratio to get a deal done. You may even get away with it once, twice, or possibly even three times. The problem is that you will be developing a bad habit and eventually you will pay the price for uncontrolled greed. It is far more difficult to correct a bad habit than to learn a new good one. Don't be greedy or foolish. Let history be your teacher. Look to the successes of others who have gone before you. Follow your intuition, your spirit, and not your ego.

The ego plays nasty tricks on us. Be the master of your ego. Learn to listen to and develop your intuition. Learn the methods properly and you will be successful. Let your ego control your behavior and you will never be fulfilled.

This isn't just me teaching and preaching. This is natural law. This is God's law. I'm making a big deal of this because it's precisely where I see many investors fall by the wayside, never to be seen again. Only the disciplined and those who focus on and live by the truth and act with wisdom and courage succeed and achieve fulfillment in this business. Now let's get back to business and learn how to perform a proper financial analysis.

FINANCIAL ANALYSIS

The following is an example of a property I owned and sold to a fellow investor. I actually sold it for $65,000 so it was an even better deal. Let's take a look and break it down.

3834 Brighton

Large up and down duplex with new and separate gas and electric, and new furnaces. Tenants pay G + E, I pay water. Residential neighborhood. List for $79,900.

Income: $1150/mo (1st fl 1BR = $450, 2nd fl + 3rd fl 3BR = $625, garage = $75) = $13,800/yr

Taxes: $695.96/yr

Insurance: $322/yr

Water: $1388.50/yr (includes sewage and garbage)

Maintenance/repair: $600/yr

Net Operating Income: $899.46/mo = $10,793.54/yr

Purchase price: $70,000, Down payment: $14,000

Loan: $56,000 over 20 yrs @ 5 %

Debt Service: $369.58/mo

Cash return: $529.88/mo = $6358.56/yr

Cash on Cash return rate = 45%, Cap Rate = 15.4%

Notice that I provide the gross income first. Then I give the basic routine expenses of the property on an annual basis. Then I provide the net operating income (NOI). This format follows closely the IRS Schedule E format. This is for a very good reason. It is a pretty good format to use when analyzing properties and it is also in the format tax accountants and the IRS use.

After the NOI, I provide a projected financing scenario based on the current lending environment. The terms may change with the economy but the mathematics are the same. This gives a prospective investor a pretty good picture of what to expect. It also allows me to project income on a cash basis and the cash-on-cash ratio. The cash-on-cash ratio is the cash income after all expenses plus debt service (loan payment of principal and interest) divided by the capital outlay to purchase the property (down payment or out of pocket cost to acquire the property).

This ratio is what you can use to compare it to returns on other types of investments like stocks and bonds. This is one of the most important ratios to look at when analyzing a property.

The next important ratio is the capitalization (CAP) rate. The cap rate is the NOI divided by the total purchase price (down payment plus principal amount of any loan) or sales price of the property. In this ratio, debt service is not factored in. So, the NOI is used before debt service is paid for.

The CAP rate is the industry standard for evaluating a property particularly from a lender's perspective. It is used to compare properties against each other.

CAP rate also reflects the relative risk of a property. So a property that has a high CAP rate may be in a less desirable neighborhood, and naturally a low cap rate may reflect a property in a good neighborhood.

The CAP rate is an inverse ratio. In other words, the lower the cap rate the more expensive the property and the higher the CAP rate the less expensive the property.

I suggest you get used to using both ratios. I personally put more emphasis on the cash-on-cash return because cash is king and I want to know how much is coming in and how much is going out.

Here is a quick resource to assist you with calculations:
http://www.rentalpropertyreporter.com/resource-center/investment-property-analyzer/

Here is another way to view cash flow analysis:

CASH FLOW ANALYSIS

Gross Income:

Est. Annual Gross Income	_____
Other Income	_____
Total Gross Income	_____
Less Vacancy Allowance	_____
Effective Gross Income	_____

Expenses:

Taxes	_____
Insurance	_____
Water/Sewer	_____
Garbage	_____
Electricity	_____
Licenses	_____
Advertising	_____
Supplies	_____
Maintenance	_____
Lawn	_____
Snow Removal	_____
Pest Control	_____
Management (offsite)	_____
Management (onsite)	_____
Accounting/Legal	_____
Miscellaneous	_____
Gas	_____

Telephone   _____
Pool   _____
Elevator   _____
Replacement Budget   _____

Total Expenses   _____
Net Operating Income   _____

Debt Service:

1st Mortgage   _____
2nd Mortgage   _____
3rd Mortgage   _____
Total Debt Service   _____

CASH FLOW: _____

TERMS

Gross Rent: The highest amount you can get monthly from the property.

Expenses: The total amount of necessary payments for the property.

Cashflow: The amount of money you pocket after all expenses and mortgage payments are paid from the rent.

If I like the return, next I determine if I like the property itself from a physical perspective.

PHYSICAL ANALYSIS

Once you have identified properties priced at or below market value for the neighborhoods they are in – and with negotiation you can get the prices down even further (more on this later) – it is time to do the physical inspection (after you do drive-bys) of the property to determine what is needed for rehab and how much it is going to cost.

I am providing a sample rehab analysis sheet for you to use in your efforts. This is by no means complete, but it is a start. I am also including a packet of several pages that you should use as you go through a property room by room. You should end up with one sheet per room including bathrooms, kitchens, basements, garages and even the outside. This way you make sure that you greatly reduce your chances of missing something.

Rehab Cost Estimate Worksheet

ESTIMATED REPAIR COSTS

DESCRIPTION	√	COST RANGE	ITEM COST	UOM	QTY	ITEM TOT
Appraisal		$200-$325 EA	$250.00	EA		$ -
Power wash Outside (Front/Back)		$1000-$2000	$1,000.00	LOT	2	$2,000.00
Exterior Paint		$2000-$6500	$2,000.00	LOT		$ -
Exterior Siding		$200-$350/SQ	$200.00	SQ		$ -
Roof (3 Ply Flat 10 Year-Shingles)		$200-$300/SQ	$200.00	LOT		$ -
Roof (Silver Coat)		$400 LOT	$400.00	LOT		$ -
Gutters (Front/Back)		$7.00/FT	$7.00	LOT		$ -
Security Doors (Installed)		$300-$600 EA	$300.00	EA	2	$600.00
Storm Doors (Installed)		$200-$250 EA	$200.00	EA	2	$400.00
Interior Doors (Installed)		$125-$175 EA	$125.00	EA	10	$1,250.00
Ceiling Fans		$75-$125 EA	$75.00	EA	5	$375.00
Miniblinds (Installed)		$10 EA	$10.00	EA	25	$250.00
Windows (Double Hung-Installed)		$200 and Up/Window	$200.00	EA		$ -
Windows (Glass Block-Installed)		$200-$300/Window	$200.00	EA	5	$1,000.00
Drywall (Installed)		$27/Sheet	$27.00	Sheet		$ -
Interior Paint (2 Coat)		$200/Room	$200.00	Room	10	$2,000.00
Carpet/Flooring		$14/Yard INSTL	$14.00	Yard	500	$7,000.00
Ceiling Tiles (Drop Installed)		$1.00/SQ FT INSTL	$1.00	SQ FT	30	$30.00
Kitchen (Complete)		$2500 AND UP	$2,500.00	LOT	1	$2,500.00
Bathroom (Tub Coat)		$900 AND UP	$900.00	LOT	1	$900.00
Bathroom (Including Tub Replace)		$2000 AND UP	$2,000.00	LOT	1	$2,000.00

Rehab Cost Estimate Worksheet

Property Address:

ESTIMATED REPAIR COSTS:

ITEM		DESCRIPTION NEEDED			UOM	cost
1	Appraisal				EA	
2	Power wash Outside (Front/Back)				LOT	
3	Exterior Paint				LOT	
4	Exterior Siding				SQ	
5	Roof (3 Ply Flat 10 Year-Shingles)				LOT	
6	Roof (Silver Coat)				LOT	
7	Gutters (Front/Back)				LOT	
8	Security Doors (Installed)				EA	
9	Storm Doors (Installed)				EA	
10	Interior Doors (Installed)				EA	
11	Ceiling Fans				EA	
12	Miniblinds (Installed)				EA	
13	Windows (Double Hung-Installed)				EA	
14	Windows (Glass Block-Installed)				EA	
15	Drywall (Installed)				Sheet	
16	Interior Paint (2 Coat)				Room	
17	Carpet/Flooring)				Yard	
18	Ceiling Tiles (Drop Installed)				SQ FT	
19	Kitchen (Complete-Rental)				LOT	
20	Kitchen (Complete-Rehab)				LOT	
21	Bathroom (Tub Coat)				LOT	
22	Bathroom (Including Tub Replace)				LOT	
23	Bathroom (Rehab)				LOT	
24	Electric (Service Line 60-150 AMP)				LOT	
25	Electric (New Breaker Box)				LOT	
26	Electric (New Funs Per Line)				LOT	
27	Light Switches/Outlets (est. 30)				LOT	
28	Plumbing 4" Main				LOT	
29	Plumbing 1" Feed				LOT	
30	PVC Sewer Line 6'				LOT	
31	Heater-Gas Forced Air (90% Eff.)				LOT	
32	Heater-Boiler (90% Eff.)				LOT	
33	Central Air				LOT	
34	Hot Water Heater (30 Gallon)				EA	

35	Property Cleanout					LOT	
36	Demo Work (3 Men)					DAY	
37	Removal-40 Yard Dumpster					LOT	
38	Post Rehab Cleaning					LOT	
39	Parge Basement (Concrete)					LOT	
40	Concrete Work (Flooring/Pavement)					SQ FT	
41	Termite Treatment (Whole House)					LOT	
42	Misc: (Detail Work, Exterminate, Etc.)					LOT	
43	Soffit Fascia					FT	
44	Landscaping					LOT	
45	Interior Trim					L FT	
46	Other:						
47	Other:						
	Total Estimated Repair Costs:						

Notes:

Legend:

UOM	Unit of Measure. How an item is priced E.G. Windows are priced per EACH Window installed.
EA	Each. Unit of Measure for per item cost.
SQ YD SQ FT SQ	Square Yard. Unit of measure used for carpet. Includes installation.
LOT	Square Foot. Unit of measure used in flooring other than carpet. Includes installation.
	Square. Unit of measure used in roofing and siding 10 x 10=100sq ft which equals 1 square. Includes installation.
	Lump Sum or Flat Price for work performed. Includes installation.

Making Offers & Closing

This is where the rubber meets the road. You have come a long way and now it is time to make the offer. You cannot violate the maximum allowable offer (MAO). If you trespass beyond this line you will be tempting fate and less profit.

The MAO is the most you should offer for a property. MAO is the ARV of the property less your 30% profit margin, then less your rehab costs. So, if you have a property with an ARV of $100k, and subtract the 30% profit margin, that leaves $70k. Then if your rehab costs are $20k you subtract that from $70k to arrive at an ARV of $50k.

I suggest starting out offering less than $50k. Depending on the market I would offer from 5-20% less than the MAO. In a market where there is a lot of inventory I would offer as much as 20% less than MAO ($40k in this case). In a market of tight inventory I would offer 5% less than the MAO or $47.5k in this case.

ARV is arrived at by looking at comparable sales (comps) from the area. Either you or your realtor needs to be the expert in the area in which you are investing. I cannot emphasize how important this value is. If you project too low you will not get your offer accepted. If you project too high you risk paying too much for the property. You have to get it right. Period.

The following is a chart you can use in your efforts:

Maximum Allowable Offer (MAO)

	ARV
-	Less Costs (30%):
-	Less Repairs:
Equals	MAO

Starting Offer

	MAO
-	Less 15%
Equals	Starting Offer

TERMS

ARV: After Repair Value. This number is derived from Comps, CMAs, and other appraisal tools.

Costs: These are the costs to get into (and sometimes out of) the property. The table below depicts the cost breakdown. Costs average around 10% and include commissions to Real Estate Agents, carrying costs, and closing costs.

Repairs: These are the estimated repairs. Use the supplied Rehab Worksheet to get your initial estimate.

MAO: Maximum Allowable Offer. This is the theoretical maximum you can pay and NOT leave any of your money in the deal after refinancing. This is NOT a requirement to do a deal, however what is acceptable to leave in will be different for everyone depending on your own cashflow and financial ability.

Starting MAO: Get this number by subtracting another 15% from your MAO. This is a decent starting point to begin your negotiations. If you get no counter offers at starting MAO, you will need to increase your initial offer. Market conditions will always impact starting MAO.

Before going over the forms to use let's look at a plan for you to follow when going on your hunt:

STEP BY STEP INSTRUTIONS FOR BUYING RENTALS

This is the exact plan I follow when I make my investments. It is the plan I use when teaching several hundred students, and it is the plan I follow when I teach real estate agents how to work with investors. It is a good plan. Follow it.

1. Establish your investment goals. At this point you need to have available cash or credit to continue.

2. Set up your search criteria on the MLS system.

3. Initially you will get an email with a link to the MLS system. The first property matching the search criteria will be shown with a drop-down box at bottom left allowing you to scan forward to other listings. You will receive the "FULL" listings. This first email will consist of several hundred listings.

4. Next, you will separate the good from the bad. Your objective is to narrow the list down to about 30 properties.

Compare the list price to the market values for the area. The list price should be below the market value.

Look at the photograph(s) of the property, the lot size, room sizes, and other characteristics. This will take a few passes. As you narrow the list also use the county website for further research. This is a process that you will get better at with experience.

For multi-units, experience in my market area shows I should get $400-500 for 1-bedroom apartments, $450-650 for 2-bedroom apartments, $600-750 for 3-bedroom apartments.

Tax costs can be obtained from the listing. Insurance should be 0.5% of value annually (on a $100,000 property that would be $500 per year).

I try to keep the price-per-unit to $35,000 or less per 3-bedroom unit, $30,000 or less per 2-bedroom units, and $25,000 or less per 1-bedroom unit.

> *NOTE: different areas will have vastly different pricing models. Study your area and make adjustments accordingly.*

Other variables include the condition of the property (Turn Key versus Rehab).

Trust your instincts and focus on what you think are the best deals. Eliminate the rest. You will get better with experience.

5. The resulting list of 30 or so properties is your drive-by list. Now you will drive by the properties to further narrow your search down to 10-15 properties.

6. At this point you narrow the list down further. This will typically result in 7 final properties.

7. Now you will schedule an appointment to go see the properties.

8. After viewing the properties, you should have a list of 4 or more that you will fill out the MAO, Cashflow, and Cost Sheets for.

9. Decide which properties to make offers on.

10. Fill out the "Offer to Purchase," and make a photocopy of your hand money check.

11. Now you make the offer(s)!

FORMS TO USE

Always use Association of Realtors Forms when making offers.

There are plenty of late night gurus out there who preach that you should use a 1-page "Intent to Buy" or some other short form for extending what may or may not be an offer. Don't do this. You are wasting everybody's time, including yours.

Aside from the obvious problem of its validity, especially in a court case should that happen, using anything other than pre-approved Association of Realtors sales agreements puts you at a competitive disadvantage. And that is not acceptable. You want every competitive advantage possible.

Just for a moment, step out of your buyer's shoes and step into the seller's shoes. Now imagine you as the seller receiving multiple offers on your property – which often happens with investment real estate. One of the offers is this little 1-page "intent to offer" with no hand money check but rather a promise of a hand money check should you accept its short and incomplete terms. The other offer is on the Association of Realtors Sales Agreement form, completely filled out, all terms identified and there is a hand money check as well. This is a legally binding agreement. Which offer are you going to take more seriously? Exactly!

You will get much further negotiating with a more substantial and official-looking sales agreement than you will with one that looks like maybe you don't care so much. Not only are you in a better negotiating position, you are in a better legal position should trouble arise. With a real agreement of sale there is far less ambiguity, if any. Also, you can still put in your contingencies for financing (should you choose to do so), inspections, appraisals, verification of income and expense data for the property, or whatever you want to have in your favor.

Always remember that when you are making an offer on a rental property, you should always make the offer contingent on seeing the current owner's financials on the property including all income and expense data for the last three years. No exceptions! The only time you can't do this is when you are buying a foreclosure property.

You also want to see current leases, any contracts the current owner has for services like pest control, property management, laundry, etc. You also want a contingency on seeing every single unit in the building you are buying. This is especially important in case you didn't get to see all the units before you made the offer.

When you are making your offer and there are multiple offers, or there is a "highest and best" scenario, you can use one of my favorite tricks:

Let's say there is a "highest and best" scenario and your intuition tells you to go to full price on the property and the full list price is $99,900. You may be tempted to offer the list price or even $100,000. Go ahead and do that but add an additional amount of say $159. In other words your offer will be $100,159. This way if you are bidding against others and there happens to be another educated investor who sees the merit in offering full price, you will get the property for $159 or less because you outsmarted the competition.

On the first round of negotiating, if you are the only offerer, let them respond to your initial offer. Then don't respond right away. Instead, wait until the last minute to make them sweat a little. Then come back with a counter offer that moves up only a little. You want to create the impression that you want the property but are already at, or very close to, your magic number. You leave the door open a little but not much. You don't want to lose a good deal over pennies. Also, in your counter-offer, make it an unusual number. For example, instead of coming back with $120,000, come back with $118,743.67. They may think you are weird but your real estate agent will explain that you have done your homework down to the penny and you know your business and what the property is worth. If it goes another round then you can waive one of your less important items, like the lawn mower you asked for. I always look for a few odds and ends to throw in my offers that I can then use later as throw-aways to get the deal done at a price acceptable to me.

CLOSING

The Big Day is approaching – another income-producing asset to be added on your balance sheet.

In most states, the buyer of a property gets to choose which company will perform the closing on a real estate transaction. Sometimes a lawyer does the closing and sometimes not. It depends on the state.

The closing company (sometimes called the Settlement or Title Company) is essentially assigned the task of transferring ownership of the real property from the current owner to the new owner. Among other things they will have the current owner sign the deed over to the new owner. They will research the current title history of the property and order and purchase title insurance for the new owner.

NEVER, EVER buy a property and not buy title insurance. I used to own a settlement company and I only had one client not buy the title insurance – and two years later when he went to sell the property, Murphy's Law struck. I don't care what anybody tells you, always get title insurance. The closing company also prorates rents and taxes, assigns leases and transfers security deposits.

The most important function has to do with title insurance though. The closing company is actually a title insurance salesperson. They purchase for you the buyer a title policy from one of the shrinking numbers of title insurance providers.

Either the title insurance company itself will do a title search or the closing company will hire a title searcher to do the search and provide a title report. This report will identify all of the current liens on the property that need to be satisfied before a new title policy will be issued and ownership of the property transferred to you.

As you might guess, it is not a perfect business. Murphy's Law is alive and well and there are situations where a defect in title may surface later on. This, my friends, is why you need title insurance. Don't be a fool. Be cool. Buy title insurance.

The next most important type of insurance you will need is Home Owners Insurance. I like to use independent insurance brokers because they have all the connections, can get the best deals, do all the work for you and get paid by the insurance companies rather than you. Some insurance companies will not insure some rental properties or they will at a tremendous cost.

There are three basic types of insurance, sometimes referred to as "A" form, "B" form and "C" form. "A" form is bare bones fire insurance. No bells and whistles here. The "B" and "C" forms cost a lot more but provide more coverage. You can get lost rent coverage, for example if you have a tree fall on your property and your tenant(s) has to move out while repairs are being made, you can receive money from the insurance company that will compensate you for lost rent until your property is inhabited again by a renter. When you are first starting out you may want to have "B" or "C" form coverage depending upon your personal circumstances. Always check with your insurance agent to discuss the pros and cons. After you have a lot of units under your belt and you have a pretty good track record of performance you can lower your coverage to the "A" form and in essence self-insure yourself against lost rent.

Over all the years I have had hundreds of properties. I can count the number of claims on one hand. I had a house fire one time and the whole thing was covered by insurance. It didn't cost me a dime. I also had what I call as-is coverage. This means that the insurance adjuster makes an estimate on what it will cost to get your property back up and running – and when he does he will discount it for depreciation. I always got coverage for the maximum value amount possible on this type of policy. Essentially, if I had a house that was worth $80,000, I would insure it for $100,000.

Another type of insurance you might need is flood insurance. Always check to see if the property you are buying is in a flood plain. You'd be surprised. If you are buying with a mortgage (shame on you) your lender will tell you if it is in a flood plain. If you are in a 100-year flood plain you will definitely want flood insurance and lenders will require it. If you are in a 500-year flood plain you should still get it. It costs less. A lender may or may not require it. They will let you know.

I had two 100-year floods occur with a two-week span in 2004. If I hadn't had flood insurance, that event would have wiped me out and it would have been nearly impossible to recover. You never know, and as a result you should get the insurance. It is government controlled. It doesn't matter where you buy it. It is all the same.

When you have your closing scheduled it is time to call and get utilities put in your name so you have electric, gas, and water on the day of closing – or the day after if you are buying a foreclosure.

The last thing you will do prior to closing is the Walk Through. ALWAYS, ALWAYS do a walk through. I bought a foreclosure once and I didn't do a walk through prior to closing. It was too inconvenient and I'd never had a problem before. Then Murphy showed up in a big way. I went to the house after the closing and one of the biggest trees I had ever seen was lying across my yard and the two yards on either side of me. It was huge and it took out fences, dog houses, toys, lawn furniture, grills, you name it. Guess who had to pay for it? You guessed it. Had I done the walkthrough, heck even if I'd just driven by, I would have seen it in time – and the banks would have had to take care of it, or reduce the price of the house to compensate me for it.

I had another student drive by a house he'd just bought hours before only to find an empty lot. The house had burned down a week before and had already been completely cleared. His student was the proud owner of a vacant lot that was worth only a fraction of what he'd just paid. He owned it. Period! No recourse. No rewind. Just a lot of sadness and self-pity.

Rehab and Rent, Flip, or Lease Option

REHAB

Knowing what to rehab, how much you spend and how far you will go with it is a moving target. Always keep in mind that you are not living in this house, the tenants are. You need to rehab according to the market that your rental property is located in. This means the socio-economic market.

You shouldn't put $50/yd carpet in a rental that is located in an upper low-end neighborhood. Likewise you shouldn't put indoor/outdoor carpet in the living room. This is a skill you will develop over time. My intention here is to help you shorten the learning curve and avoid as much expense as possible.

So let's go over the basics. First, we'll discuss carpet since we mentioned it above. In these rentals, use a good brand name like Shaw carpet. Get a neutral color like Candy Truffle. I call it the color of dirt. And it looks nice! Get the lowest grade or weight. Then put a middle-grade pad underneath. This is one of the secrets. A better pad will help the carpet last longer. The color will hide a lot of crud. It is appealing to the eye. It is a 10-year warranty carpet and is standard in the rental business.

When it comes to painting, always use a good paint, at least as good as Behr. Stick with one color for the wall surfaces, like off-white satin, and one color for all the trim, like white semi-gloss. I like the two-tone look and I always use semi-gloss on the trim. You can use flat on ceilings and even walls if you'd like. The challenge with flat paint on walls is that it doesn't clean well and you'll have to repaint more often.

You can also use a more appealing very light neutral color on the walls other than off-white. The two-tone look is appealing and it really doesn't cost that much more.

Hiring a pro to do the painting is a must. They're better and faster than you and me. And your time is much more valuable than theirs. You will use that time to find more deals.

When it comes to plumbing fixtures, don't make the mistake that everyone else makes when they first start out – buying cheap plumbing fixtures. If you pay $29 for a kitchen faucet, you will get what you paid for – CRAP. There's an old saying in plumbing: "If it ain't heavy, it ain't good." If you buy a plumbing fixture and it is loaded with plastic, it will be a waste of your time and money.

I like American Standard products. The product you and I get off the shelf at Home Depot is the same one the plumbers get at the plumbing supply house. This is not true of other manufacturers. Also, the American Standard warranty is like gold. No fuss, no muss. If you have a problem they take care of it. You won't have a problem though. Their products stand up to a lot of use and abuse.

Don't go cheap on windows. For rentals I use American Craftsman. They are good, double-hung, double-pane, and all vinyl-clad windows with a good long and solid warranty. If you get the cheapies you will be wasting your time and money.

My favorite subject is contractors. Okay, it's not my favorite subject. This is one of the worst parts of the whole business. It's hard to find good contractors and they don't last forever. I have had contractors I've known for years turn bad on me. At the first sign of trouble – like with women, trucks, alcohol, drugs, money or health – they seem to disappear into the dark side quite rapidly. Not all of them do this but an alarmingly high percentage relative to society at large.

I have friends who are contractors. I love them like brothers. But when %@#$ happens, I have to cut them off. They can harm you as much as they can help you. Always remember this: when you are hiring contractors, even if you have solid referrals, you must do a background check on them just like you do with tenants. Always make sure they are insured and bonded. Ask for these credentials. If they screw something up and they are not insured, the liability will fall directly to you as the owner of the property. This is not something you should take a shortcut on. Period!

I had a pair of contractors working with me for years. They became friends of mine. They were twin brothers and worked well together. One was the straight man and one was the booze-swigging, whore-mongering derelict who I don't even think had a valid driver's license. They were some of the first guys I ever hired. I hired the straight man and he later brought in his brother. I still should have checked him out. What I discovered after years of good work was a little bit of fraud. Nothing major but I decided not to take any chances.

I caught them cheating on supplies. They would buy more than enough supplies and charge me for it, then return the excess to Home Depot after the job was completed. It may not sound like a big deal – especially since we are only talking about a few measly dollars and cents. However, my knowledge of human nature, and the propensity of people to keep taking when they get away with a little taking, dictated that I act and act swiftly to send a message to everybody else working for me.

I had another guy try this on me prior to this occurrence. He was dumb enough to turn in a receipt for some lumber that he'd already charged me for. He didn't turn in the receipt before and thought he could use it on his next job. The problem was that he had 4x4 pressure treated lumber on there to the tune of $400 and the current job was an inside kitchen job requiring no pressure treated lumber. What an idiot. He must have assumed I didn't check receipts. I did.

I have friends who have been ripped off by their own family in business. One such situation involved over $100,000! You can never be too sure. Embezzlement and employee theft is a huge problem. My parents owned a business before they retired and had an accounting category just for theft. And it was about 10% of business. That is ridiculous. But it is real. You need to have systems to track your income and your expense. Expenses will already eat you alive if you're not careful. Throw loss-due-to-theft on top of that and it's no wonder so many people go out of business.

You can find good contractors. They are out there. Always ask for references. Look at other work they have done. Ask their prior customers how the contractor was when it came to keeping to schedule and budget and how well they communicated. Start new guys off small before you give them big jobs. Look at their appearance. Do they look like they are living the clean life or do they look like hell? Who do you want to give the keys to your property?

Whenever you are involved in a big job – more than a few thousand dollars – don't pay all at once. Give the contractor a little supply money up front. Then give them a little more when they have the basic work done. Then give them another payment when they are near completion. Hold on to the last payment until the job is complete to your satisfaction. No excuses here. If go to the final walk through and the contractor says, "Oh, I'll come back tomorrow and finish that little bit myself," do not give him the last of the agreed upon payment. If he is good to his word, he'll finish completely and then you can pay him the rest. A lot of investors fall prey to this gimmick. Even if it is innocent, it is still a problem. Don't do it!

RENT, SELL (FLIP), LEASE OPTION

There is always more than one way to make money!

I have seen more than a few investors buy and remodel a rental property with the intention of renting. Nothing wrong with that! That's who I wrote this book for. However, many investors get to this point and wonder if they can just sell the property and cash in big now while it looks so good. I say, yes you can, maybe.

If you start out on the rental path and later want to try to sell, that is not a problem. If it doesn't sell, keep it. You bought it as a rental anyway! On the other hand you cannot buy a house that you intend to flip, then remodel it and try to profit by renting. It may work in certain circumstances, but not very often. If you are remodeling to flip a house you will use better materials – paint, carpet, and cabinetry. The ends will not justify the means if you rent. Your property will likely be over improved. You cost basis will likely be higher because you bought in a better neighborhood. Generally speaking, if you bought a property to eventually rent then you should usually stick with the plan.

There is a hybrid approach to cashing in that works really well in a tight money market. (A tight money market is a market in which borrowing money is a little tougher than usual.) The basic concept is that of a Lease with an Option to Buy. This is actually two different disciplines.

Also, notice I did not say "Rent to Own." *Never* do a rent to own. When you rent to own, you are earmarking a certain portion of the rent to be counted as part of the purchase price of the house. This gives the tenant an equitable interest in the house which is a loose form of at least one of the seven rights of ownership. (What this means to you is that if the tenant stops paying rent or you have to evict them for any reason you will not be able to.) The way the law works in these matters is that you will have to foreclose on the tenant because of their equitable interest in the property. An eviction may take about one month. A foreclosure will take at least a year or more in most cases. It depends on the state. What matters is that you put yourself in a very risky position with a rent to own. A lease option is not as risky.

A lease option is really two transactions. One transaction is to rent the property to a tenant. This is strictly a lease standing on its own two feet. The option is really a document where you, the optionor, are giving the optionee (your tenant) the right to purchase the property at a later date. They have to purchase this option from you for a fee. The option fee is non-refundable. If they don't exercise their option by a certain date you can either extend the option period for another fee or choose not to extend it, and they simply remain as tenants if that is what you want.

If they do not pay their rent you can evict them because the option fee they paid you does not count toward the purchase price of the house. They just purchased the *right* to purchase the house at a later date. The fee they pay you covers the risk you take by taking your property off the market for the option period. The price is usually locked in so you have the risk of not realizing any appreciation in that period of time. You also assume the risk of normal wear and tear on your property. And if that's not enough, you are doing the tenant the favor of giving them time to get their finances in order enough to secure a loan to pay you off.

During this time you will be their biggest creditor. One of the big advantages to this is that if they don't end up buying, you keep the option fee and can try the lease option again. I have had houses I lease-optioned three times before they sold. I came out the winner, not just because I got to keep the option fee, but also because I can charge more rent on a lease option and the tenants generally take better care of the property when it's their intention to buy. So even when a sale doesn't go the whole way through – a situation most non-investors see as a failure – you still win!

Investing in rental properties can be a lot of fun. Every day is different. Every property is different. Every customer is different. You can make a lot of money and buy your own freedom. I did. I retired from the corporate world after investing for five years. I know guys who have done it in less. I have taught many investors who have gone on to create immense wealth and income by doing just what I did. I hope you will, too.

As you begin to grow your portfolio you will be confronted with the question: "Should I self-manage or hire a professional property manager to take care of the day to day operations of my growing rental property portfolio?" The answer is: "It depends." Ha. I used to get frustrated when lawyers would give me that answer to my questions. I am OK with you self-managing for a while so you can learn the ropes and get to know what it takes to manage rental properties. However, remember that every hour you spend managing your properties is one less hour you have to do what will really make you the big bucks and that is… Invest! Also, what about precious time with your loved ones?

So, what I suggest is that when you see the strains on your time and relationships developing, it is time to consider bringing on a professional property manager. I did early on and I knew what to expect from the property manager based on my own personal experience. It turned into money well invested. In fact, I went on to build my own property management business as a result. But that's another story for another time. In the next section you and I will be going over this big crazy business of property management. Are you ready? Let's go!

For more information visit:

https://bit.ly/2WCChJG

For a limited time, get 1 month FREE membership
to our Silver community where you have access to
free tools, contracts, Real Estate Statistics, and
Expert Insider Information including personal interviews,
and other books for FREE!

Turning Rental Problems Into Real Estate Profits

Your Anxiety Threshold

I believe every beginning investor must go through some really trying experiences in order to test their mettle and push through perceived barriers of stress and anxiety. I was no exception even though I have a pretty high tolerance to stress.

The third property I bought was 49 Grant Street in Etna. Over the years this property was a real cash cow. To this day I can't understand why. The lady I bought it from said the same thing. I was in for a rough ride from the day of closing (actually before).

The seller delayed the closing so she could collect unpaid rents. This should have been my first warning. Fortunately, I poured over all of the property documentation including the leases, where I discovered that she had collected the last month's rent up front. No one else knew this and she didn't disclose it. So what would have happened is that I would not have been credited with that at the closing had I not discovered it. When the tenants' leases were up they would not have paid the last month's rent – pointing rightly to their leases. The seller, of course, had conveniently forgotten this little tidbit of information.

This should have been my second warning. When we went to close for the second time, the title company had information from the municipality that there were outstanding water and sewage charges. The seller insisted she had paid them. She convinced the title officer, but not me. The title officer insisted on closing – which meant I would have been in breach had I not closed.

The time of this second closing, as required by the seller, was at 5:30 in the afternoon, after the municipality had closed for the day. How convenient for the seller. That should have been my third clue.

As it turned out, I fought the title company for nearly a year to clean up the delinquent and unpaid water and sewage. For those of you who are new to investing in real estate, water and sewage are typically lien-able items, which means they don't care who owns the house or who used the water – if it's not paid they place a lien on the house, so whoever owns it at the time wins the "prize" and inherits the problem.

I know we are entrepreneurs and we don't have "problems" – we have "challenges." Well, I'm telling you this was a problem!

This was all just the beginning. It turned out the nice little man on the first floor who was the single parent of the cute little girl in kindergarten, was also a professional deadbeat and tenant from hell. His cute little niece and her fiancé lived on the second floor. But that's okay, because I had a crackhead on the third floor. He was a social guy, so he shared some of his crack with the cute young lady on the second floor who quickly became what is known as a "Crack Ho." I didn't know what the H@#$ crack was or how bad it was… but I would a few years later.

Anyhow, back to Mr. Wonderful (I changed his name to protect the guilty) on the first floor. Trying to get rent out of this guy was like trying to extract a molar from a bull by going through his ass. It was difficult and messy. Oh, I'm stubborn. I got my rent, but not without a lot of work.

This was my first experience. Of course I learned a lot of lessons. I must have had this guy in court three or more times. Each time he would come up with the money at the last possible moment. I finally beat him, but not without him causing me a lot of extra work and getting me so agitated with his games that I nearly resorted to violence.

In the meantime, because the second-floor girl was spiraling downward into the dark world of crack addiction, she lost her job. While her fiancé was still working trying to make ends meet, she resorted to having sex with crack dealers in order to get her fix. Her fiancé eventually found out and kicked her out, then moved out himself.

At one point I went over to the property to make a repair and assumed she was home. I knocked and yelled but to no avail. I eventually let myself in, and when I got close to the bedroom I thought someone might be in bed. So I yelled again. This time the girl, buck-naked, jumped up from her near coma sleep and screamed. I screamed too and got the heck out of there. Luckily, I didn't get in trouble for that and I learned a valuable lesson:

> *Never enter an apartment on your own if you suspect someone is there and no one answers your calls – especially if you are of the opposite gender.*

The third difficult requirement was to rid myself of the zombie on the third floor. This at first appeared to be difficult, but ultimately I got a lucky break. The guy got hit by a car in front of the house. One evening I went over to the property to see the third-floor tenant after making arrangements and leaving a reminder notice on his apartment door. When I arrived, I knocked and yelled numerous times. I knew he was there and so I eventually opened the door and walked in. Sure enough, about three of them were there. None were moving. Lights were on and so was the television. I tried to wake the ringleader but he wouldn't budge. He wasn't dead and he wasn't asleep. He simply believed that he could either: a) fool me into believing he was dead, b) fool me into believing he was in a non-waking form of sleep, or c) thought he could make himself invisible.

He and his two genius cohorts eventually opened their eyes. They finally realized I wasn't giving up. I had him sign an agreement that stated that he was to vacate the apartment by the weekend if he could not make good on his rent. He signed it and he moved out the following weekend.

In the process he got hit by a car in front of the house. He refused medical attention and we never saw him again. *Hallelujah!*

Now, as the new sheriff in town, I was able to clean house and refill it with nice young female tenants – complete with jobs and checking accounts.

The next several years were good times for this property and profitable for me. But not without a cost to myself. While all the aforementioned circumstances were taking place, I had hit my wall at the time. It was my first real test dealing with tenants and I eventually prevailed.

However, one fine day in October as the leaves were changing colors I had to get out of there. I don't mean the location where I was at the time but rather the state of mind I was in. I was either having a nervous breakdown or an anxiety attack. I told my wife Susan we had to go somewhere, anywhere. It was beautiful outside and I wanted us all to go together – Susan, me, Annie, and Andrew. We hopped in the car and I just started driving. We eventually found our way to Squaw Run Park, near where we lived. We got out and started walking down a path – any old path would do. The kids kept looking at me and Susan, not understanding what we were doing. Quite frankly, neither did I.

They kept asking what we were doing there when they could get at least one more swim day in at the neighbor's pool before the weather turned too cold. I don't even know if I answered them. I was numb. It all seemed so surreal. I knew they were there but I was not engaged with them, or anyone, or anything. While walking, I spotted a rock and just sat down on it and melted. I remember faintly hearing Andrew ask Susan, "What's wrong with Daddy?" I don't remember what Susan said, but no matter. I was having my moment. And it worked. I eventually came out of the fog and we went back home.

From that moment on I was able to handle whatever ridiculous tenant problem (I mean "challenge") that came my way. I was always able to keep things in perspective and I kept my cool for a lot of years. Oh, I eventually grew tired of outsmarting deadbeat tenants and found myself lowering to their standards of uncivil language and treatment. That's about the time I realized I needed professional property management. But that's another story for another time.

For the moment, I was determined to profit from my real estate, my way. I had to learn the hard way. There were plenty of ways to learn how to buy rental property, but not much was available to guide me once I owned it. I eventually got so good that I started my own Property Management company.

Would you like to learn from my lessons without having to repeat them yourself? Good. I wrote this for you!

Getting Started Managing Your Own Rentals

This business, like all other businesses, is about systems. You have to buy, create, or otherwise implement and follow profitable, efficient, and affordable systems. You must master all of these systems, or as you grow, hire others who are masters themselves. And these systems must be integrated with each other so there is no duplication of effort. They must work seamlessly together.

The beautiful thing about a good system of systems is that it allows you to grow your portfolio with as much profit and as little pain as possible. Keep in mind that a system that works well for 100 or fewer rental units may not work well for a portfolio of a thousand or more units. So whenever you install a new system, make sure you are taking care of today's needs as well as having one eye on tomorrow.

Also, there may be times when you simply replace what you have with a better system. Currently, I like the Property Ware Property Management System. It works very well no matter how large your portfolio is. The software is priced according to the number of units you have and it works well for people managing their own units and for professional property management firms. (What I'm talking about here is a software system that integrates and ties together the other systems needed to profitably operate rental properties. The other systems – or more appropriately processes and procedures – involve marketing, advertising, bookkeeping, managing maintenance and repairs, screening tenants, leasing, evictions, turnovers, capital improvements, selling, buying, networking, and public relations.)

THE BUYING PROCESS

There are a lot of factors to consider.

Area

In the world of real estate there are a lot of different types of areas – commercial, industrial, retail, agricultural, and of course residential. With the world of residential real estate there are two basic types of areas – owner occupied and rental. Within the world of rental real estate there are single-family homes and multi-family homes. There is of course some crossover. (In other words, within the world of single-family homes there are homeowner occupants and renters. Within the world of multi-units there are owner occupants and there are renters.)

In the world of rental properties, I strongly recommend that new investors drive by different neighborhoods before buying. This is because in the rental community there are different grades of properties and neighborhoods. At the very bottom there is government housing. At the very top there are luxury homes and apartments. In between there are low-income, moderate-income and middle-income housing.

While I was aggressively growing, I focused on moderate-income housing. It provided the greatest rental income relative to price. The properties and neighborhoods in less desirable areas are too much trouble. To be sure, there are plenty of good people who are not as financially fortunate as you and me, and there are plenty of bad people who are more financially fortunate than you and me. The point here is that in the least desirable areas, you will have more problems with criminal activity. You will have more people who are not working. You will have more single mothers trying to make ends meet all on their own. All of this puts you farther down the line when it comes to paying for everything that folks in these areas have to pay for. It also means that when the S@&! hits the fan, they will leave you and your property in shambles without care for you. They will leave all of their crap. Not only will they not clean, they will leave a lot of extra disgusting filth for you to clean. In these housing areas, you may think you're getting a good deal. You are not. Stay away. *Run away!* Run as fast as you can.

Screening

Screening is perhaps the most important activity relative to your ability to profit in the rental business, once you have acquired a rental property. Your profit shows up in the form of Net Operating Income (NOI). You would have to really screw up to not make money. The easiest and most common way that people screw up is to lease your rental to the wrong people. An effective screening process is what is required in order to minimize your risks and mistakes, and maximize your successes and profit.

It is better to have a vacant unit than to have a bad tenant. Not only is a bad tenant more likely to not pay rent (on time or at all), but a bad tenant is also more likely to be a filthy dirty pig and even damage your rental unit. So not only will you likely *not* collect your rent, you will likely lose money due to filth and damage. All the while, you will have to pay taxes and insurance, principal and interest (if you have a loan), and perhaps even utilities like gas and electric, or at least water and sewage.

The negative effects of having a bad tenant can be quite devastating. This needs to be taken very seriously.

One of the easiest ways to screen tenants is to use NTN – National Tenant Network. If a prospective tenant is not paying other people, they will likely not pay you either. Furthermore, if they are getting (or have been) evicted, it is likely for a very good reason. Believe the current landlord, not the tenant, when it comes to why they are being evicted.

In fact, you not only want to check current landlord references, you also want to find and check prior landlords for the history of the prospective tenants – do they pay on time? Are they clean and respectful of property? Sometimes current landlords will give a good reference just to get rid of a bad tenant. Beware of this trick from unscrupulous landlords.

I have had prospective tenants give me all kinds of reasons why they were getting evicted. All of the reasons were due to someone else's fault. And almost every time it was the landlord who was the jerk. The landlord didn't take care of the place so the tenant didn't think they should have to pay rent. The tenant started filing all kinds of complaints with every agency under the sun to make the landlord out to be the bad guy. Imagine that – the tenant is behind on the rent and it's the landlord who is the bad guy!

I have had prospective tenants give me fictitious references. One easy way to divulge this deceit is to ask questions. Remember, before you even entertain the thought of turning possession of your property over to someone, you should get an application and proof of income and residency. This is in the form of paystubs and a current lease. You always want current and previous landlord contact info. This is because you may not want to believe what the current landlord is telling you. Whether you are speaking to the current or previous landlord, use their lease and the application as a guide. If the tenant states that they were paying $750 in rent per month, ask the landlord on the phone to verify that the applicant is paying "$700" per month and see what they say. By asking questions in this way you can ferret out the phony landlord.

Essentially, what you are looking for are people with jobs and income you can verify and a rental history you can substantiate.

Before any of this begins though, you need to do a little marketing and advertising to get the ball rolling.

MARKETING AND ADVERTISING

There are a lot of ways to advertise your vacant rental units. But first we need to agree on terminology. People often use "marketing" and "advertising" interchangeably.

Here is how Webster's dictionary defines the two words:

mar·ket·ing: the activities involved in making people aware of a company's products, making sure the products are available to be bought, etc.

   a) the act or process of selling or purchasing in a market
   b) the process or technique of promoting, selling, and distributing a product or service
   c) an aggregate of functions involved in moving goods from producer to consumer

ad·ver·tis·ing: published or broadcast advertisements, the business of creating advertisements

   a) the action of calling something to the attention of the public especially by paid announcements
   b) ADVERTISEMENTS <the magazine contains much advertising>
   c) the business of preparing advertisements for publication or broadcast

To make it a little bit easier, to me "marketing" has more to do with learning and understanding where you own your rental properties, the prospective tenants who want to live in rental units, and determining the best pricing strategy and methods to reach out to your marketplace. "Advertising" has more to do with understanding and using the available methods for getting the right message to your market, and the process of creating that message.

Having said that, there are a number of ways to send your message to your marketplace. Here are a few:

Tenant referral program: Reward your existing tenants for referring new tenants to you. I have no problem rewarding a good tenant for bringing me a good referral. $50 has always worked for me. (Please note that I said "Good Tenant" and "Good Referral." In other words, don't promote this program to just any old tenant. Promote it only to good tenants for various reasons. First of all you are rewarding good behavior! And secondly, birds of a feather flock together. Good people usually have good friends. Just like our parents told us when we were growing up, "People judge you by the company you keep.")

Local colleges: They often have online bulletin boards you can use to advertise a vacancy. Simply locate your local colleges online. Look to see if they have an online bulletin board. When in doubt just call them and ask for instructions. They're used to it. Please note: renting to college students is a specialty. You will need a rental that is built like a fortress. You will need to have some very strict and enforceable guidelines. You will need to have parents co-sign. Always have an annual lease. The renter must foot the bill for the summer months. Have individual leases for each roommate. There are pros and cons to this approach versus having one lease where each student is held jointly and individually liable for the entire lease amount. I like the former approach because then I get four parents as guarantors instead of just one.

Craigslist: Bar none, this is one of the best ways to reach your marketplace. It's free and has a wide audience. They even have a tutorial for you.

Facebook, Twitter, LinkedIn: Use your social media network(s) to get the word out. But be careful. There are rules of etiquette that you must first learn for each one. The number one taboo is spamming your network. Never abuse the privilege of social media. If you do you will be shunned, un-friended, un-liked, un-connected, and unsuccessful!

Church: Churches usually have weekly bulletins in which you can advertise your vacancies. This works well for large congregations, but I would use it in small churches as well. Look in your church's current bulletin and there should be instructions, or at least contact information, you can use to get started.

Grocery store: They usually have a bulletin board where you can pin a flyer with tear-off phone number tabs. You need to check this regularly. Sometimes the flyers disappear. Sometimes other people will post their notice right over top of yours. If you're really lucky, all of your number tabs will be gone!

Restaurants: They often will let you put a stack of flyers or business cards near the checkout. The next time you're dining at one of your favorite local restaurants, speak to the owner or manager. Someone with the authority to act is always on duty at a restaurant. Please note that there are some other great marketing and advertising opportunities here. For example, ask the proprietor if he/she will offer a discount or free meal coupon (get several) for you to use as a reward to give your good tenants who refer other good tenants to you. Use your imagination!

Local publications: Penny Saver, Green Sheet, they're in every community and are very inexpensive. Unlike the large publications (like your big city paper), I have had a lot of success with these types of publications. Call and ask for their rules and regulations. Learn the rules of their advertising and you will master the game. Some ads you will place for 1-2 weeks. Some you will place for a year. You will also learn where in the publication to place your ads, how big, how small, special features, etc. (Hint: Any time you can have your ad placed in a box you will get better results!)

Marketing has more to do with understanding the marketplace relative to your product or service and your clientele.

You always want to keep informed about what types and sizes of rentals are in demand. I have always done well with 3-bedroom houses and 2-bedroom apartments. That's not to say that you don't want 1- and 3-bedroom apartments. You do. You just want to have the right ratio of 1's, 2's and 3's for your area.

With houses just stick with 3-bedrooms and you can't go wrong. You also want to keep informed about what rents are being asked and paid. I check the Sunday paper every week to see what others are charging for rent. I also check Craigslist regularly. It also helps to know what advertising mediums work well in your particular area. For example, everyone has heard of Craigslist. It is great. I love it. But would you believe it works well in some areas and not in others? Almost every area has a Penny Saver or a Green Sheet. I never liked the big newspapers. They were always more expensive and didn't work as well.

Advertising has more to do with getting your message to market.

Once you can afford it, you may want to have your own website. I have also put up flyers at grocery stores, churches and libraries. Your message should always appeal to consumer's emotional side. In other words, instead of regurgitating a bunch of features followed by the price, use descriptive wording that focuses on benefits. "Avoid long commutes. This newly remodeled 1-bedroom apartment is just a block from the subway," is far better than "1-bedroom apartment, downtown, close to transportation." Which phrase would you be more inclined to respond to? Never list all of the features, because you want the reader to have to call you to get that information.

Responding to Ads

When prospects do call, you now have the chance to do a little phone screening before going any further.

When a prospective tenant calls you, build a little rapport first. Give both of you a moment or two to get comfortable speaking with each other before jumping right into business. It is not only good business practice, but you may also find out valuable information while doing so.

There are certain rules about what questions you can or can't ask. For example, never ask, "How many children do you have?" Rather, ask, "How many bedrooms do you need?" You will get the information you desire, but you won't have crossed over into any gray areas as far as discrimination goes.

There is a lot more to this soapbox. I suggest you Google the latest on protected classes and familiarize yourself with the information.

Anyhow, the next thing you want to accomplish in your conversation is to see if your unit is suitable for the caller. In other words, why go any further if it turns out your unit is on the third floor and the caller needs to be on the first floor? So, once you have developed rapport, you must focus on what you have to offer – your supply – and what the caller needs – their demand. Only then, once you've determined that there is a possible match, do you discuss the particular features of your available rental unit.

At this point you want to do some more screening. In a conversational way, you want to find out where they work and how long they've been working there. You'll want to find out how long they have lived in their current home and why are they looking to move. The longer they have lived in one place the better. The longer they have worked in one place the better. Ask if they have pets and if they have roommates.

Be sure to write all of this down. It will become more important later on in the process. If at the end of your conversation you are satisfied that the caller may indeed be a good candidate, then go ahead and give them the specific address and ask them to drive by your property. This is a good test of their sincerity. If they are the real deal, they will in fact drive by your property. If they like what they see – the neighborhood – you will get a call back from them with a request to see the rental unit.

Showing a Rental

I never used to go to a vacant unit to show it to only one prospective tenant. What I did was set up two-hour time slots during the upcoming Saturday to show the vacant unit to as many prospects as I could. I would schedule them ten minutes apart, knowing there would be some no-shows. Some of the prospects will see each other. This could work to your advantage in that it will create a sense of urgency. More importantly though is your time and safety. Doing the showings this way means you will be going to the unit during the day, when other people are around. The only time I would go to a unit to meet one person is if I had already met them and they wanted to bring a spouse, boyfriend or girlfriend, or roommate – or more likely to have them sign the lease.

At the big Saturday showing I always had applications on hand. You can't refuse to give an application to anyone, but you can charge a fee. I always charge a fee to cover my time and the cost of running a credit report and background check.

Never rent on the spot! Even if they have a mountain of cash – BIG RED FLAG! – take the applications and run their credit financials, rental history, employment history and public information. Do not decide based on who you liked best, or was the best looking, or had the most cash. It is this front-runner for whom you are going to check references. Check employment and current and prior landlord references. Last but not least, compare the application they filled out with the notes you took during the initial phone conversation and look for differences. If there are any, this could spell trouble.

At the end of the day you should have a front-runner based on good solid systems and practices instead of guesswork and wishful thinking. I cannot emphasize enough how important this critical step is. It is this step, more than any other, which will make or break you and your aspirations for building a large real estate portfolio.

Section 8

Currently, I do not recommend Section 8.

Sorry, Uncle Sam. What used to have some appeal for property owners has grown into a nightmare of abuse and incompetence. Go ahead, sue me. I call them as I see them.

First thing first. *Section 8* refers to the participants (tenants), not the property. Section 8 has grown into another government fiasco where taxpayers' dollars are squandered on mountains of waste. It is a form of slavery to the tenants in the program. I know, go ahead and sue me again.

I have met young female single mothers of children from multiple fathers who came to view my rental units. I have also met their sisters who were on Section 8 too, and their mother (or grandmother) who boasted that she went on Section 8 when it first came out and has been on it ever since (and was proud of the fact!), and she made sure all of her daughters got on Section 8 when they became adults.

As you can see, there is no incentive built into this program for its participants to get out. When owners rent their properties to Section 8 tenants, they give up a lot of rights. Section 8 tells the tenants not to give you a deposit until after the inspection and lease is signed or not at all. They are forced to use Section 8 leases which can get the owner into trouble, as you will see other places in this book. The owners are forced to go through an annual Section 8 inspection and are held responsible for repairing damage caused by the Section 8 tenants.

The initial inspection doesn't occur until after the property has been held for the tenant, thereby holding the owner hostage. The rents are below market value (they used to be at, or even above market value, in some cases). I remember when they lowered what they would pay on a single-family home, not because of market conditions but because Section 8 determined tenants would have to pay higher gas and electric bills in a single-family home. Duh! However, single-family homes are more valuable than apartments and do command higher rents in the marketplace.

If you do rent to a Section 8 tenant it will be months before you receive your first rent check. To their credit, they do make it retroactive. However, in the meantime won't you have bills to pay?

It used to be that if a Section 8 tenant broke the terms of the contract by not paying their portion of the rent, or by causing damage, if you evicted them then Section 8 would kick them out of the program until they made good on their debt.

But that's not all. You'll have to submit paperwork six months in advance of a lease renewal to raise your rent. Section 8 will conveniently lose this paperwork. You won't know until the deadline has passed when you can submit paperwork again. You'll have to go downtown to wait in line with all the deadbeat tenants just to get an answer because you won't get one over the phone – and that's even if you get someone on the phone.

Not so anymore. Now we as owners have no leverage and yet we give up control. No, this is not a good deal for property owners. When someone approaches you about renting your property to a Section 8 tenant, run. *Run far away and run fast.*

The following will illustrate why the Section 8 program, and all subsidy programs, are inherently flawed.

About ten years ago, Section 8 implemented a homeownership program. I was thrilled. Here we have a way to help those who really do deserve help to acquire short-term subsidy and also provide some incentive to get off the program – and instead of paying rent perpetually, make mortgage payments and become a homeowner.

On paper it looks great. I'm an entrepreneur and an idealist (and yes, even a dreamer). I readily volunteered to sell one of my newly renovated houses to a Section 8 tenant who was on the home ownership program. And guess what? It worked. I sold a nice little brick 3-bedroom home, in a nice neighborhood to a great hardworking single mother of three who wanted to stop receiving subsidies and raise her children in a nice neighborhood. This was awesome.

Now I was going to help all of my single mother Section 8 tenants in single-family homes to buy those very same homes. What I discovered though is that Section 8 had to discontinue this program – not because of funding – but because of a lack of willing participants.

I learned this after I had unsuccessfully attempted to help other participants to buy instead of rent. Time after time I got the same response: "Why would I give up a good thing when I get my rent paid for me? If I buy a house I will lose my subsidy." Exactly! Folks, we do not have a moral obligation to *give* someone a fish. (Well okay, maybe one fish). But we do have a moral obligation to *teach* others how to fish. And thus the inherent flaw. These folks have no incentive. We take it away from them by continuing to *give* them fish instead of requiring that they *learn* how to fish.

And it's the same with every other kind of subsidy program that is allowed to go on indefinitely.

You know one of the worst things about this whole program is that because these participants have no skin in the game, they feel no obligation to care for your property like proud people should. I have seen more properties dirtied, abused, and damaged by people who have their deposits and rents paid for them by other people. Have you heard enough?

Charitable Organizations

Now that you have a vague idea of how I feel about Section 8, let me tell you how I feel about private organizations that help people (temporary help) get on their feet.

I like them. I like them a lot.

Back in the late '90s I bought a house from a local Pittsburgh non-denominational church. One of their members had bequeathed a duplex to them in their will. The church didn't want it and I did. So I bought it.

I used the biblical teaching about being a good custodian with treasures, and struck a good deal for myself and solved the church's problem, too. Anyhow, after I bought the house, the listing agent (Austin Decimone, since deceased, bless his heart – a good man, a man of God and good friend) called and asked if I had ever thought about renting to refugees.

I could do my part to help a worthy cause. I said yes and that I would lower the deposit requirement and the amount of rent to help.

It turns out we were helping to sponsor Bosnian refugees. As you might remember, Bosnia was caught in the middle of an attempt at genocide by one of the former Soviet satellite states. It was horrible and I was glad to help.

Fast-forward ten years to the Bevan Place apartments. This is an eighty-unit apartment complex a few miles south of Pittsburgh – the crowning jewel in my vast apartment empire. My property manager was approached by a representative of the Jewish Community League. I agreed to meet with the rep at the complex to discuss her wish to place Burmese and Nepalese refugees in our complex.

I must tell you that as long as I can remember some of my best friends have been Jewish. God bless them all. When I was a child, Johnny Rose and I were thick as blood. In fact we were (and if I remember the rules correctly, still are) blood brothers. We were like peanut butter and jelly. Johnny's mom and dad, Norma and Ben, took me in like I was one of their family. They even took me on vacation with them. They taught me a lot by their actions. I will always love Norma Rose. Norma, if you're reading this, I love you like you were my own mother. For all of you out there who are not Jewish or don't have Jewish friends I feel sorry for you. (The Jewish race has suffered more than any other human race and they live successful and fulfilling lives in spite of their painful history. They are masters of business and money in ways you can only appreciate if you yourself are informed about matters of business and money. You should read a book by Rabi Daniel Lapin, titled *Thou Shalt Prosper*. You will understand better the biblical teaching of money and dispel some of the lies you have been told about it.)

Anyhow, back to the Jewish Community League Refugee Program. This program does not give more than one fish. It is designed to teach refugees from Burma and Nepal to fish for themselves. Thus they are responsible for their own rent after one or two months. And guess what? These tenants are some of the best at promptly paying their rent.

So yes, I like this program. It was designed intelligently by people who understand human nature – and that is why it works. These participants have incentive to succeed and be independent, partly because they know they will have to fish.

The Lease

Use a lease that will stand the test of legal challenges.

Let's get this squared away right in the beginning of this section. Please ignore all of the FREE leases you can get over the internet. Sure, you can use anything that is in writing. But you should know that *Real Estate Law is the only law that requires contracts to be in writing in order to be enforceable*.

There's an old saying in Real Estate and that is: "If it ain't in writing, it ain't REAL!" And that is true in the practical and the legal sense. Oral leases aren't worth the paper they're not written on. Get it? Don't listen to the old timers who say, "I never get it in writing because that way if they screw up I can just boot 'em out." What a joke. If you have an oral lease and you have to go to court you will be S.C.R.E.W.E.D. – PERIOD!

Okay. Now that we have that out of the way, the next question is what lease to use. Listen to me and do not ever be swayed on this. Always, and I mean ALWAYS, use a lease that is from your state's Board of Realtors. This lease has already been PRE-approved in the court system. It will stand the legal assault from tenant's attorneys all the way to the Supreme Court.

There are cases you can look up where a Court of Common Pleas Judge threw out a Section 8 lease because he didn't recognize its validity in his court. In a Commonwealth, the judge is the law. What I mean is that it doesn't matter what your contract says… the judge can disallow it, disapprove of it, overrule it, and make you start all over again. How about that?

Even a lease from the Department of Housing and Urban Development may not stand up in court.

Now, when you show up in court and you have a lease from your state's Association of Realtors, the judge knows it is already pre-approved up through the ranks and he must accept it. Have I stated clearly enough what lease you are to use?

Here is where it gets even better. You can add addendums to your lease, and I think you should. The reason is that the lease mentioned above is considered a neutral lease. In other word, it favors neither the landlord nor the tenant. The *free* leases you get on the internet are usually slanted one way or the other. The really long ones are usually landlord friendly. The really short ones are usually tenant friendly. It doesn't matter though, because you're not using those leases.

As a result of the state's Association of Realtors leases being neutral, there may not be enough legal language in them to cover all of the oddities and entities in the world of rental real estate. So, I am going to give you a sampling of some of my rules and regulations. Use them at your own discretion. I make no claims as to their legality. And you must know that any contract – in order for it to be legal – must not run contrary to federal, state, or local laws.

Okay, here you go:

Rules and Regulations

The following Rules and Regulations apply to the rental unit, including building and grounds. Violation of the following rules and regulations shall be construed as a breach of the terms and conditions, and a forfeiture, of lease agreement.

Landlord, at landlord's option may end this lease agreement, by notice in writing, and tenant may have no further right to possession of rental unit. These rules and regulations apply to tenants and any and all guests of tenants.

1) Use and Occupancy – Rental unit shall be used solely as a private residential dwelling and occupied solely by those persons listed to be occupants on Tenant's rental application and/or lease agreement.

2) Illegal Drugs – Tenant shall not keep, store, possess, use, or sell illegal drugs of any and all kind.

3) Firearms – Tenant shall not possess, store, or discharge (fire) any type of firearms or other deadly weapon of any kind at any time on said property.

4) Assignment and Sublease – Tenant shall not sublet, rent, assign, or transfer possession in part or whole to any other person or entity.

5) Alterations to Rental Unit – Tenant shall not make alterations of any kind to rental without prior written permission of Landlord.

6) Plumbing – Tenant is solely responsible for clogged commodes, sinks, tubs, and all other plumbing repairs caused by negligence of Tenant, or Tenant's guests.

7) Waterbeds – Tenant shall not have or use waterbed(s) in rental unit without prior written permission of the Landlord.

8) Pets – Absolutely no pets are permitted on the property unless otherwise authorized by Landlord and stated in lease. Violations will result in a $25.00 penalty fee per month per pet and possible termination of lease by Landlord. Tenant is responsible for any and all damages caused by their pets.

9) Fire Hazard Material – Tenant shall not keep, store, possess, or use any fire hazard material in rental unit or on rental property.

10) Locks/Keys – Tenant shall NOT change lock(s) to rental unit.

11) Dangerous and Hazardous Conditions – Tenant must notify Landlord immediately of any condition that currently exists which creates a hazardous or dangerous situation for the Tenants and their guests, residents in the neighborhood, and/or to the rental property.

12) Local, County, State Laws – Tenant shall follow and abide by all Local, County, State, and Federal laws at all times in rental unit.

13) Cleanliness – Tenant shall keep rental unit in a state of cleanliness at all times.

14) Pests, Rodents & Insects – Tenant is responsible for keeping rental unit free of all pests, rodents, and insects at all times. In case of infestation, tenant is responsible for pest treatment.

15) Noise – Tenant is responsible for keeping all noise including voice, radio, TV or otherwise at reasonable levels at all times. Quiet hours are after 10 P.M. and before 8 A.M. Sunday through Thursday and until 11 P.M. on Friday and Saturday. Local ordinances regarding noise supersede.

16) Upkeep of Grounds – Tenant is responsible for the upkeep of grounds including pick-up of litter, cutting grass, removal of weeds, and trimming hedges unless otherwise stated.

17) Garbage – Tenant shall be responsible for the proper disposal of all garbage according to local ordinances. Tenant is responsible for providing their own garbage cans and that they meet local ordinances.

18) Tenant shall keep the utilities on, and the utilities shall remain in their name for the entire duration of the lease. Under no circumstances (except for an emergency) shall the Tenant shut off the utilities or have them transferred to the Landlord prior to the end of their lease. Failure to comply with this rule will result in a $50.00 fee per utility, plus any

activation fees charged by the utility companies. Important note: shutting off or transferring the utility prior to the end of the Tenant's lease does NOT eliminate the Tenant's responsibility to pay the utilities.

19) Tenants on occasion may have overnight guests. Under no circumstances shall anyone move into the residence without prior written approval from the Landlord. All occupants must be approved by the Landlord.

Security Deposits

Get as much as you can and that is allowed by law.

NOTE: I am not a lawyer. I suggest you get a copy of, and read, the most recent version of the Landlord-Tenant Act.

If you are the unfortunate soul to end up with a bad tenant in spite of your efforts to avoid them in the first place by proper screening, then having a deposit may be your only financial safety net. I am willing to bet that 95% or more of all landlords collect only one deposit and that it is equal to one month's rent. This is what most real estate investors will do who are managing their own properties, but not you.

You certainly should collect the equivalent of at least one month's rent for damages should they occur. The sad news is that this is hardly enough to cover the cost of, well… almost anything these days. So how do you protect yourself?

One way is to collect the equivalent of one month's rent for damages and then collect the equivalent of one-half of one month's rent for cleaning. I call this a cleaning deposit – which is separate and unique from a security deposit to be used for damages.

Another way to protect yourself is to collect all of your deposits and your first month's rent up front, and in addition to that, you can collect the last month's rent up front as well. This is particularly important if you are renting to a tenant who may have passed the screening process but your intuition is telling you there is something to be cautious about.

There are other deposits you can collect that deal with pets and smokers and they will be discussed later.

When it comes to deposits, you need to be aware of some pretty serious laws. *Security deposits are not your money.* They are the tenant's money. You are assuming the role of caretaker for that money while the tenant is in a lease to rent one of your properties. *Security deposits must be held in an escrow account.* This account is typically a checking account. If the account earns interest, you have to pass this interest on to the tenant when they vacate your rental property.

After you hold a deposit for 2 years you have to begin accruing interest on the money. Some landlords send this to their tenants every year on the anniversary date of their lease. Others hold it until the tenant leaves and pays them at that time.

You are allowed to raise your deposits until the tenant has been there for 5 years.

When a tenant vacates your property you have 30 days to return their deposit to them. If you keep any portion of the deposit you have to provide a written explanation of why you kept some of the tenant's money and what it was used for.

I know some landlords who insist on doing their walk-through alone, without the tenant being present. Please keep in mind that if the tenant requests their presence during your walk-through you have to let them.

You should use a walk-through form that lists all of the pertinent items in each room. Fill this out and have the tenants sign it. I suggest you take pictures, too. This is very important. You cannot be too careful. Judges are notorious for being hard on landlords and easy on tenants when it comes to this subject.

If a tenant sues you over a security deposit, you better have your ducks in a row. The law allows them to sue you for treble (triple) damages. In other words, if the tenant's security deposit is $1,000, they can sue you for $3,000. See why this is such an important topic?

REMEMBER: I am not a lawyer. I suggest you get a copy of, and read, the most recent version of the Landlord-Tenant Act.

Pets

Which is better – a "No Pet" policy or a "Pet Profit Policy"?

Oh, I can hear it now. You're saying, "I don't allow pets and I never will."

I used to have a No-Pet policy, too. For years. And for years, I had tenants who kept pets. I evicted these tenants when they defied me. I love pets. I really do, as long as they are my own.

After years of busting people who either didn't read the lease, or didn't understand or even remember it, I decided to take the lemon and make lemonade. At first, I instituted a Pet Deposit and tailored it to the species and size of the pet. I would charge as much as one-half a month's rent for a Pet Deposit. I then added additional rent for pets. And yes, I once again tailored to the species and size of the pet. I found I could get anywhere from $25 to $100 more per month for pets. Here's the one you'll really like – I also charged an additional application fee for Fido or Fuzzy.

This brings up an interesting point. I advertised my vacancies as Pet-Friendly. This way I knew at the outset if applicants had pets, because they let their guard down when they read the ad. I didn't advertise my full pet policy though, only that I allowed pets.

If they got to the screening phase of the transaction I would introduce the pet policy. This did two things. First, the bad pet owners would turn and walk the other way. They probably knew Fuzzy or Fido would be trouble and they knew that since I knew about the pet, they couldn't conceal the fact that they had animals. Secondly, the good pet owners already expected to pay extra for pets. And they love their pets so much they will willingly pay with no hesitation. Furthermore, these pet owners love their pets so much that they are usually very good pet owners. They keep their pets clean. They clean up after their pets. And they train their pets.

So, as a result of my profit-laden pet policy, I end up with the best pet owners – who pay more money for renting my property. Over the years I made far more money on pets than I ever had to shell out for new carpet! It's like built-in profit-packed pet insurance. All the pet owners subsidize the few who cause damage.

You know, I hope none of my former tenants are reading this.

One final thought. There are certain pets that your insurance company will deny coverage for you, as the property owner, if a lawsuit is filed as a result of a prohibited breed of dog harming another. These breeds are Pit Bulls, Rottweilers, Doberman Pincers, and German Shepherds. There may be others, so make sure you check with your insurance carrier to be certain. Also, *don't mention these breeds to applicants until after they have told you what breed they have*. Otherwise they may lie to you. Or, they may have a mixed breed and think it is okay. It is not okay. A dog that is part Pit Bull is still prohibited. Landlord beware!

Smokers

Smokers can do some serious damage to your property. Do you let them in or keep them out? If you let them in, how do you protect yourself?

Personally, I think smoking is one of the dumbest habits a human can form. Don't get me wrong. I didn't say smokers are dumb. I know plenty of awesome people who smoke.

They just have at least this one dumb habit. In fact, I used to smoke. That was before I realized how disgusting it was.

You know the putrid smell of the breath of someone who has been smoking and drinking coffee? Now imagine French-kissing that person. I'm sorry. I didn't mean to make you vomit. You get the point.

If you rent to smokers you are going to have to deal with the smell of smoke for quite some time. The smell gets in your drapes, in your carpets, and even in the wall and ceiling surfaces.

I remember one Christmas getting a package from my sister in the mail. In it were all the presents for myself, my wife, and my children, Annie and Andrew. When we opened the lid of the box, the smell of smoke came pouring out. Now, imagine that the box had been away from Kelly's house for about a week. Just imagine what her house must have smelled like. And that is the point.

If you allow smokers in your properties you may have to go as far as bleaching the walls, priming, and repainting because if they are there long enough, the nicotine will leave a yellow film on the walls and ceilings.

When you are interviewing a prospective tenant you will be able to tell if they are a heavy smoker. You will smell it on their breath, in their hair, and on their clothes. If you are uncertain, follow them to their car. Heavy smokers smoke in their car. When they open the door you will smell the stale odor of cigarette butts.

Smokers aren't bad people, though. They just have a bad habit. The larger issue is that they can also burn holes in your carpet, and in worst-case scenarios burn your house down. There have been many a house fire caused by a smoker falling asleep with a lit cigarette in hand.

Some smokers are light or social smokers. I have no problem renting to them because they generally will smoke outdoors. In any case, if you rent to smokers, be sure to collect an additional deposit – and while you're at it, charge additional rent, too!

By the way, these practices do not implicate you for discrimination. Smokers are not a protected class.

Protected Classes

Discrimination is against the law. Remember the Landlord code: "The only color that matters is GREEN!"

NOTE: I am not a lawyer. I suggest you get a copy of, and read, the most recent version of the Civil Rights Act and your State and Local discrimination laws, too!

Protected classes are classes of people who are protected by Federal law against discrimination. What you need to know is that you can't keep someone who falls into one of these protected classes from renting your property simply because they fall into one of these protected classes.

The obvious classes are: race or color, national origin, religion, sex, age, familial status, and disability. This is based on the Civil Rights Act of 1964 which has been amended. Remember, you will have to know your State and Local laws, too.

One area that tends to trip up unknowing landlords has to do with service animals, typically guide dogs. If you have an applicant for one of your rental properties, you cannot keep someone out if they have a pet and that pet is a service animal.

I have seen other landlords get tripped up when it comes to those who are handicapped. This gets complicated because the law has different applications to different size buildings, how many floors you have in a particular building, how many people are in the building and the cost of a project, to bring a property into compliance with ADA guidelines, relative to the overall value of the building.

Relax. You won't be required to make a third-floor studio apartment ADA compliant if you are a small operator. Some disabled citizens may try to strong-arm you into spending a lot of money because you have to rent a third-floor studio to them. This is not the case.

Furthermore, there are ADA grants for handicapped individuals to use to build wheelchair ramps, safety bars in showers and tubs, etc. You don't have to spend a dime. And they are required to return your property to its original condition when the disabled tenant moves out.

I will tell you though that sometimes a handicapped-accessible property is worth more than GOLD! Check with your local ADA chapter and see what the demand is for handicapped-accessible properties in your area.

I have seen cases where rents are three times the prevailing rate for handicapped-accessible properties. This could be a golden opportunity for you to do something good in your community and profit as well.

Maintenance and Repairs

Once you have made a wise choice of buying a duplex and you have followed the time-tested method of placing tenants, you have to run your rental operation as a business – managing income and expenses, the bottom line! Once you get money coming in you will feel really good. The hard part will then be keeping some of it – profit!

Expenses can eat a hole in your profit faster than a wood chipper can eat a small branch. You can't ignore expenses any more than you can ignore income. Maintenance and repairs are the silent consumers of your income. Second only to a vacancy, not much else can eat away at your profit.

I always pre-conditioned tenants as to what I expected from them and what they could expect from me.

Their basic obligation is to pay rent to me on time every month without fail and to keep my property clean and in the same condition that it was in when I granted possession to them. Of course they and their guests are not to cause any destruction of any kind.

My primary obligation is to provide a safe, clean, and reliable home that is up to code. That's it. In order for me to do this, I may from time to time be required to maintain or repair something in the home. I am not obligated to make improvements based on their wishes, change colors, add features that were not there when they first took possession, or entertain any other request that is not deemed necessary to provide a safe, clean, and reliable property that is up to code.

If a tenant or their guests causes damage then they are responsible for getting my property back to the condition it was in before the damage. Please note: I do not want them to make the repair. I will determine who makes the repair. They will, however, be responsible for paying for the repair.

I wish I had a nickel for every time a tenant called in a maintenance request to repair damage that they or their guests caused. Actually, I have had these calls enough times that it is a serious enough subject for discussion.

I have had calls from tenants who informed me that their two boys, eight and nine years old, were chasing each other down the hallway, when one boy tackled the other and the two crashed into the wall at the end of the hall and put a huge hole in that wall. The tenant, the two boys' mother, said that I needed to repair the damage so that she would have a nice place instead of living in a dump!

On another occasion, a single elderly tenant called in a maintenance request to unclog her kitchen sink. When I cleared her drain, my drain snake was covered in grease from end to end. I told her to never, ever dump grease from frying chicken down the kitchen sink! A few months later she called again with another clogged drain. This time it was the toilet. This was an old house with notably old plumbing. However, she had dumped enough grease over time to clog the commode, too. When I confronted her and reminded her of my instructions to her a few months ago to not dump grease down the drain she replied that she did not dump grease down the kitchen drain like I told her – so she decided it was okay to dump the grease down the toilet. She paid for that repair and subsequently vacated the apartment because in her words, "It's just too many rules around here!"

Needed maintenance and repairs may come from other sources too, like those resulting from occupancy or code enforcement inspections. You may also receive maintenance and repair requests as a result of leasing to tenants who receive some sort of subsidy such as Section 8.

The point here is that you will from time to time be required to demonstrate that your rental property is safe, clean, reliable, and up to code. Local municipalities are often not as strict as federal entities. However, there has been a big push the last few years to have all municipalities adhere to the BOCA, the uniform body of building codes.

Keep in mind that while you may feel that getting a list of required repairs from one of these entities is a burden you didn't expect when you bought your rental, it is something you will want to accept and embrace. Make these guys part of your team. Rely on them to help you stay in their good graces – and more importantly keep your property safe, clean, reliable, and up to code. Do not run or hide from them. This will only infuriate them – and remember, they have the power to help you succeed or not.

There have been times when I would contact an inspector first before beginning a project where I had some uncertainty. What I learned is that they appreciate the opportunity to be brought in before work has begun, and they are able to help me through the process easily while avoiding problems down the road that I may not have foreseen if not for the inspector. They will not *break* the rules for you, but if you treat them with respect they will help make your investing and your life easier.

Next, let me ask you: Are you going to perform the maintenance and repairs on your rental properties yourself, or are you going to hire someone else to do them?

Since you're reading this book I can only assume that you're thinking, "Hey Gary, I bought this book so I could get the answers to questions like this from you." The right answer is, "It depends."

I can give you some guidelines. Generally speaking, I encourage my students not to perform their own maintenance and repairs. This is something that is usually to your advantage to pay someone else to do who is better at it than you are. It also frees up your time to focus on making better owner-level decisions.

Usually, if you are starting out investing, you are also still working a regular job or are heavily involved in running an already existing business.

I have had a lot of students who are tradespeople closely related to housing though, so in their case it may make sense for them to be involved at some level in maintenance and repairs.

I have also had students who are retired or are not working full time at the moment. To these folks I say, "Go ahead." Make your own maintenance and repairs, so long as you know what you're doing, and someone other than your mother can vouch for the fact that you do in fact know what you are doing.

Keep in mind that every minute you spend performing maintenance and repairs is another minute you could and maybe should be spending with your loved ones, or even finding the next great real estate investment deal. Just for the record, I did do a lot of my own maintenance and repairs early in my investing career. Some of it made sense. Other times, after much wasted time, energy, and money, I regretted it and called a pro to make things right.

Nuisance Calls

I love my tenants. They make me rich. But man, can they be a nuisance sometimes. I'm sure you've had these folks, too. They call every time the wind blows. They call when the neighbor's dog barks. They call when they realize their furniture doesn't match the paint and carpet – and so they want you to replace the paint and carpet.

I have had these folks myself and I decided to put a stop to it. You guessed it! I came up with a nuisance call policy. If they called me with three nuisance calls, I started to bill them every time they called after that for anything that wasn't important.

I had one family who kept calling about their furnace, and the HVAC guy kept telling me nothing was wrong with the furnace… so on the third call I went with the HVAC guy to the property. We walked in and you'd have thought we were in the tropics. I mean, it was hot! I asked the mother what the matter was and she pointed to the thermostat. It was turned all the way up to 90 degrees. The temperature was maxing out at 85 degrees. I told her she was going to burn out the furnace and that it wasn't designed to redline all winter long.

I asked her why she wanted it so hot. She told me that she and her family liked to run around naked and they got cold in the winter. After containing myself, I told her we were going to lock her thermostat at 78 degrees – too hot for me, and well above the 72 degrees that is generally deemed the high end of the healthy range of temperature in climate-controlled environments in the winter – and that they should put some friggin' clothes on.

I told the HVAC guy that if they called again that he should not go over there. I would enforce my nuisance call policy. And on top of that, if she burned out my furnace I would sue her in stupidity court for being stupid.

One of the most humorous scenes that ever unfolded for me involved a new tenant who had just moved in to one of my newly remodeled single-family homes. After a few days, she called and said there was a huge problem with the tub. I asked if it was leaking and she said no. I reminded her that everything was new including the tub, and couldn't imagine what could be wrong. She said I simply had to come see for myself. Now this place was nice – huge kitchen, huge main bathroom, all new carpeting and new fixtures everywhere.

When I arrived at the house the next day, she led me to the bathroom along with her two daughters and one son. We could all fit in the cavernous bathroom at the same time. She took me over to the tub and pointed at it and said, "Do you see that?" I responded that I was looking at a perfectly good tub. She said the tub was small. I informed her that the tub was a standard size that could be found in millions of homes all over the United States of America!

She put her hands on her hips and proceeded to tell me how she couldn't fit in the tub because her butt was too big and so were the butts of her two daughters. All the while her two daughters stood watching with their arms crossed and looking blankly at me while the son bobbed his head up and down in agreement, scratching his chin and repeating, "Yeah."

I will confess that her rear end looked as if two large pumpkins had been shoved down the back of her black spandex tights. The material was stretched so thin that you could plainly see her bare ass trying its best to rip those tights wide open. I'm usually pretty good on my feet but I honestly could find no way to respond to her with a dignified answer and at the same time keep a straight face.

Of course I did not replace the tub. What could I replace it with? A hot tub? I didn't charge a nuisance fee either. I think I got more than my money's worth in the form of entertainment. The point here is that people will waste your time in a lot of different ways and you should be prepared for just about anything.

Building and Improvements

Capital improvements are what you do to your property that is not expensed in the year you do the work but rather depreciated over time like the building itself.

It therefore ads to the cost basis of your property and therefore should add to its value. An example of this would be a new roof or new windows or new siding.

Replacing a faucet would be an expense. Replacing a tub would be a capital improvement.

Capital improvements are expected to be made to your property in order to keep it from becoming obsolete and less desirable as a rental unit. When you buy a rental property you should project what you believe will be required in 1, 3, 5, 10 and 15 years out. I also recommend that you create and make regular deposits to a capital improvement account.

You may think of this as an expense item because you make regular contributions to it. However, when you use these funds they are not categorized as expenses on your tax return. Rather, it will increase what you can claim for depreciation.

I recommend that you have a frank discussion with your tax accountant when you first get into the real estate investment business to determine a strategy that works for you.

Bookkeeping

No matter what other systems you have in place there is one that you must absolutely have software for and that is bookkeeping.

I promise that even if you start out doing this manually, you will evolve to using a software system. The easiest way to do this is to use QuickBooks. It is widely accepted in the industry. All tax accountants have it and use it. It is stable and well supported. It is well designed with you in mind, and it is easily adaptable to the world of property management.

You don't have to know anything about accounting, although if you have learned dual-entry accounting it certainly helps you understand the how and why of entering debits and credits for every transaction.

I encourage you to hire a local bookkeeper for a few bucks to come to your house, help you get it installed and show you the three most important things you need to do – entering deposits, paying bills, and reporting. There is more to know but you must learn these three right away, and you will have time to learn other features and functions that will serve you well.

The reporting is where you will be able to see in an instant how well your real estate portfolio is performing. Obviously, income must exceed expenses. In other words, expenses must be less than income. I know I just said the same thing and only reversed the order. However, as obvious as this philosophy is, it is the number one reason businesses fail. They simply spend more than they earn. And you cannot keep a business going for long by doing that.

The sole business reason for getting into business in the first place is to make a profit. Income minus expenses equals profit. Period. End of story.

You do want to be more fulfilled than you will be by simply pursuing profit. You agree and so do I. But what I'm talking about here is the requirement for you to be, while in business mode, a good, worthy and responsible custodian for the resources God has given you. This includes people and relationships, natural resources, and of course money. In fact, it is a natural law that the degree to which you receive, utilize, and benefit from all that God has given you is directly, precisely, and perfectly proportionate to the degree to which you are a good, worthy, and responsible custodian for these very same resources. God and our world will not give you more than you are responsible for. In fact, God and the world will take away from you that which you do not take care of. The good news is that all you desire is already laid out in front of you. You simply must be responsible for that which you desire and it shall be yours to enjoy! I would reread these last few sentences if I were you.

Life in the Trenches

FIRE!

Sometimes life has a lot of irony in it, and sometimes it can be humorous even within the context of what would normally be considered a not-so-humorous situation. My wife and her business partner were trying to get a new business of theirs off the ground. In their effort to get publicity, they had a rather larger banner created that was to be hung from an existing business sign frame in front of the building from which they rented office space. It was on a busy road named Mt. Royal Boulevard.

Almost directly across the street was the local fire company. Since we knew some of the local firemen from different companies in the area, we asked if they could be of assistance by using one of their ladder trucks to hoist one of their guys in the cherry picker and help secure the banner to the top of the sign frame. So far so good.

I was helping. The husband of Susan's partner was helping. We had our weekend warrior toolkits spread out in the grass. It was a beautiful Friday in September and rush hour was winding down. A lot of the guys from the fire company came over to shoot the breeze along with those who were helping us and a few curious neighbors. As you might imagine, the firemen had their radio transmitters turned on and strapped to their waists or shoulders. As a result all of bystanders were in easy earshot of the goings on in the area in the way of fire and other emergency calls.

And that's when it happened.

Talk about an awkward moment. A fire call came out over the radios of all the local fire companies including the one we were with at that moment. I couldn't make out the details with all the static and other background noise but the firemen were used to that and were able to decipher the information.

One of the men asked another close by what the call was about. The second firemen said, "House fire, 3144 Sorento in the city."

3144 Sorento in the city? I owned a rental house at 3144 Sorento in the city. Now keep in mind, among all the people who were there and all around me, I was the only one who knew I owned this particular property. (Oh, they knew I owned a lot of rentals but of course didn't know the specific addresses.) So even though I was surrounded by people, I felt very much alone – for the moment.

Within a minute, my Property Manager called to tell me one of my houses was on fire. I told her I was well aware, and she wanted to know how in the hell I knew, when she had only just gotten the call from the local police. You see, the Property Manager got all of the calls, not me – one of the benefits of having a Property Manager. After reviewing what facts we had available to us at the time, we determined the Property Manager would go to the property since I was already surrounded by firemen, while she lived only a few minutes away.

When she arrived at the house, the local news crews were already there. Just my luck, a really slow news day. The Property Manager knew to keep a low profile and not allow the press to get her in their clutches (at least until all the facts were gathered).

I was fortunate enough that she was able to get close enough to the reporter who was interviewing my tenants. During this time, she overheard and saw some pretty revealing dialogue and gestures. The tenants consisted of a husband, wife, and three small boys – an infant, a three year old and an eight year old. The mother was being interviewed at the time and she was singing like a bird. Meanwhile the husband was tugging on her arm and trying to shut her up!

What the Property Manager gathered was that the three boys had all been upstairs in the parents' bedroom while their mother was downstairs in the kitchen talking on the phone. The mother heard one smoke detector sound and she called upstairs. It just sounded to her like the boys were rough-housing, so she yelled for them to settle down. Then a second smoke detector sounded and at that point she ended her phone call and ran upstairs to find smoke billowing out of her room. The three boys had already found their way to the hallway. She grabbed them, ran downstairs and out the back door, then called 911.

When asked how it all began she informed the reporter – and hence all of Pittsburgh – that her eight year old had climbed up the entertainment center in her room to grab a cigarette lighter that was on the top shelf.

The first moment of grace and mercy was that the entertainment center hadn't toppled over and caused great harm to the eight year old and potentially the other boys, too. Feeling lucky and a little mischievous, I guess, the eight year old proceeded to light the nearest curtain on fire to see what would happen.

The curtain went up in flames quickly, fell out of its rings and dropped to the floor, where it caught the carpet on fire and spread to the other curtain and of course any other combustible article in its path.

Fire spreads fast and the resulting smoke is not like the white smoke of a campfire. Oh no. This smoke is thick and black. In fact, in a lot of house fires, most of the damage is from the smoke and the water used to put out the fire, and not from the flames themselves.

By the time the fire company arrived, the fire had spread through the second floor. The house is on a hill so one truck was on the low side and the other was on the high side. A larger ladder truck with the cherry picker elevated two firemen to the rooftop where they proceeded to rip through the brand new roof I had just put on, with their axes. This was so they could stick the fire hose in there and saturate absolutely everything. They also ripped out a couple of new windows.

When it was all over, the tenants were not able to salvage any personal belongings. Everything was damaged by the smoke and ultimately the water. The Salvation Army put the family up in a temporary shelter and gave them vouchers for clothing.

The house was still standing but needed a major rehab to be put back into service. It would be a few months at least.

The insurance adjuster came out the following day and confirmed that the fire was caused by the eight-year-old boy. He also gave an estimate of $80,000 for the restoration. My insurance policy would cover it. However, I informed the insurance company that because I was in the real estate business and owned a lot of properties that, other than the initial treatment for smoke and a few other specialized efforts performed by specially trained technicians, I was able to have my guy do the remodeling at a much lower cost than their estimate called for. They allowed me to do that and pay myself a 10% general contractor fee – but not profit in any other way. It was a win-win for everyone and the insurance company saved a lot of money.

Upon completion I had a more valuable home and was able to charge more rent. I eventually sold the house for a tidy profit, partly due to the remodeling work that would not have occurred if it had not been for the fire.

Last but not least, not a single soul was lost or injured in what is usually deemed a very bad experience.

A LITTLE HUMOR

Not all human drama stories are bad. Some can be a little funny.

About one year after I bought 205 S. Ohio, I got a call from the second-floor tenant complaining about the first-floor tenant. I learned to usually ignore the first call from one tenant about another. They often worked it out themselves and whenever I did get involved I usually regretted it. (For the record, I don't recall ever regretting having ignored the first phone call from one tenant complaining about another one. Please keep in mind that what I am referring to here has to do with my own tenants' relationship to one another. Not one of my tenants with a non-tenant neighbor.)

The next day the second-floor tenant called again to complain about the first-floor tenant. He sounded a little more serious this time and said that other neighbors were upset and were considering calling the police.

I thought I should gather a little intel on the situation at that point. I called the second-floor tenant back and got his voicemail. I left a message and decided to call the local police to see if there had been any complaints filed against my building or my tenants. I was informed that a few of the neighbors had in fact called to complain about the guy on the first floor hanging around in the nude. I assumed they meant that he was in his apartment and just happened to have the shades up so people could see inside. "No big deal," I thought. But I also decided to do a drive-by to see if it was a real problem, and perhaps instruct the first-floor tenant to close the blinds or put some clothes on.

Well, wouldn't you know that as I approached the building my first-floor tenant just happened to be sitting outside on the front steps leading up to the front porch. Good, that would make it easy for me to strike up a conversation about a somewhat awkward subject.

As I approached, it became obvious there was a bigger problem there. He was buck-naked outside on the front steps.

Okay now. Did I deserve this? Was this some kind of a joke? I didn't sign up for dealing with middle-aged nude people who look like what they're wearing – nothing – needs to be ironed. Baseball cap on and smoking a cigarette.

I asked him what the H@#$ he was doing sitting out front with no clothes on so that everyone could see. He answered by telling me that he had a right to do as he pleased and if others were offended that was their problem and not his. He wasn't doing anything to anybody.

I kept my cool and refrained from laughing. I explained to him that he was sitting on the front steps – the only way to get into the building – and that other than violating some very obvious public nudity laws, some people were just downright disgusted.

He was actually in the way of anyone from the second or third floor being able to get to their apartments without having to pass right by him, thus being privy to his privates!

He rebutted by saying that his privates were kept between his legs, and with his knees drawn together no one could see anything.

Now I was going from amused to disturbed. I actually had to tell the man that even though he had his knees drawn together that by-passers had absolutely no problem observing his family jewels from the side!

Of course, this had never occurred to him.

I told him that regardless of what he thought, I was prepared to file for eviction if I received a third complaint, or the local police fined me as the property owner due to nuisance complaints.

I never heard anything more on the subject.

I love crazy people. I had one elderly lady, 80+, who refused to cooperate on anything at any time. I actually grew to like her over time, but boy, she sure drove me nuts.

She used to climb this big maple tree in our front yard in order to trim branches that were growing too close to the porch roof. The neighbors would cringe every time they saw this. I used to tell her every time I saw her not to do it, because I would have to ask her to leave if she did it again.

She just said, "You're not going to get rid of me, young man. I pay my rent on time."

Darn it, the old girl had me right where she wanted me.

She didn't have a computer and she didn't even have a phone. Whenever she called she would go to a local pay phone and call from there and leave a message. Normally, she would write these encrypted letters that she put together from words she cut out of old magazines she got for free. She would tape them all onto a scrap piece of paper. The sentences took the form of old Western Union telegrams – something like "Rent enclosed. STOP. Tenants upstairs noisy. STOP. Faucet leaking. STOP. Thinking of kicking me out? STOP!"

I remember the first time I went to meet her to raise her rent. She met me at the door with her old lease from the old owner, which I did inherit, but was exercising my right to raise rents. Her copy of the lease form was totally butchered with all of her own cut and pasted words from magazines. It looked like a grade schooler's project gone bad.

The really funny thing is that her former landlord, the lady I had bought the house from, was an attorney. The tenant had simply worn her down with her incessant banterings about what the lawyer could and couldn't do, so the previous owner just gave up.

The tenant's deceased husband had been a college professor and the tenant herself was a very learned person.

Her husband may have been smart academically, but he left her penniless. She had all her worldly possessions, a whole household full, crammed into her apartment.

By the way, I did not get my rent raise. The tenant was "having none of that, young man," and I went away with my tail tucked between my legs.

Before you judge me, I must tell you that the next time I went to raise rent, I was dealing with a pretty young lady named Dawn. I flirted with Dawn and she flirted with me and I got my rent raised without any argument at all. Eat your heart out, guys.

EVICTIONS

Note: I am not a lawyer. I am not telling you what to do here, or how to do it. I suggest that you seek the advice of an attorney. Now if you choose to read my thoughts on the matter then please continue to read further.

In spite of your best efforts to place the best tenants in your rental properties, you will run into trouble every once in a while. You might as well accept it now because it will happen to you.

What matters is what you do and how you do it.

Actually, you always have to measure the what and the how against your Why – your Big Why.

For now, suffice it to say that this is a critical part of your business and you need to study the rules of the game. Remember, when you master the rules of the game, you master the game. Every state has its own Landlord/Tenant law. I wish I could tell you that they are all similar but they are not. New York is tough on owners and easy on tenants. Florida is easy on owners and tough on tenants. These are of course very general statements. I have lived most of my life in Virginia and Pennsylvania. You would think that Pennsylvania would be more tenant-friendly but actually it's Virginia.

It really doesn't matter. What matters is that you want to get your own set of your state's Landlord/Tenant Law. If you pay an attorney to do the legal work for you I still encourage you to get a copy of the law and study it.

A lot of mistakes that rental property owners make are because the owner made a technical error. In other words, the owner did what they believed was the right thing to do, when in fact it was the wrong thing to do in the eyes of the law.

Part of the Landlord/Tenant Law describes the rules of the eviction process.

You have to know how late a tenant is in paying rent before you can file a complaint with the local court – usually a magistrate. It will also stipulate that you must provide a notice to the tenant that you will file a complaint if they don't pay their rent in a certain period of time – usually 10 days. It also provides for the possibility of a waiver of notice in your lease. This means that if you have a waiver of notice clause in your lease, and if your tenant is late on the rent, you do not have to give them notice of your intent to file. You can simply file on the date where the required time has elapsed since the due date of the rent.

All rents should be due on the first of the month. Don't argue, just do it. I know people will move in on different days of the month. When that happens, have them pay a full month's rent anyway and have the last month in the lease be the month when they pay the prorated rent.

Once you have filed the Landlord/Tenant complaint with the local magistrate in the district where the property is located, the court will assign a hearing date for you and your tenant to appear and state your case. This is usually 1-2 weeks from the date you file. In that time you should continue to try to collect your rent. Time is money. You also want to make sure you have all your ducks in a row.

I know that you do because you have been a good property owner and you follow the rules of the game that you intend to win. Remember, you were not born to lose. You were born to win. You are a winner and if someone crosses you, use the rules and play your game. You may lose a battle here and there, but you will win the war.

Always keep things in perspective. For every bad tenant, you will have 10 or 100 good ones. Honor the good. Prosecute the bad. God is on your side when you play with honor and integrity. You are bigger than this single negative experience. You will win and you will move forward and get a better tenant the next time, and you will have learned another valuable lesson, further strengthening your aptitude and your attitude.

Assuming your tenant hasn't paid the rent you will meet them in court, if they even appear. They often do not. It's a losing battle for them. The only reason you may end up on the wrong end of a judgment is that you took a shortcut or made an error. And you won't do that. I have never lost a Landlord/Tenant case – ever – in 32 years, hundreds of units, and thousands of tenants.

Oh, I had a few good challengers along the way. There are a lot of career tenants out there and they also study the law. They know all the loopholes. They may resort to trickery, lying or deceit. Most judges want these cases in and out quickly, and as long as you have your documentation in line and the tenant cannot prove they paid the rent, you will get the judgment in your favor. The tenant may put up a fuss, complaining that you're a lazy, no-good landlord and their apartment is a dump and should be condemned. How ironic. The judge had never heard that before. Imagine that. You upheld your end of the bargain. They didn't. And you're the jerk. Relax. The judge has heard it all before.

In the judgment, you will get possession of your property and back rent. Now guess what. The judge doesn't go and get it for you. You have to do that. In the judgment, the tenant will have a period of time to cure the judgment – usually 10 days. If they don't, at the end of 10 days you will have to go back to court and execute an order of judgment of possession. When you do that, the tenant will have more time to make good on the rent – usually 10 days. If they don't, on the 11th day a local constable, or sheriff in some localities, will post a notice at the property announcing the date of eviction. This is the date that the constable or sheriff will show up to remove the tenant(s). You must be there and change the locks. At that point the tenant cannot re-enter the premises or they could be charged with trespassing.

There are a lot of variables here. They may really have to be physically removed and leave all of their crap behind. You have to deal with all of that crap. There is no case law that describes how long you must hang on to all of that crap before you can dispose of it, either. Some judges say it is 7 days, some say 10 and some say 30. The bottom line is that you have to allow the evicted tenant some time to get their crap before you get rid of it. Make sure you get this timing from the judge! If you screw up here, you open yourself up to more legal trouble. People can be very sensitive about their crap!

It is very rare that you have to go all the way through an eviction process. Usually tenants pay up in the first phase of the process. Those who don't often leave on their own. Of those who don't pay their rent and don't leave on their own, you have to experience one of the more distasteful events imaginable.

BELLEVUE POLICE OFFICER

Beware the wolf in lamb's clothes!

I admit it. I was fooled. I fell for the "my husband can't be here, he's a police officer and is on duty" routine. Oh, he was a Bellevue police officer alright. And he was in trouble. I just didn't know it.

He and his wife and four children were needing a larger place because their fourth child had just arrived and they needed more bedrooms. Trouble started right away. Rent was late. Cell phone numbers were no longer any good. When we would go to the apartment we found only children, the oldest in high school. The youngest, a mere infant.

We had gone all the way to the end of the eviction process and I met the local constable at the apartment to do the deed. The children were all there. Once again, no parents and no heat either. The place was cold. We got the teenager out of bed, gave her a cell phone, and told her to start calling. She finally got hold of their old old landlord who came over with his van to get the children.

Still no parents, the old landlord made some comment about, "What kind of America do we live in when we evict small children in the middle of the winter?" I must admit I had a moment of pause to question the scene. It was then that the constable retorted with, "What kind of America is it when people are allowed to have children, then leave them to fend for themselves in the cold?"

It turns out the father, the Bellevue police officer, had become addicted to crack. And there it is – my old nemesis, crack. I will not give up the fight. I will not give in or walk away. I will do my part to beat this evil, one human at a time.

I hope you learn from this story that even if Mother Teresa shows up to rent one of your apartments you still must follow the rules and perform due diligence on her and any prospective tenant, regardless of who they are.

DEATH!

The Real Estate rental business is a relationship business.

You will learn a lot about human nature and you will be part of a lot of human drama. Of your real estate holdings, you will also continue to experience more and more of the human drama that is part of life. And part of life is dying. People are born, they get new jobs, they get fired, they get married, they get divorced, they have babies, they buy houses, they grow old and they die.

Even though you have to run your properties as a business, you are part of people's lives whether you like it or not. As such you will need a little knowledge, wisdom, and guidance when experiencing the human drama and how to navigate your way through it and how it affects your business.

The first time experiencing any of these events can be a little trying on your patience and a test of your emotional intelligence. Perhaps the most uncomfortable life event is the end of life itself (as far as we know in the earthly sense), that is, death.

In 2005, one of my favorite tenants died in her first-floor rear apartment at 416 North Home Avenue. I really liked her, not just because she paid her rent on time and kept her apartment clean, but because she was such a nice, sweet person. And she made cookies for me!

I was at home in the evening when my Property Manager called to inform me that Evelyn had died. I was sad to hear the news and asked if the manager knew of any arrangements for a viewing and/or funeral. She said, "Not yet, because Evelyn is still in the apartment."

That's when I realized the weight of the moment. The coroner was at the apartment with the police and they had called my Property Manager.

One of Evelyn's friends had become concerned because she hadn't heard from her in a few days, so she decided to pay a visit. When she arrived at the apartment she couldn't get an answer to the front door. Thankfully, Evelyn lived on the first floor and so she had a kitchen door, too. Evelyn's friend went to the back door and couldn't get an answer there either.

Evelyn very rarely went anywhere, so her friend considered this unusual and decided to look in the windows. That's when she saw Evelyn laying on the kitchen floor surrounded by what looked like a dark puddle. She grew frantic and started screaming, which prompted the second-floor tenant to come to her kitchen door directly above Evelyn's to see what was the matter.

The second-floor tenant called 911 and the local police were dispatched. They forced their way into the apartment and found Evelyn's body. After checking for vital signs and calling for the local EMT they secured the area. With a puddle of blood like that and an obvious head injury they thought there may have been foul play.

The EMT squad confirmed that Evelyn had been dead for a couple of days and called the coroner. The apartment was then quarantined until the coroner released it to access from others. Together, while all of these folks were there, they ruled out foul play.

From what they could see, Evelyn had fallen and struck her head on the corner of the stove which caused the injury and the blood flow. They further believed that she'd fallen because she had a stroke or heart attack. They don't believe she knew what hit her. I'm glad. She was a good woman and I believe that God called her home and she didn't suffer.

One of the challenges was that we had no next of kin to contact. Through some search and the help of the coroner's office, we were able to locate Evelyn's only child, a son.

He was very cooperative with us and everyone else. There are certain rules in place when it comes to landlord/tenant law in regard to the death of a tenant. The bottom line is that Evelyn's son had control of the apartment for the moment. He had 30 days to gather his mother's belongings and hopefully clean and leave the apartment in good shape. He actually had everything done by the following weekend.

The other challenge is the cleanup of the scene of death. This isn't something that a regular cleaning should or would do. It is considered a bio-hazard. There are certain products and techniques used to properly clean a death scene, because there are bodily fluids involved. This needs to be taken seriously because a new tenant will eventually move in and you are obligated to provide a safe, clean, reliable property that is up to code.

We were lucky. The coroner could have kept the apartment unavailable for as long as he wanted. Then Evelyn's son could have taken much longer to do what he had to. Under the circumstances we could have asked her son to make up for lost rent and this is precisely where you must exercise your emotional intelligence and make decisions that are good for business and ones you can live with. One of my tests is: "What would I want to happen if my own mother were involved?" The answer to this question may be what guides you in your words and actions in a situation like this. I can't give you the answer. This is something you'll have to look inside yourself for and look to God for wisdom and guidance. I simply want to give you the parameters and allow you to be a little more prepared in advance for these events, especially death.

ACTS OF CHARITY!

As you grow your real estate holdings, you will also continue to experience more and more of the human drama.

These experiences will test your meddle, and more precisely they will test your will power as a business person and as a compassionate person. First and foremost, you are a member of the human race and as such you have certain obligations to your fellow man that sometimes transcend personal needs and wants. For example, if you see a child in need or in danger, it doesn't matter whether the child is yours or not, you will feel an urge to help that child. If you don't then I question your conscience and you need to go away!

Several years ago, I rented a first-floor 1-bedroom apartment to a young man named David. David was a good looking, clean cut, all-American guy, who was educated at Northwestern University. He was what I consider a slam dunk of an applicant.

The first few months of his tenancy went very well. He was always respectful and had a cute little girlfriend who usually stayed with him. So far so good. Then after a while David started paying his rent late. At first I gave him a mild but certain warning, and then he paid his rent. He stated that he had simply forgotten. Then it happened again and then again and again. And each time he paid later and later and he began to become distant with me.

Of course I smelled trouble. I would visit him and I noticed that his physical appearance started to deteriorate. I finally had enough and told him I was going to have to evict him. I tried to give him every chance I could.

On the day of the hearing, I met David in the lobby of the courtroom and we exchanged idle chatter for a few moments. Then out of concern and the lack of my ability to understand what just didn't seem reasonable, I asked David if there was something I just was not seeing, something I just didn't understand. That's when he hit me with the bomb shell. David informed me that he had become addicted to crack.

At first I was furious. You see, I had dealt with crack addiction and its devastating effects years before with my brother. I'd seen firsthand how this addiction destroys individuals and families. More importantly, though, I had seen how the love of God and family and sheer willpower and determination of one individual and his family could beat this scourge and rebuild a family.

My brother had been broken in every way a man can be broke. He lost his job. He lost his house. He lost his wife and daughter. He lost his car. He even lost his dog. He lost everything including his freedom. Then I saw the miraculous hand of God at work in my brother, in me, and in all our family. My brother beat the 800-pound gorilla. He went on to earn a bachelor's degree in nursing from the University of Virginia, one of the finest schools in the nation.

Now get this. My brother was not a kid. He was in his thirties. He went on to work in the clinical psychology ward at UVA Hospital, serving those who had pre-existing psychological conditions combined with an addiction. He went on to help others through AA who were struggling like my brother had with his own addiction. Out of the destruction and devastation that addiction had brought upon his life, he rose from the rubble and gave tenfold, maybe a hundred or a thousand or more times to help others.

Now back to David.

The judge had called me and David to his chambers and we began to walk down the hallway. As we approached the judge's chambers, my anger and frustration turned to compassion. I remembered what my brother had gone through and I saw in David the same potential – for not only recovery from addiction, but for a beautiful life.

As we walked into the judge's chambers, the judge started in on his usual routine – having us stand, give the oath, and then sit. I already knew this judge and he was a known hard-ass on property owners and regardless of the circumstances always sided with the tenants. He was eventually relieved of his duties for being caught on film during court hours at a local bar getting drunk, fondling women, and getting in fist fights. He brought shame to his family of three generations of judges.

Anyway, as we sat down I raised my hand and interrupted the judge. I asked David if I could tell the judge what he had told me in the lobby. David consented and so I proceeded to tell the judge that David had informed me that he was addicted to crack and as a result had lost his job and the only money he had went to buy more crack. I then proceeded to ask the judge for leniency on David and to allow me a little time to help him.

I don't think I could duplicate the look on that judge's face if I wanted to! He was stunned and I'm sure thoroughly confused. Anybody else in the world would want their money! And I did too, but I saw an opportunity there to retrieve a soul right out of Satan's den and deliver David back to his family and the world of light and love.

The judge told me he would grant me possession of the apartment as a failsafe and would waive any other claims against David for 30 days while I tried to help David out of the mess he was in.

David and I walked out of that judge's office together, and I'm sure David was just as astonished as the judge. He probably figured that there wasn't anybody like me on the planet who would do such a thing. Little did he know of the promise to God I had made years before.

I told David to go home and pray while I figured out what I was going to do. After I had also prayed, I felt compelled to reach out to David's parents. You know the old saying: "The apple doesn't fall far from the tree?" I figured that David's parents were good people based on my first impression of David. I was right. I got David's parents' home phone number from his rental application and I called them that afternoon.

His father answered and I introduced myself and told him the purpose of my call. After going over the events of the day and explaining that I felt called to help David and others just like him, David's father paused. Then he stated that he always knew there would be someone out there who would help them. He presumed, after what I had just told him, that I must be that person.

David's father then went on to tell me his son's history. David was in fact an awesome kid, shy, very intelligent, sweet and compassionate. His father told me how when he'd gone away to college they were proud of him but worried that he was so far from home, and that he might not be able to resist temptation on his own.

He did in fact begin to use crack while in college. They had tried numerous treatment programs but none had made any real or permanent change for David. They would get him clean, then he would fall back into the same or a similar crowd and begin using again.

You see, crack isn't something you try once. I believe it is the most addictive drug and perhaps the worst drug scourge to hit the human race – even more so than heroin.

I mentioned a few programs I was familiar with. His parents were familiar with some of the same. They had a few others and one in particular was very expensive and supposed to be the be-all and end-all... and even that hadn't worked.

They had burned through an incredible amount of money, and even though they sometimes felt like giving up, they just couldn't.

I told them the story of my brother and had a suggestion. I called my brother and asked him to come to Pittsburgh to help me help this young man. Just like with my own brother's situation, I didn't know exactly what I was going to do, but I simply allowed myself to be led by God.

David's parents agreed to meet me at their son's apartment with David and my brother. We met the following Saturday and right there in the kitchen of my little apartment (that David was now moving out of), David and I had a heart to heart talk.

I told him that I knew we were dealing with the drug and not him. I also knew that even though the drug had taken over his body and mind, the light of his Spirit still shined. I could detect a little flame in his eyes. I told him I knew the real David was in there. I told him that it was his Spirit that we would work with, and not give any credit to the drug for anything.

I told him about my brother and that we were there to help and see him through to the other side of recovery. No matter what. I was not born to lose. I was born to win. I knew that we were in a tough fight and that we would win because God was on our side, and God was looking out for all of us.

Just like with my brother, I did not fear the drug and the evil that was behind it. Our Heavenly Father did not make us weak. He made us strong. Our strength comes from Him. Defeat is not an option. I think David got the point that I was determined and that I wasn't going anywhere until we had succeeded.

David went home with his parents and we stayed in touch throughout his recovery.

About a year later, David was in the final step of the AA recovery program. Good timing and good fortune, too. My fellow scout leaders and I were looking for someone who could come speak to our Boy Scouts about drug abuse and its devastating consequences. I suggested David and told them his story. They were a little nervous. They just wanted someone to talk about pot and booze. Crack and all that went with it might be a little extreme for our Boy Scouts. But they did agree to hear David, first just among the adults, so I arranged for David to come see us and talk to us.

About ten adults sat around in a semi-circle while David spoke. Man, you should have seen these guys… sitting on the edge of their seats, leaning forward, wide-eyed and totally subdued by what David was telling them. Some of the adults were speechless.

The ones who regained their composure and did speak, gave David their heartfelt thanks and praise for what he was able to convey in his talk. It was unanimous. David was to come to the next scout meeting to speak to our boys.

I set out to implement a marketing campaign to not only have all of the scouts there, but their parents, too. This was going to be amazing. And it was.

The next week, David came to speak to our boys. It was a full house.

All the guys sat in a circle around David. Now keep in mind, David was one of them. He was young and looked even younger. A man in his 50s would not have had the same connection with these boys.

When David started speaking, the whole room went silent. He commanded attention not by his words but by his presence. I never saw so many teenage boys sit so still and so quiet for so long. You could have heard a pin drop. Their eyes were glued on David and so were their parents'.

We had done a really good thing. David had done a really good thing. The meeting ran on much longer than usual. The boys were filled with questions for David – real life questions. I was never so proud of my scouts. And I was immensely proud of David.

My brother and I both knew what David had been through, what it took to reach where he was today, and what remained ahead for him. He would go on to help many more people in his life. David had a true gift to share with others and it is God's intention for him to do so.

Oh, one more thing. David has a pathological stutter. Imagine that.

ACTS OF GOD!

Every once in a while something happens that changes the way you see the world.

In September 2004, my wife Susan and I were going to Chicago for the weekend for a much needed reprieve from the hustle and bustle and to celebrate our 16th wedding anniversary. When we left Pittsburgh that Friday afternoon there was a little rain coming down. In fact, it had been sunny earlier in the day. The forecast was for maybe an inch or so.

After our flight landed and we made our way to our condo, Susan turned on the news. There was nothing startling and only a brief mention of heavy rain in Pittsburgh.

Within a moment I decided to turn on my cell phone which had been off during the flight. I discovered a voicemail from Roger, one of my maintenance men. He left a very brief message and in an excited voice said, "Hey Gary, the Blarney Stone is under water up to the awning. You better check 49 Grant." And that was it. I couldn't imagine what was going on.

I decided to call one of my tenants, Jessica, who lived on the second floor of 49 Grant. She didn't answer so I called her place of employment, the North Park Club House Lounge. Whoever answered hung up immediately, so I called back and as soon as he answered I said, "Don't hang up. I'm Gary Wilson. I am Jessica's landlord. I'm in Chicago and need to find out what is going on with her apartment in Etna."

The excited voice on the other end of the phone said, "Etna? Etna's underwater. There's water coming in the back here and *I gotta go!*" and hung up.

Pretty soon no calls were going in or out of Pittsburgh due to the overload on the land and cell phone networks. I could do nothing. No other tenants could contact me because they couldn't get calls out. The news in Chicago was not very informative.

Imagine how the weekend for Susan and I was going to go. We decided to go ahead and stick with our plans to fly back on Sunday. Even if we wanted to go back the next day, it wouldn't have mattered. The National Guard had locked down Etna and every other little township and borough that got flooded.

It turns out that this was one of those freak meteorological events that occurs every 500 years. Two weeks prior, the remnants of a hurricane from the Gulf of Mexico had made its way up the Ohio Valley and dumped a lot of water on Western Pennsylvania. There was enough other rain in the intervening weeks to keep the ground saturated. On this particular Friday, the remnants of another hurricane was following the exact same path up the Ohio Valley and passing right over Pittsburgh – dumping about an inch of rain.

Had Mother Nature stopped there, I might not be writing this particular part of the book. However, Mother Nature had more in store for the Steel City. Some very powerful thunderstorms popped up in the late summer humidity and dumped a mother-load of rain in a very short period of time right on top of Pittsburgh – and that was the water that broke the proverbial dam.

The Allegheny and Ohio Rivers overflowed their banks and into several small and struggling little boroughs and townships. It was disastrous for an area that was already struggling financially.

Millvale, right next to Etna, had just finished revitalizing its downtown business area utilizing government grant money. It looked great. But now it was all under water. What a waste. Some of the local small businesses gave up and moved on. Some of them had been there in the late '80s when a similar flooding event occurred. In any case, many of them had lost everything.

Susan and I flew back to Pittsburgh on Sunday afternoon. Flying over Ohio and closer to Pittsburgh, we could see how flooded it was. The Ohio River is formed by the convergence of the Allegheny and Monongahela Rivers (and according to some, another underground river) at what is known as "The Point" in Pittsburgh – hence the term Three Rivers. We began to see farmers' fields that had flooded, then felled trees floating down the river, and then more debris – pieces and parts of sheds and porches and trash cans and all kinds of stuff that filled the river from bank to bank.

When we flew over Mt. Washington and "The Point" came into view, the sight hit us right between the eyes. Sitting in and around the basin that forms the famous fountain were large boats – speedboats, houseboats, you name it. The river was still swollen, and you could see hundreds of boats torn away from their moorings upstream had converged and were clogging the rivers where the bridges and The Point are. It was like something only Hollywood special effects could come up with.

All we could hear on the plane were gasps and cries of disbelief.

We finally landed and made our way home. On the way past Millvale and Etna, travelling north on Rt. 28, we could see our way up into the boroughs and partially see the real damage. It was only the beginning.

I woke up while it was still dark outside on Monday morning. As you might imagine, I hadn't sleep too much. Keep in mind, because of congestion on the phone networks, I still hadn't spoken to my tenants in Millvale or Etna. So, I dressed in work clothes and boots, loaded every tool I could into my trusty 4-wheel drive, 4-door Toyota Tacoma and prepared for the unimaginable.

At the last minute, I decided to pack the deeds to all of my properties in Millvale and Etna. I didn't know why. It was just intuition. And it was a good thing I did.

When I got to Etna the National Guard was not letting anybody in except emergency crews, verified relief agencies, and finally, property owners. It was the first day that they were letting property owners back in.

The first house I went to was 48 Cherry Street, a 3-unit building and what I believed was the lowest lying property in Etna. It was also where my longtime and most favorite tenant – the elderly Italian mother of 100 and grandmother of 1,000 – Virginia Miles, lived. I loved that woman. Every time I would go to work on her apartment she would fatten my skinny butt up with her homemade cooking! She had a dog I titled "the hairy watermelon."

She fed that dog human food, so much that his belly dragged on the ground when he walked!

When I climbed up the front steps I could hear a lot of commotion. There were a handful of Shaler area school teachers who had volunteered to help local citizens in the school district who had been impacted by the flooding. I knew a few of them and they all knew my two children Annie and Andrew.

What I saw next was heart breaking. The water had just made it to the first floor – Virginia's apartment. The flooring was destroyed. The worst part though was the fact that the basement had been completely submerged. Those teachers were doing their best to haul out (by sheer brute force) several old refrigerators and freezers. What made it more difficult was that the basement steps had been knocked off their footing when the big (floating) appliances had bashed into them during the flooding. Everything in there, Christmas decorations, old collectables, clothes, toys, had been destroyed. Virginia kept her head and was a positive influence on everyone there who otherwise would have been in tears.

My plan that day was to assess the damage in all my properties and get them back up and running ASAP. Three had flooded as a direct result of the overflowing rivers. A few more had sewage backing up into the basements (even though one of them was a few hundred feet uphill) due to the sewage system being overwhelmed. In all, I had 12 tenants uprooted.

Turns out GOD had a different plan.

On that first day, it became obvious that I wasn't going to be repairing or replacing any electric panels, furnaces, water tanks, flooring or walls – or anything else for that matter. I called in Roger who agreed to work for free just to help these folks. We worked until sunset. We had to stop at that point because those areas had no water or gas or electric service. The utilities had all been shut down for safety reasons.

Around dinnertime I called Susan to tell her I wouldn't be home until after sundown. Those folks simply needed all the help they could get.

Leaving my tenants and all of the citizens of Etna and Millvale that night was more than I could bear. I was going home to a beautiful house with a beautiful family, virtually unaffected by the mayhem, and leaving those poor, desolate folks alone in the dark with no electricity or water or functioning toilets.

Mercifully, Mother Nature blessed us all with a few weeks of beautiful weather in which to work. I thanked God Almighty for all that I had, and vowed to do everything I could to help those people.

I went back every day for the next several days. The first few days we helped as many people as we could to salvage any belongings we thought could be saved. Gradually more and more people were cleared to help, like folks from churches near and far.

On Wednesday, I ran into a pastor of a church from my in-laws' hometown. He was sitting on the front steps of a neighboring property and wiping mud from 100-year-old photos of the elderly resident who lived there. We introduced ourselves and looked at the photos, and then back at the poor old women who had been wearing the same clothes for five days now, covered in mud. We both looked back at each other and started crying. This was ground zero. Electric panels and water tanks didn't matter at this point. In the beautiful mid-day sunshine, in Etna, Pennsylvania, on that particular Wednesday in September 2004, what mattered most was the call to help from thousands of innocent folks who had lost their precious sentimental belongings – and whose lives had changed forever.

I managed to repair or replace everything that had to be addressed eventually. I got every unit ready to reoccupy and inspected for clearance. I got all the units reoccupied as well. You know, what still amazes me to this day is that I lost only two tenants. One was young and only taking care of herself. The other was paraplegic and needed immediate facilities. Everyone else came back.

I got some of the best Christmas cards ever that year. Every one of my tenants told me the reason they came back was because of me. It wasn't the apartment. It was because they appreciated how much I had cared for them in their time of need.

My life has been blessed a hundred-fold as a result of that natural disaster and the opportunity it gave me to answer God's calling and just help my tenants and the other citizens of Etna, Millvale, and Sharpsburg, Pennsylvania. Susan and I had to curb our lifestyle as a result. You see, I had retired from the corporate world the year before (at the ripe old age of 40). We had no other source of income… but today I am a rich man in many more ways than a big bank account. What many other folks consider a very negative event I see as a blessing.

In the end, everything turned out alright, and even today, tenants I haven't rented to for a decade still stop me in the grocery store to give me a hug and tell me how much they miss me.

* * *

I decided to close this section with the flooding story because I want you to assess who you are and where you are right now. Is what you are doing aligned with God's intention for your life?

This has nothing to do with what you *do*. It has everything to do with *how you do it* and more importantly, *why you do it*. I suggest looking at yourself in the mirror and asking some deep probing questions. Can you serve your fellow man in the activities you are currently engaged in?

As a result of my real estate investing, I have built a successful Real Estate Brokerage Company named Win Realty Advisors. I have built a successful Property Management Company named Win Rental Management. I have built a Title Company named Win Settlement Services. Through it all, and as a result of my business ventures, I have started and shared in more friendships than I can count. I seek to serve first before being served – and as a result I believe I am one of the most fortunate men in the world. As the famous Zig Ziglar taught us, "Help as many people as you can to get what they want, and as a result you will get plenty of what you want."

I hope you can see now, after reading this, that you can do many things to improve your odds of experiencing the pleasure of profiting… without the pain… with your rental properties.

I will tell you that if this book puts a little fear or anxiety in you, then remember you can do what I eventually did and turn the daily responsibilities over to a professional property manager. In fact, I created my own property management company and started offering property management services to other investors just like you. I named it Win Rental Management because, with the policies and procedures I developed, it results in more deposits and more rents being collected, and reduced expenses… so everybody wins.

May God bless you, your family, and friends and your business ventures in peace and prosperity.

PS. I've enclosed a sampling of some of the policies and procedures from Win Rental Management that you can use as a guideline in managing your properties and even managing the manager when you decide to make that move.

POLICIES AND PROCEDURES

WIN RENTAL MANAGEMENT POLICY & PROCEDURES

Unrented Units

Complaints

Security Deposit/Escrow Account

Maintenance Calls

Signing Out Keys – Agents

Signing Out Keys

Lease Renewals

Move Out Services/Walk-Through Sheet

Occupancy Permits

Advertisement of Vacancies

Filing Judgments/Evictions

Rental/Utilities Collections

WIN RENTAL MANAGEMENT POLICY & PROCEDURES

UNRENTED UNITS

POLICY: Win Rental Management screens and places new tenants into vacant units.

GOAL: To rent vacant units in an effective timeframe

PROCEDURE:

1. Assess any units that are not rented in one month.
2. Get feedback from person showing the unit.
3. Contact owner with any suggestions to improve property.
4. Make improvements as necessary (as approved by owner).
5. If property does not rent within 3 months from the date it was marketed, Win Rental Management will charge the owner only ½ of the first month's rent instead of the full month's rent for renting the unit.

NOTE: Remember location, condition of property, and seasonal limitations are also determining factors when a unit does not rent quickly. Win Rental Management cannot be legally liable for any rents while unit is vacant.

NOTE: Owner does not pay any management fees while unit is vacant.

WIN RENTAL MANAGEMENT POLICY & PROCEDURES

COMPLAINTS

POLICY: Win Rental Management will promptly address any issues and/or concerns.

GOAL: To effectively address any complaints and/or concerns

PROCEDURE: When Win Rental Management receives a complaint and/or concern by mail or by phone:

1. The Win Rental Management staff member tries to handle the situation.
2. If the staff member was unable to resolve the situation they would go the Operations Manager.
3. The Operations Manager will go over the situation and either:
   a) Advise the staff member on how to address the situation
   b) Address the situation personally
   c) Consult with the Broker

WIN RENTAL MANAGEMENT POLICY & PROCEDURES

SECURITY DEPOSIT/ESCROW ACCOUNT

POLICY: All security deposits received from tenants are put into an escrow account as required by real estate licensing laws and regulations, until the termination of any lease. These are held at the following location:

> First Commonwealth Bank, Central Office
> Indiana, PA 15701

GOAL: To follow real estate licensing laws and regulations

PROCEDURE: Legally the tenant is to give a written 30-day notice when vacating the property. If a tenant does not comply, they forfeit their security deposit.

Once the property is vacant, Win Rental Management will complete a walk-through of the apartment or house that was rented.

If the property has been left in the same condition as when it was first rented (the move-in date), the tenant will receive their full security deposit back in the form of an escrow check within the state-allotted time of 30 days from the date on the walk-through form.

If there is any damage to the property (general cleaning, repairs, carpet cleaning, etc.), Win Rental Management will clean and or do repairs needed to make the apartment ready for the next tenant. This is deducted from the security deposit and the owner will receive the remainder of the monies with written documentation of deductions.

If the tenant has not reimbursed Win Rental Management for prepaid utilities at this time, these will also be deducted from the security deposit.

*PLEASE SEE STATE RULES AND REGULATIONS FOR ESCROW ACCOUNTS

WIN RENTAL MANAGEMENT POLICY & PROCEDURES

MAINTENANCE CALLS

POLICY: Win Rental Management receives maintenance calls and distributes to various sub-contractors.

GOAL: Completing maintenance calls in a timely and responsible manner

PROCEDURE: Tenant places maintenance call to Win Rental Management Team. A member of the Win Rental Management Team takes the calls and fills out a work order with the following information: tenant's name, phone number, address, date, and description of issue.

The Owner of the property is contacted. If it is an emergency and we are unable to get in touch with the owner, the emergency service will be done and owner will be billed.

Maintenance calls are screened to make sure tenant is not responsible for the repair. Priority is assigned to work order based on the following: safety issue (security or personal harm), and whether the issue could cause further property damage.

Work order is assigned to sub-contractor based on field of specialty and possible response time.

Sub-contractor contacts tenant to set up an appointment to assess situation and/or make repairs.

Emergencies are fixed immediately.

* For maintenance and repairs greater than one month's rent, the sub-contractor will deal directly with the owner.

WIN RENTAL MANAGEMENT POLICY & PROCEDURES

SIGNING OUT KEYS – AGENTS

POLICY: Win Rental Management will provide keys to Agents for the purpose of showing properties for sale.

GOAL: To provide agents with keys to show properties that are for sale

PROCEDURE: Agent contacts Win Rental Management concerning keys.

Agent comes to the office at 100 Center Avenue to pick up keys.

Agent gives a member of the Win Rental management staff a driver's license and business card.

Win Rental Management staff member makes a copy of the driver's license and business card.

Win Rental Management signs keys out for the agent and gives agent the keys.

Agent must return the keys the same day.

When keys are returned, the Win Rental Management staff will shred the copy of the driver's license, and give the business card to Lori.

If keys are not returned to Win Rental Management office, the agent will be contacted by the staff.

WIN RENTAL MANAGEMENT POLICY & PROCEDURES

SIGNING OUT KEYS

POLICY: Win Rental Management will keep a set of keys for all properties for the purpose of access into units for emergencies, maintenance calls, etc.

GOAL: To provide workers with keys to the properties for emergencies, maintenance calls, etc.

PROCEDURE:

Win Rental Management notifies sub-contractor of maintenance issue.

Win Rental Management gives sub-contractor contact information for tenant.

Sub-contractor contacts tenant to set up appointment.

If tenant is unable to be home for the appointment set by the sub-contractor, the sub-contractor will contact Win Rental Management.

Sub-contractor will go to Win Rental Management office to pick up keys for unit.

The key closets are locked at all times. During regular business hours (8am-4pm), the receptionist at the front desk will have the key for the key closets. Keys are then signed out by sub-contractor.

Sub-contractor must return the keys to the office that day and put in the key return box and sign the keys back in.

SUB-CONTRATOR MAY NOT KEEP KEYS OVERNIGHT.

The Receptionist will then put the keys away and sign them in as well.

*FAILURE TO RETURN and/or LOST keys will be at the sub-contractor's expense.

WIN RENTAL MANAGEMENT POLICY & PROCEDURES

LEASE RENEWALS

POLICY: Win Rental Management will keep a log of lease renewals.

GOAL: To keep all leases updated and current

PROCEDURE: Win Rental Management will keep a log of when each tenant's lease expires.

Win Rental Management will contact the owner to see if they want to make changes to the lease.

Win Rental Management will contact the tenant 30-60 days before expiration of lease to set up appointment with tenant.

If owner requests changes we will notify tenant.

Win Rental Management will use state-approved lease and execute lease with tenant.

Win Rental Management will have Broker sign lease.

Win Rental Management will make one copy of lease for owner and one copy for tenant.

The original lease will remain at our office.

WIN RENTAL MANAGEMENT POLICY & PROCEDURES

MOVE OUT SERVICES

WALK-THROUGH SHEET

POLICY: Win Rental Management will walk through a unit after tenant has moved out and type up a walk-through sheet to be mailed to owner and tenant.

GOAL: To perform walk-through and send security deposit

PROCEDURE: Tenant gives Win Rental Management a 30-day written notice informing us of intent to move out.

Win Rental Management informs owner of notice.

When tenant moves, Win Rental Management does an inspection of the unit.

The results are recorded and the owner is notified.

If repairs need to be done, we ask the owner who will be doing the work.

The owner is to contact us when the work is completed.

We check with the billing department to see if tenant had an outstanding balance.

The results are typed up and given to the billing department.

If a security deposit is to be returned to tenant it must be within 30 days. If the tenant does not get the deposit back, the monies will be sent to the owner.

When the unit is ready, it will be advertised.

WIN RENTAL MANAGEMENT POLICY & PROCEDURES

OCCUPANCY PERMITS

POLICY: Win Rental Management will fill out Occupancy Permits according to Borough and local laws.

GOAL: To provide local boroughs with contact information for tenants

PROCEDURE: Win Rental Management staff will contact borough to get a copy of the form.

Owner must pay any fees that are associated with the permits.

Win Rental Management will fill out the form and send it into the borough.

Win Rental Management will contact owner with any questions and/or assistance.

WIN RENTAL MANAGEMENT POLICY & PROCEDURES

ADVERTISEMENT OF VACANIES

POLICY: Win Rental Management will advertise a vacant unit to acquire potential tenants.

GOAL: To advertise vacant units when ready to be shown

PROCEDURE: (NOTE: UNIT MUST BE COMPLETELY DONE TO ADVERTISE OR SHOW)

Win Rental Management staff has Owner fill out Rental Unit Information sheet.

Win Rental Management staff walks through unit to ensure unit is ready to be shown.

If any issues are found, Win Rental Management will contact owner to have issues corrected before advertising unit.

Win Rental Management will place an ad on Craigslist and post outlets.

The ad will be posted twice a week.

Win Rental Management takes calls from potential tenants.

All calls and/or e-mails will be returned within 24 hours.

WIN RENTAL MANAGEMENT POLICY & PROCEDURES

FILING JUDGMENTS/EVICTIONS

POLICY: To collect past due rents and/or utilities from tenants.

GOAL: To collect all rent/utilities monies owed to the owner from tenants

PROCEDURE: When Win Rental Management and/or Owner have made decision, a Landlord and a member of the Win Rental Management Team fills out Tenant Complaint. The Owner is responsible for paying the fee.

*NOTE: Lease must first be checked to make sure it waives the 15-day notice posted on property.

The form is then mailed in or taken to the local Magisterial District Court. The court will then schedule a date for the hearing and send Win Rental Management and the Tenant the date and time of the hearing.

A member of the Win Rental Management Team will go to the hearing with all documentation and represent the owner.

All information is presented to the Judge.

The Judge makes the final decision and mails to Win Rental Management and the tenant.

According to the decision of the Judge, the account is adjusted and/or the tenant has 10 days to pay the balance. If tenant did not pay balance, on the 11th day, Win Rental Management files for possession. The owner is responsible for the expense.

If the tenant files an appeal, the case then goes downtown. Win Rental Management Team will recommend an Attorney for the appeal at Owner's expense. We will then have a sub-contractor contact the Constable to set up an appointment for the eviction and change the locks.

If the tenant still has personal belongings in the unit, they are given a 72-hour notice to contact the sub-contractor to retrieve their belongings.

If the belongings are not claimed, they will be disposed.

WIN RENTAL MANAGEMENT POLICY & PROCEDURES

RENTAL/UTILITIES COLLECTIONS

POLICY: The collecting of unpaid rents and utilities.

GOAL: To ensure that all rents and utilities are paid by tenants on time

PROCEDURE: All rents are due on the 1st of each month. A grace period is given until the 5th of the month according to lease.

Any rent payments that are received after the 5th of the month will have a $50 late fee applied to tenant's account, which Win Rental Management keeps.

On the 6th of the month a list of non-payers is written up by the Billing Department.

On the 7th of the month all non-payers are sent a Notice of Overdue rent by the Billing Department.

On the 10th of the month a Notice to Quit is sent to non-payers by the Billing Department.

The Billing Department also calls each tenant with any past due balances to collect.

The Billing Department contacts the owner of the property by the 15th of each month if the tenants are not current with any monies due.

The Management Team and Owner will then make the decision to take tenant to court for non-payment.

Win Rental Management will file in court on behalf of the owner at owner's expense.

PLEASE SEE FILING JUDGMENTS AND EVICTION POLICY & PROCEDURE FOR FURTHER INFORMATION.

At this point you may have started to wonder why I haven't spoken much about flipping houses yet. We're going to talk about that now. However, a little more background may give you the proper context as to why I focus on building a rental portfolio first.

Now I LOVE flipping! Cashing those big checks is fun fun fun! I am grateful though that I started out buying rentals first. I have helped a lot of people over the years build successful rental portfolios and make a ton of money flipping houses. I can tell you from a lot of experience that flipping homes and buying rentals have different risks. I can also tell you that the risks associated with flipping can cause more problems for a fledgling investor than those associated with buying rentals. Stated plainly, when a new investor has a "not so pleasant" experience on their first flip it usually knocks them off their horse for good. They never get back into the race.

However, when a new investor buys a rental first and they have an awful experience they still have ownership of the property. Even though they may want to sell it, that may take a while and in the interim they can usually rectify the situation they're currently in and as such get back on their horse – and therefore back in the race.

It is my humble opinion that it is better to build a portfolio of rentals first before you start flipping. This will allow you to stretch your risk muscles and your tolerance for stress. You will also gain valuable knowledge over time in the world of Real Estate Investing. Then, when you do start flipping you will be operating from strength, both financially and intellectually, so even if you have a bad experience flipping it likely won't knock you out of the race. You will still have wealth and income from your rentals.

Quite frankly you will also likely make fewer mistakes because you will have a greater understanding of market dynamics and know instinctively when and where to flip homes. I hope that paints the big picture for you, so let's dive into flipping and help you cash some big juicy checks! Go ahead and turn the page!

For more information visit:

https://bit.ly/2Whc0Sl

For a limited time, get 1 month FREE membership
to our Silver community where you have access to
free tools, contracts, Real Estate Statistics, and
Expert Insider Information including personal interviews,
and other books for FREE!

Flipping for Profit Without the Pain

Getting Started Flipping

Mr. Demet didn't teach me how to flip houses. I took a training course called Real Estate Riches, which no longer exists. However, I wouldn't have started (or been able to) if it wasn't for having experience with rental properties first to provide a solid foundation from which to launch a house-flipping venture.

2719 Spring Garden

So far I had used what I learned to buy rental properties. It was now time to use the tools and skills to purchase and flip a property.

The first one I worked on was 2719 Spring Garden Avenue. What an experience. It was a good looking little cape cod with aluminum siding that was set up as a two-bedroom home. I knew right away that I could make it a three-bedroom home. This is something that is very important. A two-bedroom, single-family home would not be as easy a sale as a three-bedroom, single-family home.

It was set on a large piece of property while still close to the city. It had off-street parking at the end of a long driveway. It was very private and a dream for a family with school-aged children, especially boys. Trees were everywhere. It even had a great front porch that spanned the entire front of the house.

The remodeling project wasn't that complicated. I put a new kitchen counter on the existing base cabinets and replaced the cabinet hardware. This made it look as if the cabinets were new too. I provided a new refrigerator and stove. I painted every room. I laid down new carpeting everywhere and new resilient flooring in the kitchen. The bathroom needed a new tub surround and new fixtures. The flooring and cabinetry were okay the way they were. The windows were okay too, and so was the roof.

But the landscaping needed a lot of TLC. There was a brick patio off the side of the house that we discovered while clearing brush and vines and dirt. It added a nice touch to the property. The heat was hot water radiator type and the boiler needed to be replaced as well as the hot water tank.

The basement itself was fine. We also painted the front porch and replaced the front storm door. I paid $20,000 for the house and put about $10,000 into remodeling. Not bad. But there's more.

This house was a bank foreclosure which means I bought it "as-is." I did check it out thoroughly prior to purchase and felt I knew the good, the bad, and the ugly. But what I didn't know was there was a major problem lurking underground that even a home inspector wouldn't have turned up.

After deciding to rent the house for a few years before selling (I don't recommend this for flips, though – more on this later), the new tenants started to notice a backup in the basement that only occurred after heavy water use – like laundry, a bath, etc., all at the same time. By the time we got a plumber out there, the backup had subsided. Putting a snake and camera down the drain revealed nothing.

After this occurred a third time I realized I had to get more aggressive. We decided to dig up the waste line about seventy-five feet down the driveway and tap in there with a snake and camera going out into the street. What we found was a major problem. The waste line had collapsed under the weight of the road where the curb was over our waste line. The collapse was too far down the line to see it from running a snake and camera from the house.

To make matters worse, the waste line tied directly into a major city trunk line, not an eight-inch neighborhood line but one that was nearly two feet in diameter. Furthermore, that line and my connection to it was directly under Spring Garden Road, a well-travelled street.

If that's not enough it was also on a ninety-degree bend in the road. This meant I would need to have three flag men – one at the site of the dig and one on each leg of the road – in order to coordinate traffic.

I had to pay for steel plates to cover the massive hole that had to be dug to get to the connection to the main line. I had to pay for a special connection that you just don't get at the plumbers' supply store. I had to replace every foot of new waste line up to and into the house. I had to pay for all of that excavation and gravel and new hard top for the road we just put a large hole in.

All of that cost over $20,000. When I sold the house a few years later I still turned a small profit. This is one of the reasons I like real estate so much. You can have problems like this and still make money. Real estate can be more forgiving than other types of investing.

The girl who bought this home was in her early twenties and waited tables for a living. She bought it with her boyfriend. She was able to get financing through a first-time homebuyer program for single women. I don't know that I've ever seen someone so happy as when we went to closing. She actually got money back at the closing table due to overfunding relative to her gift from the program she was in. So she walked away with money in her pocket and keys to her new home!

3344 Portola

The next house I flipped was 3344 Portola, another bank-owned property that I bought for $30,000. This house was a nice three-bedroom, all brick with a wide front porch, rear patio and nice deep backyard that had off-street parking for two vehicles.

It needed all new flooring, fresh paint, and some work in the kitchen and bathroom as well as the basement. We put ceramic tile in the kitchen this time and removed one cabinet to make it look roomier. We replaced the kitchen counter, sink, and hardware and provided all new appliances. The bathroom already had a double bowl sink and a nice tub and toilet.

The third-floor attic was finished into a nice large master bedroom. There were two other bedrooms and a den on the second floor with the bathroom. Most of the windows were already new but we did have to replace and/or repair a few.

The sliding glass door off the dining room was repaired with new glass and seals. The basement got a new powder room and was freshly painted. We also put in a new laundry station. We had quite a bit of landscaping to do including removing a tree and planting new shrubbery.

This place was looking good and was a prime candidate for a young couple or family. I put it on the market at Thanksgiving. No one thought I could sell it at that time of year. They were wrong. I put about $15,000 into the rehab and sold it for $72,000 for a nice little profit.

The woman who bought it was a Section 8 tenant renting from another landlord. She bought this home through the Section 8 Home Buyer program. They eventually cancelled the program because they couldn't get enough tenants to participate. What a shame. It was a good program and was what is needed to help stop the self-perpetuating dependency on this subsidy.

I was so excited about this program that I tried to help one of my own tenants get into it. She was one of the last Section 8 tenants I had after I eventually decided not to rent to Section 8 tenants anymore. She got well into the program and then backed out. She told me that she didn't want to take a chance on losing her home if she couldn't pay the mortgage (which was less than her rent) and she didn't want to lose her Section 8 rent subsidy.

There should be a time limit as to how long a person can continue to receive a Section 8 subsidy just like there is a limit on unemployment.

I'll give just one more example before diving into the meat and potatoes of flipping a house.

3811 Wilksboro

3811 Wilksboro was a textbook example of how to do a flip right, and also not have any surprises during rehab. I remember this one so easily not because it went off without a hitch and sold as I was putting the sign in the yard, but because the numbers were so easy to remember.

I bought 3811 Wilksboro for $25,000, put $25,000 into rehabbing it, and sold it for $75,000. That is the perfect ratio for a flip.

3811 Wilksboro started off as a three-bedroom, one-bathroom house. When I was done it was a five-bedroom, two-bathroom home. It had exceptionally large rooms, a nice large front yard, off-street parking in the rear and it was in a section of town where a lot of the city employees like to live.

It had hot water radiator heat and aluminum siding. Alcoa is headquartered in Pittsburgh, and a lot of houses there have Alcoa siding!

It had a great front porch with decent landscaping. We had to parge and paint the basement walls. We had to replace some of the windows. We had to carpet everywhere. Some of the soffit and fascia needed to be replaced. Everything needed to be painted.

I supplied the refrigerator and stove. We kept the kitchen cabinets but did replace the flooring. It had original pocket doors and awesome wainscoting in the hallway. It was a great little neighborhood and my buyer would come from across the street.

On the last day of rehab, the workers were hauling away the last of the paint cans, 2x4's, etc., and I went to put the For Sale sign in the front yard. I had intended to list it on the MLS but I never had to.

As I was using my foot to push the metal sign frame into the ground I heard a voice from across the street asking, "How much is the house being sold for?" I knew that I wanted $75,000 for it so I stated that I wanted $80,000.

He said he wanted to see the inside, so we went inside. I had never met this gentleman before but within five minutes he was offering me $75,000 for the property.

Thankfully I am a Scout Master with the Boy Scouts of America and our motto is "Be Prepared." Within one-half hour I had a fully executed sales agreement in hand.

It turned out the gentleman's sister used to own the home. She had died of cancer a short while before and the house fell into foreclosure. It also turned out that he was a carpenter. I asked him why he didn't do what I had done, and he said that he saw hammers and nails all day long and didn't want to see them when he got home.

He had kept an eye on the project and looked in the windows every evening after the workers left to see how the rehab was going. He figured he'd let me do all the work, get a little profit and save him all of the aggravation. He didn't even want the house for himself. He was buying it for his nephew, the son of his sister who had owned the house and died of cancer. He felt bad and wanted to do something for his nephew and at the same time keep him close to the family.

What a great story! Everybody won. I made a profit. The nephew got a nice house and his uncle got peace of mind. All of you reading this can experience these same kinds of stories. My hope and wish and prayer for you is that you do. Please read on.

Analyzing Properties to Flip

As with prospecting for rental properties, when you go out on your hunt for properties to flip you must keep things in perspective. First of all, you are not going to live there. What you perceive as being acceptable may or may not be acceptable to a prospective buyer.

Revisit page 47 for information about
locating and targeting properties

On the next page I have included a report based on school districts that I generate from the local MLS system. It shows me exactly what areas are selling and in what price ranges. This is excellent information to have when you are investing. If you are not a realtor (and I think you should be – please check out my free Investor-Agent book through www.MyInvestmentServices.com), then I suggest showing this to your real estate agent and ask them to create this for you on at least a quarterly basis if not monthly.

Activity in Pittsburgh Market by School District
Active and sold for previous six month - Oct. 16, 2012 - April 15, 2013

Fox Chapel Active	Fox Chapel Sold	Hampton Active	Hampton Sold	North Allegheny Active	North Allegheny Sold	North Hills Active	North Hills Sold	Pine Richland Active	Pine Richland Sold	Quaker Valley Active	Quaker Valley Sold	Shaler Active	Shaler Sold	Avonworth Active	Avonworth Sold
11	16	7	18	16	30	58	74	4	15	9	11	35	46	8	12
17	15	5	16	30	52	30	59	6	21	10	9	34	37	12	11
11	8	5	8	20	51	17	16	7	10	9	5	8	12	7	4
15	9	2	12	18	32	10	6	5	13	15	7	7	1	4	6
15	11	3	5	22	26	3	2	8	13	7	6	1	1	2	7
12	14	1	6	8	15	0	0	4	5	5	5	1	0	3	4
14	8	1	2	9	11	1	0	8	4	9	5	1	0	2	2
15	8	4	0	2	3	1	0	3	5	7	3	0	0	2	2
28	11	3	0	9	9	1	0	6	5	10	9	0	0	4	1
10	6	5	3	11	9	2	0	3	6	8	5	0	0	3	0
7	2	1	2	8	2	0	0	8	8	5	1	0	0	0	0
7	3	3	0	8	1	0	1	0	1	10	0	0	0	0	0
13	4	2	0	2	1	0	0	3	2	4	1	0	0	1	0
13	5	0	1	3	0	0	0	4	1	10	1	0	0	0	0
1	3	1	1	0	1	0	0	7	3	5	2	0	0	0	0
North Allegheny		North Allegheny		North Allegheny		North Allegheny		North Allegheny		North Allegheny		North Allegheny		NAL	NAL

FINANCIAL ANALYSIS

Before you even set foot outside your house and turn over the motor in your car you must do some financial analysis on your desktop. But before going over the forms to use, let's look at a plan for you to follow when going on your hunt. This is the exact plan I followed when I made all of my investments. It is the plan I used when teaching hundreds of students and it is the plan I follow when I teach real estate agents how to work with investors. It is a good plan. Follow it.

FINANCIAL ANALYSIS FOR FLIPS

1. Establish your investment goals. At this point you need to have available cash or credit to continue.

2. Set up your search criteria on the MLS system.

3. Initially you will get an email with a link to the MLS system. The first property matching the search criteria will be shown with a drop-down box at bottom left, allowing you to scan forward to other listings. You will receive the "FULL" listings. This first email will consist of several hundred listings.

4. Next, you will separate the good from the bad. Your objective is to narrow the list down to about 30 properties. Compare the list price to the market values for the area. The list price should be below the market value. Look at the photograph(s) of the property, the lot size, room sizes, and other characteristics. This will take a few passes. As you narrow the list, also use the county website for further research. This is a process that you will get better at with experience.

5. The resulting list of 30 or so properties is your drive-by list. Now you will drive by the properties to further narrow your search down to 10-15 properties.

6. At this point you narrow the list down further. This will typically result in 7 final properties.

7. Now you will schedule an appointment to go see the properties.

8. After viewing the properties, you should have a list of 4 or more that you will fill out the MAO, Cashflow, and Cost Sheets for.

9. Decide which properties to make offers on.

10. Fill out the "Offer to Purchase," and make a photocopy of your hand money check.

11. Now you make the offer(s)!

If you like the return, next you'll determine if you like the property itself from a physical perspective.

So, as you can see, you are going to peruse the list of properties your investor/agent has sent you according to your specifications. You will separate the wheat from the chaff according to the instructions. This may take three or more passes through the data.

Remember, it makes no sense to drive by a bunch of properties and do rehab sheets on them only to find out later that they have little chance of making sense economically. Make sure the properties you will drive by and eventually do rehab sheets for at least have a fighting chance of returning a profit for you.

Once you have narrowed your list of properties down to the best prospects it is time to do drive-bys.

PHYSICAL ANALYSIS

Once you have identified properties priced at or below market value for the neighborhoods they are in – and with negotiation you can get the prices down even further (more on this later) – it is time to do the physical inspection (after you do drive-bys) of the property to determine what is needed for rehab and how much it is going to cost.

I am providing a sample rehab analysis sheet for you to use in your efforts. This is by no means to be deemed complete, but it is a start. I am also including a packet of several pages that you should use as you go through a property room by room. You should end up with one sheet per room including bathrooms, kitchens, basements, garages and even the outside. This way you make sure that you greatly reduce your chances of missing something.

The following example is 3811 Wilkesboro Street – the one I sold for $75k. The rehab sheet states that the remodeling project would be $28,119.00. I actually cut back on what I did in the kitchen and bathrooms and made it a $25k project. I came in within $100 of this budget.

That, my friends, is a home run.

Here are the typed notes I took when walking through the house. Detailed notes will help you more accurately prepare the Rehab Cost Estimate Sheet:

3811 Wilkesboro

1. Living room:
   Minor repair
   Paint
   Ceiling light
   Carpet

2. Dining room
   Paint
   Refinish floor
   Redo pocket door

3. Kitchen
   Paint
   Install new floor
   New dishwasher
   New stove
   New frig

4. Bathroom 1st floor
   Paint
   Install floor
   Shower rod
   Med cab

5. Basement
   5 glass block windows
   Scrape & duralock basement walls
   New electric panel

6. 1st floor hallway
   Paint
   Carpet

7. Stairwell to 2nd floor
   Paint
   Carpet

8. Bathroom 2nd floor
   Paint
   New surround

9. Bedroom rear
   Paint
   Carpet

10. Bedroom middle
    Paint
    Carpet
    Install ceiling light

11. Bedroom front left
    Paint

12. Bedroom front right
    Ceiling light
    Paint
    Lay carpet
    Repair mantel

13. 2nd floor hall
    Paint
    Carpet

14. Stairwell to 3rd floor
    Paint
    Carpet

15. 3rd floor rear
    Paint
    Carpet
    Heat
    Build wall and door
    Build closet

16. 3rd floor front
    Repair walls
    Paint
    Carpet
    Add heat
    Add outlets
    Add light

17. Exterior
    Replace 2 concrete pads
    Fix rear awning
    Paint shed
    1-piece soffit

18. Yard
    Cut and clear

Rehab Cost Estimate Worksheet

ESTIMATED REPAIR COSTS

DESCRIPTION	√	COST RANGE	ITEM COST	UOM	QTY	ITEM TOT
Appraisal		$200-$325 EA	$250.00	EA		$ -
Power wash Outside (Front/Back)		$1000-$2000	$1,000.00	LOT	2	$2,000.00
Exterior Paint		$2000-$6500	$2,000.00	LOT		$ -
Exterior Siding		$200-$350/SQ	$200.00	SQ		$ -
Roof (3 Ply Flat 10 Year-Shingles)		$200-$300/SQ	$200.00	LOT		$ -
Roof (Silver Coat)		$400 LOT	$400.00	LOT		$ -
Gutters (Front/Back)		$7.00/FT	$7.00	LOT		$ -
Security Doors (Installed)		$300-$600 EA	$300.00	EA	2	$600.00
Storm Doors (Installed)		$200-$250 EA	$200.00	EA	2	$400.00
Interior Doors (Installed)		$125-$175 EA	$125.00	EA	10	$1,250.00
Ceiling Fans		$75-$125 EA	$75.00	EA	5	$375.00
Miniblinds (Installed)		$10 EA	$10.00	EA	25	$250.00
Windows (Double Hung-Installed)		$200 and Up/Window	$200.00	EA		$ -
Windows (Glass Block-Installed)		$200-$300/Window	$200.00	EA	5	$1,000.00
Drywall (Installed)		$27/Sheet	$27.00	Sheet		$ -
Interior Paint (2 Coat)		$200/Room	$200.00	Room	10	$2,000.00
Carpet/Flooring		$14/Yard INSTL	$14.00	Yard	500	$7,000.00
Ceiling Tiles (Drop Installed)		$1.00/SQ FT INSTL	$1.00	SQ FT	30	$30.00
Kitchen (Complete)		$2500 AND UP	$2,500.00	LOT	1	$2,500.00
Bathroom (Tub Coat)		$900 AND UP	$900.00	LOT	1	$900.00
Bathroom (Including Tub Replace)		$2000 AND UP	$2,000.00	LOT	1	$2,000.00

Electric (Service Line 60-150 AMP)	$500 LOT	$500.00	LOT		$	-
Electric (New Breaker Box)	$700 LOT	$700.00	LOT	1		$700.00
Electric (New Funs Per Line)	$100-$150 LOT	$100.00	LOT		$	-
Light Switches/Outlets (est. 30)	$5 EA	$5.00	LOT	40		$200.00
Plumbing 4" Main	$475 LOT	$475.00	LOT		$	-
Plumbing 1" Feed	$125 LOT	$125.00	LOT		$	-
PVC Sewer Line 6'	$275 LOT	$275.00	LOT		$	-
Heater-Gas Forced Air (90% Eff.)	$1500-$2000 LOT	$1,500.00	LOT		$	-
Heater-Boiler (90% Eff.)	$3800-$4000 LOT	$3,800.00	LOT		$	-
Hot Water Heater (30 Gallon)	$450 EA	$450.00	EA		$	-
Property Cleanout	$500-$1000 LOT	$1,000.00	LOT		$	-
Demo Work (3 Men)	$500 DAY	$500.00	DAY	2		$1,000.00
Removal-40 Yard Dumpster	$500 LOT	$500.00	LOT	1		$500.00
Post Rehab Cleaning	$200-$800 LOT	$800.00	LOT	1		$800.00
Parge Basement (Concrete)	$1000 LOT	$1,000.00	LOT		$	-
Concrete Work (Flooring/Pavement)	$6.00-$10.00/SQ FT	$6.00	SQ FT	144		$864.00
Termite Treatment (Whole House)	$500 LOT	$500.00	LOT		$	-
Misc: (Detail Work, Exterminate, Etc.)	$1000 LOT	$1,000.00	LOT		$	-
Soffit Fascia	$5.50/FT	$5.50	FT		$	-
Landscaping	$25-$2000 LOT	$2,000.00	LOT	1		$2,000.00
Interior Trim	$3.50/LINEAR FT	$3.50	L FT	500		$1,750.00
Other:					$	-
Other:					$	-
			Total Estimated Repair Co			$28,119.00

This gives a prospective investor a pretty good picture of what to expect. Not all of your efforts will pay off. This one happened to work out.

Using my search methods I usually come up with one to three properties that make sense to pursue with offers. Compare this high percentage shot approach to the shotgun method, shooting at everything that moves.

You can see why good realtors like working with me and now will want to work with you. You're not wasting their time or yours. I can get within striking distance quite a lot with less effort with my approach and make offers with confidence because they are closer to list price as opposed to making dozens of ridiculously low offers. That approach is for losers and suckers. You are neither of these. Your offers will get favorable responses and you will make a lot of money with less effort as a result.

Revisit page 62 for information about making offers and closing.

Rehab to Sell

You need to rehab according to the socio-economic market that your property is located in. As we discovered with rental properties, you shouldn't put $50/yard carpet in a flip that is located in an upper low-end neighborhood. Likewise you shouldn't put indoor/outdoor carpet in the living room. This is a skill that you will develop over time. My intention here is to help you shorten the learning curve and avoid as much expense as possible.

In most flips, use a good brand name like Shaw carpet. Get a neutral color like Candy Truffle at the lowest or middle-grade weight, depending on which end of the middle-class layer the property is in. Then put underneath of it a middle-grade pad.

When it comes to painting for flips, always use a good paint at least as good as Behr. Stick with one color for the wall surfaces like off-white satin and one color for all the trim like white semi-gloss. I like the two-tone look and I always use semi-gloss on the trim. You can use flat on ceilings and even walls if you'd like. You can also use a more appealing very light neutral color on the walls other than off-white. The two-tone look is appealing and really doesn't cost that much more.

Hiring a pro to do the painting is a must. They're better and faster than you and me. And your time is much more valuable than theirs. You will use that time to find more deals.

When it comes to plumbing fixtures, again, don't buy cheap. I like American Standard products.

For windows, I use American Craftsman. I like American Craftsman cabinets, too. Use them in kitchens and bathrooms. A lot of times you can go to the "bid room" at Lowes online and when you buy bulk you can get a pretty good discount.

Be cautious when hiring contractors!

Now you're ready to cash in on your investment! At this point you may want to use the Realtor who helped you acquire the property in the first place. This will solidify the relationship and help you grow your business with a qualified bonified team player who likes to Win!

We'll talk more about that later but for now remember a few things about selling houses. First, in any market, whatever you're selling should be at the top of the market. In the case of real estate your house should be presented in the best light possible. If you've remodeled correctly then this is not a problem.

Whenever I put a house back on the market after I've remodeled it I place myself in the mindset of the eventual buyer. I drive down the street and make notes of everything I see from the first impression including the mailbox, sidewalk, and driveway to the landscaping and lawn, and finally to the house itself – siding, roof, windows, and finally the front door. Your job is to enhance the experience your buyer will have as they go through the same steps you just went through! Then voila, you have a winner.

I am assuming of course that the inside is stellar. The big question now is: "What are you going to do with the money?" Remember, wealth isn't just a matter of how much you make but rather how much you keep. At this point you've got to exercise some discipline and be a good custodian with this new wealth so that you build a solid financial future for yourself and perhaps leave a financial legacy for your loved ones or even your favorite charity. I suggest investing these gains on flips in more rentals or building a business you've always wanted. Then you will have no problem being philanthropic! The more you grow, the more you'll be able to help others. Can I get an Amen?

Are you getting excited but wonder how on earth you are going to afford to do this? How are you actually going to pay for a property and its remodeling? One possibility is that you don't actually buy the house and remodel it. Rather you do the work to locate the investment, get it under contract, then sell the contract. That's right, you don't actually take ownership but still make some money. This is called wholesaling and we're going to talk about that next.

For more information visit:

https://bit.ly/2WyHhPm

For a limited time, get 1 month FREE membership
to our Silver community where you have access to
free tools, contracts, Real Estate Statistics, and
Expert Insider Information including personal interviews,
and other books for FREE!

WholesalingSo Everybody Wins

Why and How it Works

What is wholesaling? The short answer is that you can get a property under contract and then sell the contract to another buyer. Here is a brief explanation in practical terms.

Assume the owner of a property is Party A.

Another person, Party B, makes an offer on that property.

Party A and Party B come to terms and execute a legally binding contract for the sale of that property. So far so good!

Party B does not intend to actually buy the property. He would like to profit from his efforts in identifying a good deal so he, Party B, sells the contract he has to Party C. He does this for a fee.

In other words Party B charges a wholesale fee to Party C in exchange for Party C purchasing the rights of the buyer in the sales agreement to buy the property from Party A. Party C actually follows through and buys the property from Party A.

Graphically this looks like:

A → B = original sales agreement

B → C = wholesale deal

A → C = C buys property from A

Here are two examples of wholesale deals I was involved in. In the first example I was Party B. In the second example I was Party C.

Smithton Avenue

Smithton Avenue was my first experience wholesaling properties. It was almost accidental the way it came about. I was out looking for properties for myself. As usual I had found more than I could take on myself and was dreading the thought of deciding which one to turn loose when I got a call from one of my fellow investors who had a friend looking for an investment in my neck of the woods.

This other person was a dentist and didn't have a lot of discretionary time to spend looking for investments. I was literally standing in the very property I was to eventually wholesale to this other investor. I had gone back to the property to go over my notes and reassure myself that of all the good deals I had, this was the one I could most easily let go of and miss the least.

I knew what wholesaling was at the time. I just simply hadn't done one yet. I wanted to buy every property that I determined to be a good deal. Sound familiar?

Right after I hung up the phone with my friend, the dentist called me. We struck a deal right there on the spot. So, I got the property under control with my own offer. My offer had an assignment clause in it so that I could assign the contract to someone else. And that's what I did. I assigned the contract to the dentist and asked for and received a $2,500 fee. It was truly as simple as that. I had to do almost no work to strike that deal. Now $2,500 may not seem like a lot of money but keep in mind that at the time I knew nothing about wholesaling.

I had not yet been in a wholesale transaction. I did no advertising. The end buyer landed in my lap. All I did was locate the property and do the financial analysis on it to determine that it was a good deal. I certainly should have asked for a larger fee but being that I didn't know any better, I thought was doing pretty good by getting $2,500 for doing almost nothing.

I never even had to go to a closing for this one. The end buyer (C) bought directly from the seller (A) and sent the check for $2,500 directly to me in the mail!

There are a few lessons in here that we will expand upon further in this book but first I want to give you an example of another wholesale deal where I was on the other end.

1304 Superior

1304 Superior came across my radar screen at a time when I was investing quite heavily. It was located in a part of town that I was not completely familiar with yet but it was in my sights as an area to explore for future investing. The way it came to me was through another fellow investor who had his real estate license with the same brokerage company that I did. He and his brother, who happened to be running for city council at the time, were well-known local investors. They had come across an estate sale that involved multiple properties. They only wanted and could afford two of the three properties that were being sold as part of the estate. They had all three properties under contract as a package deal. They called me because they had heard that I was an active investor in the area.

This third property was actually pretty nice. It was completely sided with all the trim wrapped in aluminum. It sat on a large corner double lot. It had a great front porch and new windows. In other words it had great curb appeal. The inside had all the original hardwood floors, crown molding, chair rails, and hand rails. Even though it didn't have separate gas, and it was being used a single-family home, it did have separate electric and could easily be set up as a two-unit. And that's exactly what I did.

I asked the other investors what they wanted for the property. They wanted only $16,000. It took me exactly .001 of a second to accept their terms. I spent another $16,000 splitting and renovating the property. When I was all done, I refinanced it at 80% loan to value on a $75,000 appraisal. You do the math. As you can see I made $60,000 cash on a $32,000 purchase plus rehab. That's a $28,000 cash gain plus another $15,000 in equity, all because I bought a property wholesale for $16,000. In other words, all told I more than doubled my money, PLUS I had $1,200 per month in rent coming in. We actually did the entire transaction at the closing table at one time. In other words: A → B, B → C, and A → C all occurred in one sitting involving the seller (A), the wholesaler (B), and me the end buyer (C). Wholesaling has served me well in my investing.

All of you reading this can experience these same kinds of stories. My hope and wish and prayer for you is that you do. Please read on.

WHY IT WORKS

Wholesaling works because of two important factors:

1) Some people have available time but not available money, and…

2) Some people have available money but not available time.

Everyone fits in one of these two categories. There are exceptions. Some people have available time and money. Your goal is to be one of these people!

If you are in category 1 (Party B) then you can serve those in category 2 (Party C).

HOW IT WORKS

If you have a short-term memory then make sure you implant permanently what I am about to tell you. The way wholesaling works – in fact, the only way it can work so that everybody wins – is that you, as the wholesaler (Party B) must find your buyers first!

That's right. You first market, advertise, and capture and nurture a growing list of people who are interested in finding great real estate deals, whether they be flips or rentals, and have the money but don't have the time to do it.

Then and only then do you go out and find great real estate deals and get them under contract. Nothing could be more damaging to your reputation than getting properties under contract and not being able to sell the contract or follow through on the purchase of the property.

Those who teach that it is easy to get out of a contract if you can't sell it, so it is not something to be overly concerned about, are damaging to the world of investing and wholesaling in particular. This implies a lack of proper execution of the principles and if you have to break a contract then you violate the principle of "Everybody Wins." In this case the sellers (Party A) lose. And you lose too, because you will develop a reputation of someone NOT to deal with.

Don't fall into this trap. Follow the easy, simple processes that I am teaching you here and you will profit so that everybody wins! All you are doing is filling orders. Part of nurturing your buyer clients is asking them questions, listening to their answers, and understanding what types of properties they want. Then you go out and find those properties, get them under contract, and sell the contract to your buyer.

Finding Buyers for Your Wholesale Contracts?

Marketing and advertising! That's right. You market yourself as the go-to guy or girl in your area who knows how to sniff out those awesome real estate deals. You can easily market yourself by creating an impressive image on Facebook, LinkedIn, Google, Twitter, and even more social media venues. You should also create your own website. All of this is simple. It may not be easy because it does take time, but it is simple.

You advertise by sending messages through LinkedIn, and posting messages on Facebook, to those who are following you, showing them the deals you have done and promoting the one(s) you currently have. You can also use Postlets to advertise your current deals. Furthermore, you can identify, through public records, those who are regularly buying properties in your area. You can send them, through the U.S. Mail, your latest deals and entice them to sign up with you as their provider of great real estate deals. Of course you can use Craigslist, bulletin boards in your church or grocery store, and yard signs. Here is a rundown of available advertising mediums:

Craigslist – Bar none, this is one of the best ways to reach your marketplace. It's free and has a wide audience. They even have a tutorial for you.

Facebook, Twitter, LinkedIn – Use your social media networks to get the word out. Be careful how you use social media. There are rules of etiquette you must first learn for each one. The number one taboo is spamming your network. Never abuse the privilege of social media. If you do you will be shunned, un-friended, un-liked, un-connected and unsuccessful!

Church – Churches usually have weekly bulletins in which you can advertise your vacancies. This works well for large congregations but I would use it in small churches as well. Look in your church's current bulletin and there should be instructions or at least contact information that you can use to get started.

Grocery store – Usually they have a bulletin board where you can pin a flyer with tear-off phone number tabs. You need to check this regularly. Sometimes they disappear. Sometimes other people will post their notice right over top of yours. If you're really lucky all of your number tabs will be gone!

Restaurants – They often will let you put a stack of flyers or business cards near the checkout. The next time you're dining at one of your local favorite restaurants speak to the owner or manager. Someone with the authority to act is always on duty at a restaurant. Use your imagination!

Local publications – Penny Saver, Green Sheet, they're in every community and are very inexpensive. Unlike the large publications like your big city paper, I have had a lot of success with these types of publications. Call and ask for their rules and regulations. Learn the rules of their advertising game and you will master the game. Some ads you will place for one to two weeks. Some you will place for a year. You will also learn where in the publication to place your ads, how big, how small, special features, etc. Hint – Any time you can have your ad placed in a box you will get better results!

Net Listing

When it comes to wholesaling you have to beware of the rules and regulations regarding the transfer of real estate, and for the subject of this section, specifically those rules and regulations dealing with the subject of wholesaling.

In certain states, like Pennsylvania, if you are a licensed real estate agent, you can use the existing real estate rules and regulations in your state to participate in wholesaling.

If you are a licensed real estate agent you can play the role of Party B from within the context of serving as a real estate agent to Party A. This is how it works.

Assuming you are a licensed real estate agent and you are also an Investor, you can approach a seller with the concept that you will list their property for sale under the following conditions:

1. The seller determines what final sale price they would like to see.
2. You enter into a listing contract for that price.
3. You agree that your compensation will be any amount of money that is over and above the final sale price the seller is looking for.

You list the house for a price that you believe it could actually sell for. Here is an example:

The seller Party A wants $100k for the sale of his house. You the agent/investor Party B enter a listing agreement that will net the seller $100k. You advertise the house for $125k, and you sell it for $120k. The seller gets $100k and you get $20k as your commission on the sale.

If you are a savvy Agent/Investor and the buyer of this house is going to remodel it and sell for profit (flip), you can propose the buyer also sell it with you as his Agent when the remodeling is complete and the house is ready for resale.

I'm sure you can see the tremendous potential for licensed agents in states that recognize net listings.

If you are a licensed agent in a state that does not recognize net listings, or you simply are not a licensed Real Estate Agent, then I recommend you set up a LLC to conduct your wholesaling business.

At this point there are probably all kinds of questions going off inside your head. That's good. Let me show you how you can really crank up your business for massive profit and do it honorably and ethically and most of all correctly. If you are a licensee, most brokers won't want you wholesaling and most states and provinces frown upon it. That's because most people, including professionals, don't fully understand it. It is because of this that mistakes are made, people get greedy and take shortcuts or mislead, and people get hurt. So you and I have a responsibility to do our part and wholesale so everybody wins. The following diagrams and explanation will help a lot.

• *The Problem...*

A   B   C

A = House for sale

B = Wholesaler

C = Buyer

"A" would like to sell their house.
"B" gets the house "A" under contract and earns a wholesale fee.
"C" purchases the sales agreement from "B" and now becomes the buyer.
"A" then sells the house to "C".
It gets better ... MUCH BETTER!

The Secret Strategy...

Enter the Investor Agent:

D

• *The Problem...*

A   B   C   D

A = House for sale

B = Wholesaler

C = Buyer

D = Investor Agent

Now, "D" enters into an agreement to represent "B," the wholesaler. "D" finds the property "A," gets it listed for sale, thereby representing "A," AND representing "B" as the buyer, then executing a sales agreement between "A" and "B." Next, "D" finds the buyer "C" and represents "C" in purchasing the sales agreement from "B." "A" then sells the property to "C."

The Investor Agent "D" collects:

- Listing Commission from "A"

- Fee (not commission) from "B"

- Buyer Commission from "C"

AND that's not ALL!

Suppose the property is to be a FLIP.

Investor/Agent "D" then represents "C" in listing the property once it is remodeled. "D" then collects another listing commission and if "D" has a really good day, even finds the final purchaser of the property being remodeled and sold by "C," thereby collecting yet another commission…

…FOR A TOTAL OF 4 COMMISSIONS AND 1 FEE!!!

Selling the Contract

You have established a database of buyers and now you have filled an order for the buyers in your database who have indicated they want to buy this type of property. So, now you have to tell them about it. You have to sell it so that the current owner gets his price, the buyer gets a great deal, and you make a wholesaling fee – your Profit!

Remember this classic description by Bill Cosby: "If you give me a prime rib complete with a potato and sour cream and chives and a side salad served on a trash can lid I won't want what you are offering me. However, if you present this same meal to me on fine china with silverware then I will want what you are offering me."

When you are wholesaling you want to create an investor package showcasing your wholesale deal in such a way that it gets attention and appeals to your buyer(s) enough so that they will want to buy it. I suggest creating a brief portfolio with photos, a written description of the property and the surrounding area, and a pro-forma projecting financial results for the buyer of this property.

You can initially create a flyer to pique the interest of several buyers and only provide the portfolio to the buyer who is interested. You will want to showcase this juicy deal on your website and even post a Facebook ad and a LinkedIn post to attract your buyers. There is a free system called Postlets you can use to drive buyers to your website along with the Facebook and LinkedIn traffic. If you have done a good job building your database of buyers, and you have found and secured a great deal, then built an appealing presentation and communicated it to your buyers using the channels available to you, then you should make a profit for all of your effort.

Do you now see how incredibly profitable this business can be? Well it gets even better. When you have a Real Estate license it gives you the license to serve others in multiple capacities and make huge profits! What's interesting is that up until now you may have never considered getting your Real Estate license or perhaps you were dead set against it. I was, too. Let me share with you what I discovered.

We'll talk more about being an Investor/Agent in a minute but first I want to talk about using creative strategies when investing in Real Estate. Up until now you may be wondering if I ever used creative strategies when investing, and the answer is "Yes." I probably just sent a shockwave up your spine, especially if you remember some of my earlier comments. I did learn a lot from a gentleman named Carleton Sheets. He now makes his information available for free. He is one of the vanguards in the modern era of Real Estate Investing and he will tell you that he learned a lot of creative investing techniques from people and resources dating back to the 1950s. Some of those actually go back hundreds, even thousands of years.

I want you to be aware that there are creative techniques to investing. I also want you to be aware that you will have to work a lot harder to invest if you are trying to do so while not using traditional techniques or without using your own money. No matter, these are valuable in that they will stretch your knowledge and imagination and perhaps give you a few ideas to use in unique situations. I commend Mr. Sheets for making so much information available for free. I'm going to go over a few techniques that are old school and some I used when interest rates were much higher. Also, take note that you should check with your tax accountant, Investor/Agent, or even Real Estate attorney before using some of these just to make sure they are able to be used in your state or province. Some of the government programs may or may not be available in your state or province.

I think you're going to really like this section. You will certainly learn a lot so get out your pen or pencil and turn everything else off. You will need your whole brain for this. Let's do this. Turn the page.

Creative Investing Techniques

Creative Investing Techniques

For several years now I have been on a cash basis. However, when I first got started investing I used creative financing. Most investors learn these techniques early on in their investing career, like I did, as a way to avoid the cost of borrowing money from institutional lenders (banks, savings and loans, etc.) and to overcome unaffordable monthly mortgage loan payments and poor or nonexistent credit. Even people with money realize, if they can purchase property with very little or no money down and keep their monthly payments low, then they will have made a good real estate investment even better. Please note though that when you borrow or leverage too much, your equity position will be smaller and your cashflow will be lower, too!

Leverage means making the most of what you've got. This could mean borrowing from yourself or others based on a little capital and good credit, or it could mean leveraging the circumstances of a seller or yourself. When it comes to real estate investing, leverage is the use of other people's money. When the leverage is 100% (no money down), it means getting other people's money to do everything. If you invest $100,000 to purchase a $1,000,000 property, and the property generates a spendable cashflow of $200,000 per year through leverage, then you have earned two times – or 200% per year – on your investment ($200,000 divided by $100,000). If you purchased the same property "no money down," your return of $200,000 would have been infinite.

Are there people in the world who are willing to sell their properties creatively? Yes, there are. There may be more or less at different times depending on where we are in the business cycle. If interest rates are very high then you will see more sellers willing to be creative. If inventory is high then you will see the same thing.

SOURCES FOR CREATIVE FINANCING

As you progress through the individual "no money down" and creative financing techniques, you will be able to identify at least ten sources for creative financing. They are as follows:

1. The seller
2. The property itself
3. Investors
4. Partners
5. Tenants
6. Real estate agents and brokers
7. Your services and skills
8. Existing loans on the property
9. Unsecured paper and secured paper on equities (equity is the value of an asset minus any debt or money you owe on it)
10. Institutional lenders (banks, savings and loans)

A common limiting belief is that if you purchase property "no money down," the seller gets no cash. This may be true with some of the techniques, but there are others that will allow the seller to leave the closing table with cash. However, the cash does not have to be yours.

Not all sellers who are willing to be creative are in distress. In fact, when sellers are able to walk away from a closing table with cash in their pockets, you can purchase a seller's property more creatively, even though the seller may have initially been inflexible and interested in a more conventional sale.

The other important thing to remember is that, while a seller is inflexible today (or so the seller may say), that situation may well change within a few days or weeks. Sellers' circumstances, emotions, and needs change rapidly. A seller may be inflexible today but very eager to sell the proper creatively tomorrow.

All of the "no money down" techniques are described in detail, so you can apply them immediately. Eventually, you may combine different aspects from several techniques.

Since interest rates rise and fall continuously, the percentages used in these examples were selected for illustrative purposes only. The actual rate you offer will vary, depending on the current interest rates and the flexibility of the seller. The values of property are for illustrative purposes as well. A good "bread and butter" property may have a fair market value of $150,000 to $200,000 in one area of the country, and a value twice that or more in another.

Just remember, the basic premise of real estate investing is that interest rates must be – and usually are – commensurate with value.

NOTE: There can be some limiting beliefs out there that you may encounter and have to overcome. One of them is that mortgages are no longer assumable. This is not true! VA mortgages are still assumable and so are many adjustable rate mortgages!

Strategy 1: Pledged Asset Mortgage

Bankers seldom come up with creative alternatives for buying property with no money down, but several banks in the United States have.

This is a technique I have used in a number of cases. Rather than paying the traditional down payment which most banks require, some are accepting other assets as collateral. The asset may be something you personally own, or it could be provided by a family member or friend. The lender does not get the right to convert the asset to cash, unless you go into default on their loan, and they have to foreclose.

Generally, banks will not charge more than market rates for these loans, so they become more attractive. While being administered, the program uses only certificates of deposit at credit unions or federally insured banks, since they only accept pledged collateral. For an owner-occupied property, the certificate of deposit must be at least 10% of the price paid for; and that number moves to 20% for an investor loan. The original owner of the CD gets the accrued interest. Once a payment history begins, and/or the agreed upon minimum equity position is achieved, the CD is released to the person who pledged it.

I am convinced some banks – on a case-by-case basis – would be willing to accept a pledged asset, rather than a CD to a credit-worthy borrower. For example, banks are willing to accept a "pay-down" of interest rates by a seller of property. For a negotiated amount, a seller could pay down the interest rate on a bank loan for a period of several years, and the rate could be 3% or 4% below the current market rate.

Some banks allow a down payment to be gifted from a seller or a family member of the borrower. Based on the flexibility that some banks are showing, I believe there are banks which allow pledged assets other than CDs. For example, a vacant lot, a boat, fine jewelry, inventory in a business, or even accounts receivable may be considered. I knew one investor who persuaded a bank to issue a Letter of Credit to a seller, guaranteeing payment of a note he owed the seller 12 months later. This Letter of Credit was guaranteed by a mortgage on equity he had in another property.

If you do not have any cash for a down payment, then be creative in your negotiations with banks; suggest ways in which they might loan 100% of the purchase price of a property. Remember, bankers are schooled in more traditional ways of loaning money, but if you present a new and creative way – to obtain 100% financing – they may be open it.

Strategy 2: Bank Loans and Other Creative Sources of Down Payments

Banks and other types of lenders will make loans based on your signature, or perhaps, the equity you have in a car, boat, or other property. Demonstrate your ability to repay these loans by working with a few local banks. Start by borrowing small amounts and repaying the loans earlier than agreed. With this technique, building up a line of credit with two or three banks is not difficult.

You will also find the seller can be a good source to lend you the down payment. When the required down payment is only a few thousand dollars, or when you are a few thousand dollars short, a flexible seller may agree to a delayed down payment 6 to 12 months after closing. Offering the seller a high interest rate can help you do this. Many sellers would find a 12% to 15% interest rate attractive and might even spread the down payment over a longer period of time (for example, 24 to 48 months). On a relatively small amount of money, the higher interest rate does not actually cost you much more and it is tax deductible. One of my students just did this in Wisconsin!

Strategy 3: Blanket Mortgage

Another favorite of mine is the blanket mortgage. I did my first one of these with a small community bank. It was in the form of a commercial line of credit. A seller might be willing to sell "no money down," taking back a mortgage for the entire equity of a property. However, many sellers are afraid the buyer will walk away from the property before building up a substantial equity, forcing the resale of the property all over again. If this happens, sellers are concerned they will receive the property back in a condition worse than when it was originally sold.

To overcome a seller's fear, you could persuade them by offering additional collateral with a "blanket mortgage." A blanket mortgage includes more than one property. You might use equity in your home, another property, or even an automobile under the terms of a blanket mortgage.

Caution: With the blanket mortgage the seller may be taking back for a term as long as five or ten years. Since you do not want to tie up your extra property that long, make certain that the mortgage contains terms that will allow you to release your home or other property from the mortgage, after you have made payments on time for a period of 6, 12, or 18 months.

When I did my first one, the lender documented everything including a lien on all the properties under the blanket but did not record the liens and wasn't going to unless I started to get behind or go into default.

Strategy 4: Using the Broker's Commission

I generally don't like this because I am also a broker, too! However, I have been on both ends of this technique and it does work if presented properly. From time to time, you will come across a property listed by a broker that is being offered for a 10% down payment. Typically, the seller is asking for the 10% to cover the broker's commission, as well as closing costs.

Brokers' commissions are generally 5% to 7% of the purchase price. If a broker both lists and sells the property, the broker receives the entire commission. If another broker is involved, then usually the commission is split 50/50.

Borrowing a portion of the commission, or giving the broker a portion of the ownership in lieu of all or part of the commission, is sometimes possible, especially when dealing with a listing broker. If the listing broker is also the selling broker, the commission will not be split, and the broker will be in a better position to loan all or part of it to you.

If you find some initial reluctance from the broker, you might try to offer the broker a note for an amount larger than the commission. For example: if the broker's commission is $15,000, you might consider offering an $18,000 promissory note. The note might bear interest at 12% with payments of 1% per month. In other words, every month you would pay $150 to the broker. At the end of the year you would have reduced (amortized) the note by 12%, or $1,800. The note could become due and payable in five to seven years. Generating all or part of the down payment this way, is inexpensive.

Before approaching an agent or broker about borrowing a commission, it is important to understand how commission splits are handled in a real estate office. When a seller lists a piece of property with a broker, the broker's compensation is stated in the contract. It is usually computed as a percentage of the total selling price. Within a broker's office, salespeople have a splitting arrangement with the broker. Generally, the splitting agreement (50/50; 60/40, etc.) is predicated on the salesperson's annual productivity. While a seller will generally not know about internal splitting arrangements, an informed seller does know that the commission is always negotiable at the time the listing agreement is signed.

Brokers, beware! The one possible negative is when you are asked to partner with the consumer on a deal and make your commission your contribution. It all looks good on the front end but the risk may show up later if something goes wrong. If in this circumstance the consumer files a complaint and they are not a licensed real estate agent and you are, a hearing officer will often hold you to a higher standard. As a result they may hold you more accountable than the consumer.

Here is what this may look like. First, you have an agent who is creative and flexible AND knows how to work with investors – an Investor/Agent!

Broker's commission is usually 5% to 7% of the purchase price.

Initially, ask the broker to loan all of his or her commission to you, secured by a note and mortgage, at a reasonable rate of interest, say 5%.

If necessary, offer the broker a note for a slightly higher amount and at a higher interest rate.

You have reduced the amount of cash needed to purchase a property.

In several instances, I know of students who have not only succeeded in persuading the broker to take a note for his or her commission, they have actually borrowed money from the broker. In one case, the broker went into his pocket for $10,000 to make the deal work. The broker believed in the property and was to receive a $14,000 commission if the sale was successful. He wrote a check to the buyer for $10,000, and in return, he received a $24,000 note secured by a mortgage on the property.

By the way, one of the advantages of you becoming a licensed broker yourself is that you can, in most cases, share in a portion (often up to 50%) of the commission. That certainly beats borrowing! Another angle related to becoming a broker is you may intentionally choose not to share in a brokerage commission (and let the broker know this); this gives the broker further incentive to work harder toward having the seller accept your offer. If you choose this strategy, you can still try to borrow the commission. At that time, you subtly imply to the broker: If he or she doesn't want to lend you all or part of the commission, you would instead like to share in the commission.

Strategy 5: Buy Low, Refinance High

I used this technique dozens and dozens of times once I was on a cash basis. If you have access to sizable amounts of cash, this technique is excellent. You can sometimes buy properties for 75% to 80% of fair market value or less, from people who need to sell for all cash right away. I have bought properties for 50% of value using cash!

On one of the Superior Avenue properties, I was contacted by the brother of a city councilman who, like his brother, was also an investor. They asked if I could buy one of three properties they had under contract because they could only buy two. I looked at the property and quickly decided to go for it. They were closing in less than a week. I made my 50% offer and they took it. I paid very little in closing costs because the title company had already done all the work on all three properties, including the one I bought! Even after remodeling I more than doubled my investment in value, and cash flowed more than $1000 per month to boot! I also refinanced the property, getting all of my money back plus another $28,000 in cash. In other words I also utilized the prior technique!

Many professionals have cash available to invest under these circumstances. They have neither the time nor expertise to go into the marketplace to find properties like this. If you can, then enter into a working relationship with these types of people; it will generate a good yearly cashflow for yourself and your investor. A win/win situation is created for both of you.

Strategy 6: Create a Note and Sell it for Cash

Assume you locate a property that is on the market for $250,000 which has an existing $125,000 assumable mortgage. The seller has an equity of $125,000 and is asking for this amount in cash. The property has been on the market for four or five months – without selling – and the owner is getting anxious. Offer the seller $75,000 cash, contingent upon being able to locate a new second mortgage. You are, in effect, offering the seller $200,000 for the property ($125,000 mortgage assumed plus $75,000 cash). This is not at all a bad offer, considering the seller is asking $250,000, and the property has been on the market for four or five months. If the seller accepts, you will proceed to find a lender to loan $75,000 to you in return for a mortgage.

You may have to go to a private lender. Check the classified ad section in your local newspaper, or you can go to a local mortgage broker who represents private investors. Call one of these lenders; tell them you have a property that is valued at $250,000, has an existing $125,000 first mortgage on it, and you are in need of $75,000 cash. Ask them how large a note and mortgage would have to be; also inquire about the interest rate and term for them to give you the loan. Assume they respond by telling you they would need a $75,000 note and mortgage at 10% interest for a term of five years. You would then determine, by doing a financial analysis of the property, whether or not the net operating income would support the payments on this new second mortgage – with you assuming the existing mortgage. If it does, you would proceed with the transaction and buy the property with "no money down."

This is what this will look like:

Asking price... $250,000
Seller's equity.. $125,000
Property has been on the market for an extended period and the seller is anxious.

Offer the seller $75,000 cash contingent upon locating a new second mortgage.

Find a lender to loan $75,000.

Look in classifieds of local newspaper for private lenders or go to a local mortgage broker.

> Remember, if you are a Silver Level Member or higher of Real Estate With Gary Wilson, you can access the Private Lenders Report for your area on demand any time for FREE! Email Support@REWGW.com for details.

Determine, through a financial analysis, if the NOI will support the assumable mortgage and a new second mortgage with the terms required by the lender.

The seller receives cash for the equity in the property.
You have a "no money down" transaction.

Strategy 7: Defer a Portion of the Purchase Price

In some areas of the country, local real estate prices are very high, making it nearly impossible to achieve a break-even or positive cashflow. This problem can be overcome in two ways: 1) Negotiate no-interest or low-interest financing by the seller, or 2) Defer a portion of the purchase price. The latter alterative is usually easier. This works great in places like San Francisco or Vancouver, B.C.

Assume a seller has a three-bedroom, two-bath home on the market for $1,000,000. There is an existing $500,000 assumable first mortgage on the property. In return for obtaining his or her purchase price, the seller is willing to carry back a mortgage for the balance at the going market rate of interest.

The fair market rent rate on the property is $8,000. You could offer to assume the first mortgage, and give the seller a second mortgage with two notes; one note for $250,000 at a market rate of interest and the second for $250,000, also fixed at a market rate of interest but with the interest deferred for five years. At that time, the notes – plus the unpaid interest on the second note – would become due. Or preferably, the first note would stay on the property, making only the free second note with deferred interest due.

Interest on $250,000, 6% simple interest per annum, for 5 years equals $18,000 per year.

Be sure that the deferred interest on the second note ($250,000) is only accumulated, not compounded. Otherwise, you will be paying interest on interest. That could cause the unpaid balance of the $250,000 note plus interest to escalate dramatically.

At the end of six years, you could refinance, paying off the first mortgage plus both notes or – most preferably – the second note only for $250,000 plus interest. Ideally, the seller's first note for $25,000 and the second mortgage taken back would stay on the property. If the second mortgage is to stay on the property after refinancing, the mortgage would have to include a subordination clause that would be inserted at the time you buy the property and sign the mortgage.

If the rent rate will not support the first and second mortgage – for $250,000 – the interest on that note could be adjusted down, to a point where the property could support the payments. The second note would then be correspondingly increased.

Strategy 8: Deposits, Rent Credits, and Real Estate Tax Credits

I have done this a number of different ways to close on a property. At closing, you will receive a credit for unpaid real estate taxes. Real estate taxes are generally paid in arrears, meaning the seller is always behind in paying taxes. For example, real estate taxes for this year are due and paid sometime near the beginning of the following year. The buyer receives a credit for the real estate taxes, which have not yet been paid.

In the case of income property, security deposits are credited as well. Some landlords collect the final month's rent at the time of signing the lease. By doing this, this rent is turned over to the buyer at closing. Finally, the buyer receives credit for part of the rent, which has been collected in the current month. For example, if you close on income property on the 10th of the month, you will receive credit for approximately two-thirds of the month's rent. If you close on the first of the month, you will either receive the rents collected already by the seller, or you will immediately collect the rents yourself. Credits can be used to reduce the amount of cash required for the down payment.

Sometimes, these credits can be substantial. On a ten-unit building, there might be $10,000 in security deposits, an additional credit for unpaid real estate taxes of $5,000, and the last month's rents of ten times the monthly rent rate. You can see that it would not be unusual for credits on a building this size to be as much as $25,000.

You should also remember that when buying property, you will have no expenses during the first 30 days. Since mortgage payments and other expenses – such as utilities – are paid in arrears (after you use the service) and rents are paid in advance, you will have one month's rent that is not committed.

Let's say you purchase a ten-unit building on the first of the month. You receive rents in the amount of $10,000. You receive a credit for security deposits of $10,000, and you receive a credit for the last month's rents of $10,000. Assuming that real estate taxes are $5,000 per year, you receive a real estate tax credit of up to $5,000, depending on when the closing takes place.

If you are getting a new mortgage, the first payment will not be due until the 1st of the following month. You can use the second month's rent to pay the first mortgage payment. If you were assuming an existing mortgage, where the payment is due around the 15th of the month, you could talk to the lender about moving the mortgage payment ahead to the 1st of the following month. You will probably have to pay one-half month's interest, but you would benefit by receiving as much as one-half month's rent payments. This extra cash could be used for a down payment, for fixing up the property, or your own personal use. Your total credit just for these items will be $35,000!

Because of this, you have substantially reduced the amount of cash needed to close on this building. These credits may very well be enough to make this a "cash back at closing" deal.

Strategy 9: The FHA 203(b) Loan

The loan known as the FHA 203(b), is the single-family mortgage insurance program most commonly used all over America. According to the FHA official site, the FHA 203(b) "may be used to purchase or refinance a new or existing 1- to 4-family home in both urban and rural areas including manufactured homes on permanent foundations. Typically, lenders offer terms at 15 or 30 years, and interest rates are negotiated between the borrower and lender."

Borrowers who have looked at conventional mortgages and compared them with the FHA 203(b) learn several things. The 203(b) is easier to qualify for because the FHA backs the loan, giving protection to the lender.

Thanks to this protection, the FHA Frequently Asked Questions section at FHA.gov says, "…you don't have to have a perfect credit score to get an FHA mortgage. In fact, even if you have had credit problems, such as a bankruptcy, it's easier for you to qualify for an FHA loan than a conventional loan."

FHA loans do not come with zero down payment offers, but the down payment that is required is comparatively lower than many conventional loans. FHA mortgages require a down payment as low as 3.5%, which the FHA allows to come from an employer, family member, or charitable organization in the form of a gift if the borrower chooses to accept outside help for the loan.

In spite of what some assume, the FHA does not set interest rates on FHA mortgages, but according to HUD, "FHA loans have competitive interest rates because the Federal government insures the loans. Always compare an FHA loan with other loan types."

All FHA loan money comes from participating lenders and the FHA does not provide "direct financing." But it does require agency approval before a bank can issue an FHA home loan – the FHA and HUD work with lenders to ensure quality, regulatory compliance, and fairness in the lending process.

There are plenty of other FHA insured home loans available besides the 203(b), it's just one of many – but it's the first thing many borrowers think of when they want to buy a home with an FHA mortgage – even if they don't know the technical name for the loan.

Strategy 10: Home Equity Loan

This is one of the very first strategies I used when I started investing in real estate. It leverages the capital in your own home. Many lending institutions make loans secured with the equity in your home or other properties by up to 80% of their value or more. There was a time when you could get a loan of up to 125% of the value of your home. That also partially led to one of the biggest economic downturns in history! The interest rate is usually tied to the prime rate. Shop around… some lenders may offer a rate anywhere from 0.5% below prime to 4% over prime rate. Generally, you will get a better rate if you are borrowing a larger amount of money ($100,000 or more) than if you borrow a small amount.

The payoff period is often 5 to 20 years, depending upon the lending institution. Most institutions do not charge any points (the percentage of the loan the borrower must pay to the bank for making the loan – one point equals 1% of the loan amount). In addition, the originating costs of the loan are very small, and the interest paid may be tax deductible. If you get this in the form of a line of credit then you can use and reuse this source of capital over and over again!

Strategy 11: Land Contracts (Agreements for Deed or Contract for Deed)

This form of seller financing is quite popular in some parts of the country. It is most often used with the sale of vacant land or lots. In concept, it calls for the purchaser to pay for all or most of the property before he or she receives legal title. In its simplest form, a land contract works like a mortgage, except that the legal title does not pass until a predetermined and stipulated number of payments have been made.

Theoretically, it provides additional protection for the seller in the event of default. If the purchaser does not make the payments as agreed, then the land contract usually stipulates that the money paid – up to the date of default – is deemed to be rent for the period from the term of possession to the date of default. To clear the title if default occurs, a "Quit Claim Deed" should be given by the purchaser to the seller. This should be done at the time of purchase, to release the purchaser's equitable interest in the property.

When a land contract is used, the contract will call for specific dollar payments. These are usually monthly with the money applied in the following order: 1) to interest on the purchase price; 2) to any applicable charges, such as real estate taxes, insurance, and special assessments; 3) to the unpaid principal balance of the purchase price. If the contract states that the legal title will pass before the principal balance is paid in full, then a "balloon" payment will usually become due. However, the seller could take back a note and mortgage in lieu of the "balloon" payment.

Some people believe a land contract provides a legal way around due-on-sale clauses found in many mortgages. Not so. The due-on-sale clause is triggered by any transfer of legal or equitable title to real estate. While legal title is not transferred with a land contract – until the stipulated number of payments have been made – equitable title has passed.

From a practical standpoint, the due-on-sale clause is not triggered, because no deed has been conveyed and recorded, and insurance continues in force in the name of the seller. It is unlikely, but not impossible, that the lender would learn of the transaction.

Let's look at an example. Assume that you find a two-family property that is on the market for $240,000. There is an existing first mortgage of $120,000 with monthly payments of $1,000. The mortgage is not assumable. The owner is asking for $40,000 cash down, and is willing to take back a "wrap-around" mortgage for $200,000 at 8%. Let's say you are able to persuade the seller to accept $220,000 for the property. Rather than take legal title to the property and give the seller a "wrap-around" mortgage, the seller sells you the property on a land contract. Since land contracts protect a seller more, you have convinced the seller to accept a $20,000 down payment, consisting of 10 semi-annual payments of $1,000 each with no interest. You then agree you will pay the seller $200,000 at 8% interest only for five years. At that time, you will agree to take legal title to the property. With the added monthly payment for taxes and insurance, which we will assume to be $500, your total cash out of pocket will be $1,500 per month. You know that the two-family property will bring in a total income of $2,000 a month. If you add a 10% management fee and a $100 per month cost for maintenance, then you will have approximately $200 per month positive cashflow.

This is win/win for both parties. You are buying the property with little money down. The seller has the security of knowing he or she has not conveyed legal title of the property to you, and there is a positive cashflow.

If you use this technique to buy a property, there are words of warning. If the contract for deed is for an extended period of time, then a number of events could take place that might put you in a precarious position. If the property is mortgaged with a mortgage containing a due-on-sale clause, then it is possible – although unlikely – the lender will learn of the land contract sale and call the loan due, possibly demanding the loan be properly assumed with related fees and an adjustment of a higher interest rate. Your contract should contain language stating, if this happens, how you and the seller will handle this problem. A reasonable way is to have you and the seller agree to split any additional or increased costs that arise from this event.

Also, to protect yourself from the sellers' divorcing, declaring bankruptcy, becoming mentally incompetent, or dying, you should have the seller execute a deed. The deed should be held by a reputable title company. Your monthly payments should be mailed to the title company, and when the agreed upon number of payments have been made, the title company will record the deed.

At the time you enter into the land contract, a title search should be done to make certain the sellers have clear title. Then – as mentioned earlier – after the contract has been signed, the contract itself or a memorandum of the land contract should be recorded in the public records of the county, where the property is located.

In order for this to work you need a seller who does not need cash at closing but would like monthly income and little risk.

The buyer has a property for almost "no money down." In fact, with a security deposit and last month's rent from a tenant located before the closing, the buyer may even put cash in his or her own pocket.

The buyer has "purchased" a property even with bad credit.

The buyer has a positive monthly income of over $200.

The seller has a small down payment, a monthly income, and has been relieved of ownership responsibilities while getting almost all of what they asked for!

Strategy 12: Life Insurance Policy Loan

This is actually one I learned from some of my wealthier clients. The cash value of whole life insurance policies earns an extremely low return. This money can often be borrowed at rates of 6% or less. You can borrow against your policy (or the policies of others) to acquire real estate.

If a deal requires a $100,000 down payment to purchase an investment property and you have whole life insurance of your own with a cash value of $100,000, you can borrow against the $100,000 and use this $100,000 as a down payment. You can also partner with someone who has a whole life policy and offer to pay them interest for the use of their whole life insurance value.

Since borrowing against a whole life insurance policy will reduce the pay-out at the time of death, you would want to take out a term life insurance policy for the policyholder in the same amount as you borrowed. If additional peace of mind is needed for the whole life policy owner, you could take out a term life insurance policy on your own life.

You can see that this type of situation is truly win/win/win. You buy the property with no money down. The policyholder has the same amount of insurance and makes a small profit on the borrowed amount. And, the life insurance agent sold a new term life insurance policy.

Strategy 13: Lower the Price and Raise the Interest Rate

My very first mentor showed this to me. It was in the early '80s when interest rates were already very high and more people, including homeowners, were using this to buy the homes they lived in. It wasn't just used by investors. A higher interest rate may encourage the seller to accept lower prices or lower down payments or both. This will also allow a seller to postpone a portion of capital gain.

For example, a seller has a property for sale at an asking price of $500,000. The property has an existing, assumable mortgage of $250,000, payable at the rate of $2,500 per month. The seller wants $100,000 cash at close, and will extend you a loan of $400,000 in the form of a mortgage at 10% interest.

Offer the seller $450,000 with no money down. Agree to take over the loan of $250,000 and pay 10% interest on the remaining $200,000 for a period of five years. The result is a monthly interest payment of $1,666.66 ($250,000 times 10% divided by 12 months) to the seller. If you pay this per month for interest, then the entire principal amount of $200,000 will be due in five years.

If the total monthly payments – for the first and second mortgage of $4,166 per month – result in a negative cashflow, then restructure the second mortgage so only a portion of the 10% interest is paid monthly. The balance would be accumulated but not compounded, and would be due along with the $200,000 at the end of five years. Then at the end of five years, refinance the entire debt using your equity as a down payment.

Buyer has a property for "no money down." The monthly payments may be high, but restructuring the interest can help alleviate some of the burden.

The seller has received a good price and high monthly income.

Strategy 14: Move a Private Mortgage from a Senior to a Junior Position

Consider the following situation. A seller has a property on the market for $300,000. There is an existing private first mortgage on the property in the amount of $180,000.

Approach the private mortgage holder to see if the mortgage can be moved from a first position (senior) to a second position (junior) if you pay $60,000 in cash. Agree to pay the cash after a new first mortgage is secured. This will reduce the mortgage from $180,000 to $120,000. Next, get a new $180,000 first mortgage on the property; $60,000 of this will be the cash that goes to the private mortgage holder; the other $120,000 will go to the seller. This "no money down" technique works well when the private mortgage holder is not willing to discount the mortgage in return for a complete payoff.

If you own property that has a private first mortgage, you could use this same strategy to remove your equity for other investment purposes.

The seller receives $300,000 for the property and receives all cash for his or her $120,000 equity in the property.

The buyer has a "no money down" deal, a $180,000 new first mortgage, and a $120,000 second mortgage.

Strategy 15: Obtain a New Mortgage to Pay Off Existing Loans and Provide Down Payment Money

You can use this strategy when the seller owes nothing on the property, or when the amount the seller owes is not greater than 40% of the property's value. However, you must have a flexible seller willing to help finance the property. I love working with sellers who owe nothing on their property. They are more willing to listen to creative strategies.

For instance, assume the seller of a $500,000 house has an existing loan of $100,000, but they are looking for a $150,000 down payment and willing to carry the financing for the balance of $250,000 ($500,000 less $100,000 less $150,000). Simply obtain a new first mortgage for $250,000, which can pay off the existing $100,000 mortgage and give the seller $150,000. Next, give the seller a second mortgage in the amount of $250,000. The $250,000 first mortgage – plus a $250,000 second mortgage – gives the seller his or her total asking price of $500,000.

A seller who may be reluctant to accept this offer, may ultimately agree to accept an offer with more cash up front. For example, obtain a new loan in the amount of $350,000, giving the seller a $100,000 larger down payment than expected, or a total of $250,000 ($350,000 new mortgage proceeds minus $100,000 old mortgage payoff).

The seller receives total asking price and the entire down payment needed. The buyer has a "no money down" deal.

Many banks, but not all, will want you as the purchaser to put some of your own cash in the transaction. If you have none, but do have equity in another property you own, then securing the second mortgage from the seller may satisfy the bank. Basically, you would say to the banker, "I am, in effect, using my equity in another property I own to borrow money from the seller of this property, and I'm using that money for my down payment." Another alternative is you could bring in a partner who has equity in another property, which could be used to secure the seller's mortgage.

An additional solution would be for the seller to transfer the property to you "as-is," with the existing loan remaining on the property. Once the property has been deeded to you, you would then obtain a new first mortgage for $250,000 and complete the transaction as described. If you find bankers inflexible in making a new first mortgage loan under these circumstances, contact mortgage brokers. They frequently are more flexible than banks, but charge higher interest rates or more points.

Strategy 16: Rental Participation

More seasoned investors who are ready to retire are more likely to work with you using this strategy. You might persuade a seller to give you a "no money down" or low purchase, low-interest seller financing. You may even utilize a moratorium of interest, which is an agreement that no interest will be due on the seller's note and mortgage for a specified period of time. You would agree to give the seller a portion of any rental increases.

Assume you are negotiating to purchase a property that rents for $1,000 per month or $12,000 per year. Offer the seller 10%, 15%, or even 25% of any annual rental income that exceeds $12,000 per year, excluding any forfeited security deposits. This money might go toward any unpaid interest, or it might be considered a "reward" for the seller agreeing to a low-interest loan. You might do this for a period of three to seven years. In essence, the seller participates in the risk as well as the rewards of the property.

Strategy 17: Satisfy the Seller's Needs

Attempt to learn what the seller intends to do with the down payment. If it is going to be used to acquire something or pay a debt, then perhaps, you could acquire the item for him or her, and put it on your credit card. Or, you could assume a seller's liability.

The seller might be using the cash received for the property to take a trip overseas, to purchase furniture, or even buy a new automobile. You could agree to pay for the trip or furniture or even lease an automobile for the seller. The seller may have outstanding bills, which are due to a department store or a professional person, such as a doctor. By personally contacting these people or places, you arrange to assume the repayment responsibility for the debt, or a discount could be obtained by paying the debt in full. This strategy offers many possibilities.

Never jump to any premature conclusions about the seller's situation. This is a perfect example, where questioning the seller can net positive results.

As much as possible in any situation, try to gather as much information as you can. The solution will often present itself in the process of doing so!

Strategy 18: Using Discounted Bonds

If a seller is willing to assist in financing the property, then some collateral is usually required. Generally, this takes the form of the real estate that you are buying. Deep down, I am convinced that most sellers would be more comfortable having their notes secured by good quality bonds.

You'll find private corporate bonds – listed in the financial section of major newspapers called New York Exchange Bonds – and U.S. government bonds in the *Wall Street Journal*. For tax-free bonds, you'll need to contact a stock broker.

Find a good tax-free, zero-interest bond, such as a city, state, or county revenue bond, which will be due in nine or ten years. You will probably have to pay between $500 and $700 for one of these bonds, depending on interest rates at the time. But when they become due and payable at maturity in nine or ten years, they will yield $1,000. Since the bonds are tax-free, there will be no tax liability for the seller or you.

This strategy works best when you have a relatively low mortgage in relation to the property value. Let's look at the following example. Assume that a seller has a 4-family property on the market for $200,000. The existing mortgage on the property is $50,000, and the seller has $150,000 in equity. The down payment the seller needs at closing is $20,000 cash, and the seller is willing to accept a $130,000 second mortgage due in ten years.

Ask the seller if good quality bonds securing the $130,000 note would be better than a second mortgage on real estate. Some sellers will agree to the bonds. You then offer to buy the property with the $20,000 down payment due in 90 days, and the $130,000 note secured by the bonds. Ask the seller to deed the property to you with the $150,000 equity; this will secure the $150,000 you owe to the seller with equity in. Once you are the owner, obtain a new $150,000 mortgage on the property.

The proceeds from the mortgage are used as follows: $50,000 to pay off the first mortgage; approximately $70,000 to buy the $130,000 worth of bonds due in nine or ten years; $20,000 goes to the seller; and you can put approximately $10,000 cash in your pocket.

Potential problems do exist though.

First, if the bonds are taxable, then the seller will have to recognize an annual gain as the bonds increase in value. Tell the seller this. To avoid the yearly recognition of taxable gain, you may want to use zero-coupon municipal bonds.

The second problem is unless the seller is willing to take zero interest on the note, then you will have to make interest payments each year, until the bonds mature. This will not present a problem as long as you budget properly. Don't forget, you will receive cash at the closing.

It should be understood that we are not attempting to deal in an underhanded way or fool the seller. Everything should be spelled out and understandable to the seller. While the bonds are only worth approximately $70,000 today, they will be worth $130,000 in ten years – at the time the seller has agreed to receive the money. The seller's only risk is loss of the interest, which you have agreed to pay in the meantime. To overcome this, you might agree to secure the interest payments with a mortgage on another property you own. If you have the cash, you could prepay several years' interest. You could even buy a second zero-interest bond for that amount, which could be used as security for the interest you have agreed to pay. Be creative.

Seller receives $20,000 cash. The seller has bonds to secure the $130,000 note which is due in ten years. The buyer has equity in a property. Extra cash has been generated for the buyer.

Strategy 19: Using Equity in One Property to Buy Another

This requires you to create a promissory note and mortgage on existing equity you have in an asset (home, boat, investment property, automobile, vacant land, etc.), and use it as a down payment on another property.

Let's say you find a duplex that is on the market for $120,000, and there is an existing $50,000 mortgage. The seller's equity is $70,000 ($120,000 less $50,000). Create a promissory note and mortgage in the amount of $30,000, secured by equity in one of your assets. Use that as a down payment on the 2-family property, and ask the seller to take either a $40,000 second mortgage or a $90,000 "wrap-around" mortgage for the balance. ("Wrap-around" mortgages are discussed in the next strategy.) When you buy the 2-family property, you will immediately have $30,000 equity in this property because of the $30,000 mortgage, which is secured by another property that you used as a down payment.

The mortgage that you are creating on your existing asset should have a "substitution of collateral" clause, allowing you to later move that mortgage. For example, you might use equity in your own home to buy investment Property A; then, you use equity in A to buy B and B to buy C. With the substitution of collateral clause, you can move the mortgage from your own personal residence into your most recent purchase, Property C. If the seller of the 2-family property, Property A, is concerned about not receiving any cash at the time of close, then the note and mortgage can be converted into cash by selling it to someone else.

Buyer has $30,000 equity in the 2-family property and has once again bought "no money down."

Strategy 20: The Wrap-Around Mortgage

Assume the following situation. A seller has a property with a fair market value (F.M.V.) of $250,000, and an existing assumable mortgage of $150,000 at 8% interest with payments of $1,270 per month. The seller's equity is $100,000 ($250,000 less $150,000).

A classic, yet conventional, "no money down" way to buy the property would call for the buyer to assume the first mortgage of $150,000. Next, the buyer would give the seller a second mortgage for the $100,000 balance, at a mutually agreeable interest rate – suppose 10% – with payments of $1000 per month. The purchaser's total payment would be $2,270 per month.

To avoid the cost and liability of assuming the existing mortgage, offer the seller a $250,000 "wrap-around" mortgage, payable at the rate of 10% interest, with payments of $2,225 per month. On the surface, it appears to be the same proposition, but look at the actual effect.

A "wrap-around" mortgage is a new mortgage which literally "wraps" around the old mortgage. By using a "wrap-around" mortgage, the buyer makes payments on the new mortgage directly to the seller, and the seller continues to make payments on the old mortgage. Since the payments on the new mortgage are larger than on the old mortgage, the seller keeps the difference.

In the "wrap-around" mortgage example, you will pay the seller annual payments of $26,700 ($2,225 times 12). The seller will pay annual payments of $14,700 ($1,225 times 12) on the first mortgage. The seller will keep the difference, or $12,000 per year ($26,700 less $14,700). The seller's equity is $100,000, so the seller is actually netting 12% ($12,000 divided by $100,000) on the transaction. The first mortgage – because it is older and more of the monthly payment is being credited toward the principal balance – is being paid off at a faster rate than the "wrap-around" mortgage. Therefore, when the first mortgage is paid off in 20 years or so, the "wrap-around" mortgage will still have an unpaid balance of about $165,000. The seller's equity has effectively grown from $100,000 to $165,000 and, in the meantime, has earned 12% annually; a win/win situation.

The seller keeps $12,000 in interest per year for a 12% return on his/her $100,000 equity. The seller's mortgage is paid off in 20 years. The seller's equity in the mortgage has grown from $100,000 to $165,000.

Buyer accomplishes a "no money down" deal. The buyer avoids the cost and liability of assuming the first mortgage from a bank.

Strategy 21: Federal, State, and Local Real Estate-Related Programs

PLEASE NOTE: These programs come and go. This is an example of what has been available at different times. I encourage you to contact your local, county, and state agencies to determine what is possible now.

Many cities and towns have real estate related programs which can assist you. All 50 states have housing programs. Here is a list of groups of people who benefit from these loans:

- First-time home buyer
- Lower or moderate income home buyer
- Disabled or handicapped person
- Minority woman
- American Indian
- Property with an environmental hazard
- Elderly
- Delinquent on mortgage payments
- Want to build low-cost rental units
- Neighborhood needs revitalization
- Migrant farm worker
- Live in a mobile home rental park
- Want to make home more energy efficient
- Live in home with dysfunctional plumbing
- Live in property with lead paint

The question is, how do you use these various programs? It would be an enormous task (and soon outdated) to try to list every single agency in every state. But with a little effort on your part, it should be a simple task to locate all the agencies and programs in your state, in which you might participate.

How can you achieve this? You can go to your local telephone company office or library, and find the telephone directory for your state capitol. From there, you can call the office of your local State Representative, asking if they can provide the names and addresses of the housing-related agencies. In addition, look at your local telephone directory for agencies that have the word 'housing' or 'mortgage' in the name. Contact the Human Services Department of your county movement, too; they can help determine which of the local programs you qualify for and which would benefit you most.

Do this research and obtain information about every program available; your goal is to find what might assist you personally or professionally in your role as a real estate investor. These agencies want you to take advantage of their resources. You pay for these programs through tax money; isn't it time to benefit from that?

Every year, hundreds of millions of dollars in budgeted expenditures go unclaimed. This is primarily because people do not know about these programs, or they are too lazy to do some basic research. Even so, the government provides assistance in an amount of approximately $500 billion per year. The assistance takes many forms. There are loans with or without interest; there are loan guarantees for loans made through private lenders; there are grants that do not require repayment; there is unrestricted-use or specified direct payments to individuals; and there is insurance, which is designed to assure reimbursement for any losses sustained.

Be aware though, the government programs are constantly changing. Some are eliminated as new ones are added. While a given program may be technically active, from a practical standpoint, it may be inactive because of lack of funding by Congress.

Federal Government Programs

Some of the federal programs that would be most applicable are shown below along with the name of the office in Washington, D.C., that administers it and a brief description.

As of this writing here is a list of what the federal government is offering:

BASIC FHA-INSURED HOME MORTGAGE

Managing Agency

Federal Housing Administration (FHA)
https://www.hud.gov/program_offices/housing/fhahistory

Program Description

This program can help individuals buy a single-family home. While U.S. Housing and Urban Development (HUD) does not lend money directly to buyers to purchase a home, FHA-approved lenders make loans through a number of FHA insurance programs.

General Program Requirements

Home buyers or current homeowners who intend to live in the home and are able to meet the cash investment, the mortgage payments, eligibility and credit requirements, can apply for a home mortgage loan through an FHA-approved lender.

Loan Terms

Please contact an FHA-approved lender for loan term information. To find an approved lender, please visit:

https://www.hud.gov/program_offices/housing/sfh/lender/lenderlist

Your Next Steps

The following information will lead you to the next steps to apply for this benefit.

Application Process

To obtain an FHA-insured mortgage, contact an FHA-approved lender:

https://www.hud.gov/program_offices/housing/sfh/lender/lenderlist

Program Contact Information

To read more about the home buying process, go to:
http://portal.hud.gov/hudportal/HUD?src=/program_offices/housing/sfh/ins/203b--df

To contact a HUD Housing Counseling agency, go to:
http://www.hud.gov/counseling/

To contact the Federal Housing Administration (FHA), please use one of the following methods:

Visit: http://portal.hud.gov/hudportal/HUD?src=/program_offices/housing

Write:
U.S. Department of Housing and Urban Development
Federal Housing Administration
451 Seventh St., SW
Washington, D.C. 20410

Call: 1-800-CALL-FHA (1-800-225-5342) or via Federal Information Relay Service (w/TTY): 1-800-877-8339

Email: answers@hud.gov

CASH-OUT REFINANCE LOAN

Managing Agency

Veterans Benefits Administration (VBA) http://benefits.va.gov/benefits/

Program Description

The Department of Veterans Affairs (VA) *Cash-Out Refinance Loan* is for homeowners who want to trade equity for cash from their home. These loans can be used as strictly cash at closing, or to pay off debt, making home improvements, and paying off liens. The Cash-Out Refinance Loan can also be used to refinance a non-VA loan into a VA loan. VA will guaranty loans up to 100% of the value of your home.

General Program Requirements

Persons who may qualify for VA-guaranteed loans include:

- Eligible Veterans / Servicemembers
- Current Reserve and National Guard members (after 6 years of creditable service)
- Certain surviving spouses

To be eligible, the Veteran/Servicemember must have been discharged under conditions other than dishonorable and meet length of service requirements.

As a requirement for a VA home loan, the Veteran, the Veteran's spouse, or dependent child must certify occupancy for the property.

Loan Terms

Market Interest Rate, VA funding fee, and no pre-payment penalties. Maximum loan term cannot exceed 30 years. No maximum loan amount.

Application Process

To apply, you will need a valid Certificate of Eligibility (COE). There are several ways to obtain your COE:

- You may be able to obtain a COE online through eBenefits.
- If you are unable to obtain your COE through eBenefits, check with your lender. In most cases, your lender will be able to obtain a COE for you using the Automated Certificate of Eligibility (ACE) program.

For more information on this program, please visit the Home Loans webpage.

Program Contact Information

If you have questions:

- Visit the Inquiry Routing and Information System (IRIS) website to search Frequently Asked Questions or ask a question online.
- Please contact a Regional Loan Center if you have detailed questions.

To apply for benefits and view your benefit status, open an eBenefits Premium account. eBenefits is a one-stop source for information on Department of Defense and Department of Veterans Affairs benefits and services. With a free Premium level eBenefits account, Veterans, Servicemembers and their family members can conduct self-service transactions such as checking compensation and pension claim status information, enrolling in GI Bill, and obtaining copies of civil service preference letters, military records (DD214), and other personal information. For further information and to register for a free Premium level account, visit the eBenefits website.

COMBINATION MORTGAGE INSURANCE FOR MANUFACTURED HOME AND LOT

Managing Agency

Federal Housing Administration (FHA)
https://www.hud.gov/program_offices/housing/fhahistory

Program Description

Federal Housing Administration (FHA) insures mortgage loans made by FHA-approved lenders to buyers of manufactured homes and the lots on which to place them.

General Program Requirements

Buyers of manufactured homes who plan to use the home as their principal residence are eligible to apply for a home loan with an FHA-approved lender.

Loan Terms

Please contact an FHA-approved lender for loan term information. To find an approved lender, please visit:
http://www.hud.gov/ll/code/llslcrit.cfm

Application Process

To obtain an FHA insured mortgage, contact an FHA-approved lender:
http://www.hud.gov/ll/code/llslcrit.cfm

Program Contact Information

To read more about this program, go to:
http://portal.hud.gov/hudportal/HUD?src=/program_offices/housing/sfh/title/manuf146

To contact a U.S. Department of Housing and Urban Development (HUD) Housing Counseling agency, go to: http://www.hud.gov/counseling/

To contact the Federal Housing Administration (FHA), please use one of the following methods:

Visit: http://portal.hud.gov/hudportal/HUD?src=/program_offices/housing

Write:

U.S. Department of Housing and Urban Development
Federal Housing Administration
451 Seventh St., SW
Washington, D.C. 20410

Call: 1-800-CALL-FHA (1-800-225-5342) or via Federal Information Relay Service (w/TTY): 1-800-877-8339

Email: answers@hud.gov

DIRECT HOME LOANS FOR NATIVE AMERICANS

Managing Agency

Veterans Benefits Administration (VBA) http://benefits.va.gov/benefits/

Program Description

The Native American Direct Loan (NADL) program makes home loans available to eligible Native American Veterans who wish to purchase, construct, or improve a home on Federal Trust land or to reduce the interest rate.

Veterans who are not Native American, but who are married to a Native American non-Veteran, may be eligible for a direct loan under this program.

General Program Requirements

To obtain a NADL, the law requires that:

1. The applicant must be an eligible Veteran.
2. The tribal organization or other appropriate Native American group must be participating in the VA direct loan program. The tribal organization must have signed a Memorandum of Understanding with the Secretary of Veterans Affairs, that spells out the conditions under which the program will operate on its trust lands.
3. Apply for a Certificate of Eligibility.
4. The loan must be to purchase, construct, or improve a home on Native American trust land.
5. The Veteran must occupy the property as his or her primary residence.
6. The Veteran must be a satisfactory credit risk.

Commissioned Officers of the Public Health Service and National Oceanic and Atmospheric Administration are considered to be active duty members and Veterans, once discharged.

Length-of-service requirements apply, in most cases.

All prospective applicants are encouraged to first contact their local housing authority and VA to discuss their financial situation and obtain a general idea of whether or not they might qualify for a home loan.

For more information, please visit the NADL program website.

Program Contact Information

If you have questions:

- Visit the Inquiry Routing and Information System (IRIS) website to search Frequently Asked Questions or ask a question on-line.
- Please contact a Regional Loan Center if you have detailed questions.

To apply for benefits and view your benefit status, open an eBenefits Premium account. eBenefits is a one-stop source for information on Department of Defense and Department of Veterans Affairs benefits and services. With a free Premium level eBenefits account, Veterans, Servicemembers and their family members can conduct self-service transactions such as checking compensation and pension claim status information, enrolling in GI Bill, and obtaining copies of civil service preference letters, military records (DD214), and other personal information. For further information and to register for a free Premium level account, visit the eBenefits website.

ENERGY EFFICIENT MORTGAGE INSURANCE

Managing Agency

Federal Housing Administration (FHA)
https://www.hud.gov/program_offices/housing/fhahistory

Program Description

This program helps homebuyers or homeowners save money on utility bills by helping them get loans to cover the cost of adding energy-saving features to new or existing housing as part of a Federal Housing Administration insured home purchase or refinancing mortgage.

The Federal Housing Administration's (FHA) Energy Efficient Mortgage (EEM) program recognizes that lower utility costs can help a homeowner pay a higher mortgage to cover the cost of energy improvements. Under the program, persons may add the cost of energy-efficient improvements to their loan amount.

General Program Requirements

The borrower must qualify for the portion of the loan used to purchase or refinance a home. Borrowers are not required to qualify on the portion of the loan used for making energy-efficient upgrades. All FHA-approved lenders are eligible to offer EEM to persons who are purchasing or refinancing with an FHA-insured mortgage.

Borrowers must qualify for a home purchase or refinance under FHA's minimum credit requirements. The energy-efficient improvements must be cost-effective, meaning that the total cost of the improvements must be less than the energy saved over the expected life of the improvements.

An estimate of energy savings must be determined by a home energy rating report that is prepared by an energy consultant using a Home Energy Rating System (HERS). The cost of the energy rating report and inspections may be financed with the cost-effective energy-efficient improvements.

Application Process

To obtain an FHA insured mortgage, contact an FHA-approved lender who is participating in this program: http://www.hud.gov/ll/code/llslcrit.cfm

Program Contact Information

To read more about this program, go to:
http://portal.hud.gov/hudportal/HUD?src=/program_offices/housing/sfh/eem/energy-r

To contact a U.S. Department of Housing and Urban Development (HUD) Housing Counseling agency, go to: http://www.hud.gov/counseling/

To contact the Federal Housing Administration (FHA), please use one of the following methods: Visit: http://portal.hud.gov/hudportal/HUD?src=/program_offices/housing

Write:
U.S. Department of Housing and Urban Development
Federal Housing Administration
451 Seventh St., SW
Washington, D.C. 20410

Call:

1-800-CALL-FHA (1-800-225-5342) or via Federal Information Relay Service (w/TTY): 1-800-877-8339

Email: answers@hud.gov

HOME MORTGAGE INSURANCE FOR DISASTER VICTIMS

Managing Agency

Federal Housing Administration (FHA)
https://www.hud.gov/program_offices/housing/fhahistory

Program Description

Through Section 203(h), the Federal Government helps survivors in presidentially-designated disaster areas recover by making it easier for them to get mortgages and become homeowners or re-establish themselves as homeowners.

General Program Requirements

Individuals are eligible for this program if their homes are located in an area that was designated by the President as a disaster area and if their homes were destroyed or damaged to such an extent that reconstruction or replacement is necessary. Insured mortgages may be used to finance the purchase or reconstruction of a single-family home that will be the principal residence of the homeowner.

Loan Terms

Please contact a Federal Housing Administration (FHA) approved lender for loan term information. To find an approved lender, please visit:
http://www.hud.gov/ll/code/llslcrit.cfm

Application Process

The borrower's application for mortgage insurance must be submitted to the lender within one year of the President's declaration of the disaster. Applications are made only through a Federal Housing Administration (FHA) approved lending institution.

To obtain an FHA insured mortgage, or lookup lender information, contact an FHA-approved lender: http://www.hud.gov/ll/code/llslcrit.cfm

Program Contact Information

To read more about this program, go to:
http://portal.hud.gov/hudportal/HUD?src=/program_offices/housing/sfh/ins/203h-dft

To contact a U.S. Department of Housing and Urban Development (HUD) Housing Counseling agency, go to: http://www.hud.gov/counseling/

To contact the Federal Housing Administration (FHA), please use one of the following methods:

Visit: http://portal.hud.gov/hudportal/HUD?src=/program_offices/housing

Write:
U.S. Department of Housing and Urban Development
Federal Housing Administration
451 Seventh St., SW
Washington, D.C. 20410

Call:1-800-CALL-FHA (1-800-225-5342) or via Federal Information Relay Service (w/TTY): 1-800-877-8339

Email: answers@hud.gov

HOME REHABILITATION MORTGAGE INSURANCE

Managing Agency

Federal Housing Administration (FHA)
https://www.hud.gov/program_offices/housing/fhahistory

Program Description

Section 203(k) insurance enables homebuyers and homeowners to finance both the purchase (or refinancing) of a house and the cost of its rehabilitation through a single mortgage or to finance the rehabilitation of their existing home.

General Program Requirements

All persons who can make the monthly mortgage payments are eligible to apply. Cooperative units are not eligible.

Loan Terms

Please contact a Federal Housing Administration (FHA) approved lender for loan term information. To find an approved lender, please visit: http://www.hud.gov/ll/code/llslcrit.cfm

Application Process

To obtain an FHA insured mortgage, contact an FHA-approved lender: http://www.hud.gov/ll/code/llslcrit.cfm

Program Contact Information

To read more about this program, go to: http://portal.hud.gov/hudportal/HUD?src=/program_offices/housing/sfh/203k/203k--df

To contact a HUD Housing Counseling agency, go to: https://entp.hud.gov/idapp/html/hecm_agency_look.cfm

To contact the Federal Housing Administration (FHA), please use one of the following methods:

Visit: http://portal.hud.gov/hudportal/HUD?src=/program_offices/housing

Write:
U.S. Department of Housing and Urban Development
Federal Housing Administration
451 Seventh St., SW
Washington, D.C. 20410

Call: 1-800-CALL-FHA (1-800-225-5342) or via Federal Information Relay Service (w/TTY): 1-800-877-8339

Email: answers@hud.gov

HOME AND PROPERTY DISASTER LOANS

Managing Agency

U.S. Small Business Administration
http://www.sba.gov

Program Description

The U.S. Small Business Administration (SBA) is responsible for providing affordable, timely, and accessible financial assistance to homeowners and renters located in a declared disaster area. Financial assistance is available in the form of low-interest, long-term loans for losses that are not fully covered by insurance or other recoveries.

Homeowners may apply for up to $200,000 to repair or replace their primary residence to its pre-disaster condition. The loan may not be used to upgrade the home or make additions to it, unless as required by building authority/code. In some cases, SBA may be able to refinance all or part of a previous mortgage (not to exceed $200,000) when the applicant does not have credit available elsewhere, has suffered substantial disaster damage not covered by insurance, and intends to repair the damage. SBA considers refinancing when processing each application. Loans may also be increased by as much as 20% of the verified losses (not to exceed $200,000) to protect the damaged real property from possible future disasters of the same kind. Secondary homes or vacation properties are not eligible for home disaster loans; however, qualified rental properties may be eligible for assistance under the business disaster loan program.

Renters and homeowners alike may borrow up to $40,000 to replace damaged or destroyed personal property such as clothing, furniture, appliances, automobiles, etc. As a rule of thumb, personal property is anything that is not considered real estate or a part of the actual structure. This loan may not be used to replace extraordinarily expensive or irreplaceable items, such as antiques, collections, pleasure boats, recreational vehicles, fur coats, etc.

General Program Requirements

In order to qualify for this benefit program, homeowners and renters must have sustained physical damage and be located in a disaster declared county.

Loan Terms

Disaster survivors must repay SBA disaster loans. SBA can only approve loans to applicants with a reasonable ability to repay the loan and other obligations from earnings. The terms of each loan are established in accordance with each borrower's ability to repay. The law gives SBA several powerful tools to make disaster loans affordable: low fixed interest rates, long-terms (up to 30 years), and refinancing of prior real estate liens (in some cases). As required by law, the interest rate for each loan is based on SBA's determination of whether an applicant has the ability to borrow or use their own resources to overcome the disaster.

The SBA can provide up to $200,000 to homeowners to repair or replace their primary residence. Homeowners and renters are eligible for up to $40,000 to help repair or replace personal property. There are no upfront fees or early payment penalties charged by SBA.

Application Process

Apply online for disaster loan assistance at your own convenience through SBA's secure Disaster Loan Assistance website. You may also send completed applications to:

Processing and Disbursement Center
14925 Kingsport Road
Fort Worth, Texas 76155

Disaster victims can also apply in person at any FEMA-State Disaster Recovery Center or SBA Disaster Loan Outreach Center and receive personal, one-on-one help from an SBA representative. To find a location near you or help applying by mail, please contact our Customer Service Center at 1-800-659-2955 or by e-mail at DisasterCustomerService@sba.gov.

Homeowners and renters applying for assistance in a Presidential disaster declaration must first register with FEMA either online at www.disasterassistance.gov or by phone at 1-800-621-3362.

Program Contact Information

For more information about the program or questions on how to apply, please visit: https://disasterloan.sba.gov/ela/Information/HomePersonalPropertyLoans

Or contact the program at: 1-800-659-2955, or disastercustomerservice@sba.gov

INDIAN HOME LOAN GUARANTEE PROGRAM

Managing Agency

Public and Indian Housing (PIH)
https://www.hud.gov/program_offices/public_indian_housing

Program Description

This grant provides and operates cost-effective, decent, safe and affordable dwellings for lower-income families through an authorized local Public Housing Agency (PHA).

General Program Requirements

In order to qualify for this benefit program, you must be Native American/American Indian, need aid in obtaining decent, safe, and/or sanitary rental housing, and characterize your financial situation as low income or very low income.

Application Process

Please visit the Participating Lenders List to find an Approved Section 184 Lender.

Once you find an approved lender, they should prepare the documents and submit them to the Office of Native American Programs (ONAP) in Denver, Colorado.

Program Contact Information

For more information regarding this program, please visit the Section 184 Indian Home Loan Guarantee Program page on HUD's website.

You may also call 1-800-561-5913, or visit the Office of Native American Programs (ONAP) website.

INDIAN HOME LOAN GUARANTEE PROGRAM (SECTION 184)

Managing Agency

U.S. Department of Housing and Urban Development http://www.hud.gov/

Program Description

This program provides home ownership opportunities to Native Americans, Tribes, Tribally Designated Housing Entities (TDHEs), and Indian Housing Authorities on Indian land, through a guaranteed mortgage loan program available through private financial institutions.

General Program Requirements

In order to qualify for this benefit program, you must be a Native American/American Indian in the process of buying a home that will be your primary residence. You or your family member(s) must also be enrolled in a federally recognized American Indian tribe or Alaska Native village.

Loan Terms

Fixed Rate Financing with market rate of interest. Length of loan is 30 years or less. Payments are made monthly. The maximum loan amount is 150% of the Federal Housing Administration (FHA) lending limits for the area. There are no prepayment penalties.

Application Process

A list of the U.S. Department of Housing and Urban Development (HUD) approved 184 lenders for financing homes is available online: http://portal.hud.gov/hudportal/HUD?src=/program_offices/public_indian_housing/ih/homeownership/184/borrowers

Program Contact Information

For more information, please visit HUD's Office of Native American Programs website.

You may also call the program office at: 1-800-561-5913

INTEREST RATE REDUCTION REFINANCE LOAN (IRRRL)

Managing Agency

Veterans Benefits Administration (VBA) http://benefits.va.gov/benefits/

Program Description

A Department of Veterans Affairs (VA) Interest Rate Reduction Refinance Loan (IRRRL) can be used to refinance an existing VA loan to lower the interest rate.

IRRRLs do not require credit underwriting and may include the entire outstanding balance of the prior loan, to include closing costs and up to two discount points. Please note that some lenders may require additional credit requirements for loan approval. Therefore, VA encourages you to contact multiple lenders to determine the best loan option to fit your needs.

General Program Requirements

Persons who may qualify for this refinance loan include:

- Eligible Veterans
- Active duty Servicemembers
- Current Reserve and National Guard members (after 6 years of creditable service)
- Certain surviving spouses

To be eligible, the Veteran/Servicemember must have been discharged under conditions other than dishonorable and meet length of service requirements.

As a requirement for a VA home loan, the Veteran, the Veteran's spouse, or dependent child must certify occupancy for the property.

Loan Terms

Veterans can negotiate the interest rate with the lender on all loan types. A VA funding fee must be paid unless the Veteran is exempt due to receipt of disability compensation. The funding fee can be paid in cash or rolled into the loan. The Veteran, the spouse, or the child of an active duty Servicemember must certify their intent to occupy the property. VA does not require an appraisal to refinance a loan.

Application Process

For more information on this program, please visit the Home Loans webpage.

Program Contact Information

Visit the Inquiry Routing and Information System (IRIS) website to search Frequently Asked Questions or ask a question online, or contact a Regional Loan Center if you have detailed questions.

To apply for benefits and view your benefit status, open an eBenefits Premium account. eBenefits is a one-stop source for information on Department of Defense and Department of Veterans Affairs benefits and services. With a free Premium level eBenefits account, Veterans, Servicemembers and their family members can conduct self-service transactions such as checking compensation and pension claim status information, enrolling in GI Bill, and obtaining copies of civil service preference letters, military records (DD214), and other personal information. For further information and to register for a free Premium level account, visit the eBenefits website.

LOAN MANAGEMENT

Managing Agency

Veterans Benefits Administration (VBA) http://benefits.va.gov/benefits/

Program Description

For Veterans or Servicemembers who have a VA-guaranteed conventional or sub-prime loan, the Department of Veterans Affairs (VA) has a network of eight Regional Loan Centers that can offer advice and guidance during times of financial hardship.

Borrowers may visit the Home Loans Information page, or call toll free: 1-877-827-3702 to speak with a VA Loan Technician. However, unlike when a Veteran has a VA-guaranteed home loan, VA does not have the authority to intervene on the borrower's behalf for conventional loans. It is imperative that a borrower contact his/her mortgage servicer as quickly as possible when faced with financial hardship.

General Program Requirements

Persons who may qualify for VA-guaranteed loans include:

- Eligible Veterans / Servicemembers
- Current Reserve and National Guard members (after 6 years of creditable service)
- Certain surviving spouses

Commissioned Officers of the Public Health Service and National Oceanic and Atmospheric Administration are considered to be active duty members and Veterans, once discharged.

Length-of-service requirements apply, in most cases.

Loan Terms

The mortgage servicer has the primary responsibility for servicing the loan to resolve the default. When VA decides additional information or action is needed, VA initiates contact with the Veteran to offer financial counseling, discuss loss mitigation options that have been considered, and sometimes serve as an intermediary between the Veteran and mortgage servicer to negotiate a resolution to the default. VA then helps the servicer and the borrower to arrange an appropriate loss mitigation option, such as:

- Repayment Plan: The Veteran may pay a regular payment plus part of the delinquency each month over a period of time until the loan is brought current;
- Special Forbearance: Temporarily suspend payments to allow the Veteran time to sell the property or reinstate the loan;
- Loan Modification: Provide the Veteran a fresh start by adding the delinquency to the loan balance and establishing a new payment schedule;

- Refunding: VA can consider refunding (purchasing) the loan and modifying it to make the payments more affordable to the Veteran;
- Compromise Sale / Short Sale: The Veteran sells their home for an amount less than what is owed at current market value with VA paying the difference, up to the maximum guaranty on the loan; or
- Deed-in-Lieu of Foreclosure: The Veteran voluntarily deeds the property to the servicer to avoid the foreclosure process, with VA paying the difference between the payoff and the net property value.

For more information on this program, visit the Home Loans Information page.

Program Contact Information

If you have questions:

- Visit the Inquiry Routing and Information System (IRIS) website to search Frequently Asked Questions or ask a question online.
- Please contact a Regional Loan Center if you have detailed questions.

To apply for benefits and view your benefit status, open an eBenefits Premium account. eBenefits is a one-stop source for information on Department of Defense and Department of Veterans Affairs benefits and services. With a free Premium level eBenefits account, Veterans, Servicemembers and their family members can conduct self-service transactions such as checking compensation and pension claim status information, enrolling in GI Bill, and obtaining copies of civil service preference letters, military records (DD214), and other personal information. For further information and to register for a free Premium level account, visit the eBenefits website.

MANUFACTURED HOME LOAN INSURANCE

Managing Agency

Federal Housing Administration (FHA)
https://www.hud.gov/program_offices/housing/fhahistory

Program Description

Federal Housing Administration (FHA) insures mortgage loans made by private lending institutions to finance the purchase of a new or used manufactured home.

General Program Requirements

All buyers who meet credit requirements and plan to use the manufactured home as their principal place of residence are eligible for the program.

Loan Terms

Please contact an FHA-approved lender for loan term information. To find an approved lender, please visit: http://www.hud.gov/ll/code/llslcrit.cfm

Application Process

Buyers of manufactured homes may apply for a loan through an FHA-approved lender or through a lender's approved manufactured home dealer.

To obtain an FHA insured mortgage, contact an FHA-approved lender: http://www.hud.gov/ll/code/llslcrit.cfm

Program Contact Information

To read more about this program, go to:
http://portal.hud.gov/hudportal/HUD?src=/program_offices/housing/sfh/title/manuf14

To contact a HUD Housing Counseling agency, go to: http://www.hud.gov/counseling/

To contact the Federal Housing Administration (FHA), please use one of the following methods:

Visit: http://portal.hud.gov/hudportal/HUD?src=/program_offices/housing

Write:
U.S. Department of Housing and Urban Development
Federal Housing Administration
451 Seventh St., SW
Washington, D.C. 20410

Call: 1-800-CALL-FHA (1-800-225-5342) or via Federal Information Relay Service (w/TTY): 1-800-877-8339

Email: answers@hud.gov

PROPERTY IMPROVEMENT LOAN INSURANCE

Managing Agency

Federal Housing Administration (FHA)
https://www.hud.gov/program_offices/housing/fhahistory

Program Description

The Federal Housing Administration (FHA) makes it easier for consumers to obtain affordable home improvement loans by insuring loans made by private lenders to improve properties that meet certain requirements. Lending institutions make loans from their own funds to eligible borrowers to finance these improvements.

General Program Requirements

Eligible borrowers include the owner of the property to be improved, the person leasing the property (provided that the lease will extend at least 6 months beyond the date when the loan must be repaid), or someone purchasing the property under a land installment contract.

Loan Terms

Please contact an FHA-approved lender for loan term information. To find an FHA-approved lender, visit: http://www.hud.gov/ll/code/llslcrit.cfm

Application Process

To obtain an FHA insured mortgage, contact an FHA-approved lender at: http://www.hud.gov/ll/code/llslcrit.cfm

Program Contact Information

To read more about this program, go to:
http://portal.hud.gov/hudportal/HUD?src=/program_offices/housing/sfh/title/title-i

To contact a HUD Housing Counseling agency, go to:
https://entp.hud.gov/idapp/html/hecm_agency_look.cfm

To contact the Federal Housing Administration (FHA), please use one of the following methods:

Visit: http://portal.hud.gov/hudportal/HUD?src=/program_offices/housing

Write:

U.S. Department of Housing and Urban Development
Federal Housing Administration
451 Seventh St., SW
Washington, D.C. 20410

Call: 1-800-CALL-FHA (1-800-225-5342) or via Federal Information Relay Service
(w/TTY): 1-800-877-8339

Email: answers@hud.gov

RURAL HOUSING LOANS

Managing Agency

U.S. Department of Agriculture http://www.usda.gov/

Program Description

Direct and guaranteed loans may be used to buy, build, or improve the applicant's permanent residence. New manufactured homes may be financed when they are on a permanent site, purchased from an approved dealer or contractor, and meet certain other requirements. Under very limited circumstances, homes may be re-financed with direct loans. Dwellings financed must be modest, decent, safe, and sanitary. The value of a home financed with a direct loan may not exceed the area limit. Assistance is available in the States, the Commonwealth of Puerto Rico, the U.S. Virgin Islands, Guam, American Samoa, the Commonwealth of Northern Mariana's, and the Trust Territories of the Pacific Islands. Direct loans are made at the interest rate specified in RD Instruction 440.1, Exhibit B (PDF) (available in any Rural Development local office).

General Program Requirements

In order to qualify for this benefit program, your property must be located in an eligible rural area. Applicants must have very low, low, or moderate incomes. Very low income is defined as below 50% of the area median income (AMI); low income is between 50 and 80% of AMI; moderate income is below 115% percent of AMI. Families must be without adequate housing, but able to afford the housing payments, including principal, interest, taxes, and insurance (PITI). Qualifying repayment ratios are 29% for PITI to 41% for total debt. In addition, applicants must be unable to obtain credit elsewhere, yet have an acceptable credit history. You must also be a U.S. citizen or permanent resident.

Loan Terms

Direct loans are repaid over 33 years or 38 years for applicants whose adjusted annual income does not exceed 60% of the area median income, if necessary to show repayment ability. Payment assistance is granted on direct loans to reduce the installment to an "effective interest rate" as low as 1%, depending on adjusted family income. Payment assistance is subject to recapture by the government when the customer no longer resides in the dwelling. There is no funding provided for deferred mortgage authority or loans for deferred mortgage assumptions.

Guaranteed loans are amortized over 30 years. The promissory note interest rate is set by the lender. There is no required down payment. The lender must also determine repayment feasibility, using ratios of repayment (gross) income to PITI and to total family debt.

Application Process

Interested applicants should contact their local USDA Rural Development field office for more information.

To apply for Direct loans obtain Application Form (RD 410-4) (PDF) and Release Form (RD 3550-1) (PDF).

Program Contact Information

For more information, contact your Rural Development office at: 202-720-4323

RURAL HOUSING: FARM LABOR HOUSING LOANS AND GRANTS

Managing Agency

U.S. Department of Agriculture, http://www.usda.gov/

Program Description

The Farm Labor Housing Loan and Grant program provides capital financing for the development of housing for domestic farm laborers. Farm Labor Housing loans and grants are provided to buy, build, improve, or repair housing for farm laborers, including persons whose income is earned in aquaculture (fish and oyster farms) and those engaged in on-farm processing. Funds can be used to purchase a site or a leasehold interest in a site; to construct housing, daycare facilities, or community rooms; to pay fees to purchase durable household furnishings; and to pay construction loan interest.

General Program Requirements

Loans are made to farmers, associations of farmers, family farm corporations, Indian tribes, nonprofit organizations, public agencies, and associations of farmworkers. Typically, loan applicants are unable to obtain credit elsewhere, but in some instances, farmers able to get credit elsewhere may obtain loans at a rate of interest based on the cost of federal borrowing. Grants are made to farmworker associations, nonprofit organizations, Indian tribes, and public agencies. Funds may be used in urban areas for nearby farm labor. (This is the only Rural Housing Service rural service area exception.)

Loan Terms

Loans are for 33 years at 1% interest. Grants may cover up to 90% of development costs. The balance may be a Farm Labor Housing Program loan.

Application Process

Upon publication of a Notice in the Federal Register, a two-stage application process is used. In stage one, applicants submit a pre-application, which is used to determine preliminary eligibility and feasibility. Pre-applications selected for further processing will be invited to submit an application. The pre-application consists of SF-424.2, "Application for Federal Assistance (For Construction)" and the information listed in exhibit A-1 or A-2 of Rural Development regulations, 1944-D, as applicable.

Program Contact Information

For more information, please visit the Farm Labor Housing Loan and Grant program website.

To find out about availability of farm labor housing in your locality, contact your local Rural Development field office using the Office Locator Tool.

RURAL HOUSING: HOUSING REPAIR LOANS AND GRANTS

Managing Agency

U.S. Department of Agriculture, http://www.usda.gov/

Program Description

The Rural Housing Repair Loans and Grants program provides loans and grants to very low-income homeowners to repair, improve, modernize, or to remove health and safety hazards in their rural dwellings. Loans are arranged for up to 20 years at 1% interest.

Grants may be arranged for recipients who are 62 years of age or older and can be used only to pay for repairs and improvements to remove health and safety hazards. Loan/grant combinations may be arranged for applicants who can repay part of the cost. Very low-income for this program is defined as below 50% of the area median income.

General Program Requirements

In order to be eligible for the loan program, you must be a homeowner who has very low income, and you must be a U.S. citizen or permanent resident who lives in a rural area. In order to be eligible for the grant program, you must meet the above requirements, and also be aged 62 years or older.

Loan Terms

Loans of up to $20,000 and grants of up to $7,500 are available. Loans are for up to 20 years at 1% interest. A real estate mortgage is required for loans of $7,500 or more. Full title services are required for loans of $7,500 or more. Grants may be recaptured if the property is sold in less than three years. Loans and grants can be combined for up to $27,500 in assistance.

Application Process

To apply for a loan or grant online go to http://www.sc.egov.usda.gov, or you may contact your State's Rural Development field office using this office locator tool: http://offices.sc.egov.usda.gov/locator/app.

Program Contact Information

For more information about the housing repair loan program, visit: http://www.rd.usda.gov/programs-services/single-family-housing-repair-loans-grants

More on Rural Development Housing & Community Facilities Programs at: http://www.rd.usda.gov/programs-services

---

Other "no money down" strategies focus on using promissory notes to create cash. There will be situations where the seller must receive cash at closing, and there will be instances where it is possible for you to leave the closing with cash in your pocket. You may be re-reading the aforementioned, wondering how you provide cash to the seller when you have none.

Some sellers are in a position where they are not able to sell their properties, unless they actually receive cash at the closing. If you are using one of the strategies which does not allow the seller to receive cash then you might not be able to buy the property, unless you can show how to convert your offering note into cash. Let's look at several ways that the seller might accomplish this.

Strategy 22: Collateralize the Paper

The note could be taken to a bank – with whom the seller has a good banking relationship – and pledged as security for borrowing money. While the seller may be paying 3% to 4% more than the amount of money received from you in interest, this is a negotiable point. Ultimately, if he or she collateralizes the note, then you may have to pay the seller the same interest rate that the seller will have to pay to a bank.

A variation of this strategy would involve you creating a note and mortgage on property which you currently own and have equity. In turn, you could use that note and mortgage as collateral for money.

Strategy 23: Create Multiple Notes Using One Note as Collateral

Suppose you have purchased a property, and you have given a $20,000 promissory note to a seller. If the seller does not need the entire $20,000, the seller could write a smaller note or several notes, using the $20,000 note as collateral. One new note might be written for $4,000, and it could be sold at a discount of 30% to generate $1,400 in cash. Another second new note for $4,000 could be used by the seller as a down payment to buy real estate. The seller of the two new notes would still have the original note for $20,000; they would continue to receive the interest income from it, and in turn, he or she could pay the interest on the two $4,000 notes. $12,000 of that note would be unencumbered and movable, possibly using it as collateral for additional notes.

Strategy 24: Sell the Paper at a Discount

There is an active market of investors eager to purchase notes at a discount. The sale of a note at a discount is not difficult, depending on its interest rate, terms, the credit-worthiness of the maker, and the strength of the collateral. This process is known as discounting a note. Remember, when you have a note that is paying a lower interest rate than current prevailing rates you will have to sell the note at a discount. On the other hand if you have a note that is paying a higher interest rate than current prevailing rates then you can sell the note for a premium!

Strategy 25: Use the Paper as a Down Payment to Purchase Real Estate

You, the buyer, might give the seller a note for $20,000, which is secured by a mortgage on the real estate you are purchasing from him or her. The seller could then use the note at its full face value to purchase another property.

As discussed, many sellers of property are glad to receive paper that is secured by real estate. The seller to whom you are giving the note will find it easier to use that note as a down payment than they might suspect. Once the new property is acquired, the seller could use any number of ways to take cash out of the equity in the new property.

Strategy 26: Sell the Income from the Note

Most people are aware when they receive a note, they have an asset in the amount of the note. What most people do not realize is that they really have two assets. One is the note itself, and two is the cashflow that comes each month or year from that note.

Assume that you gave the seller a $24,000 promissory note, bearing interest at 10%, payable $2,400 per year. That $2,400 per year income – which the seller is receiving – could be sold at a discount, or the seller could sell several years' worth of income at a discount to generate cash. This strategy would leave the primary asset, the $24,000 note, untouched.

Investors who purchase "streams" of income like this, are generally looking for a minimum of 20% return on their investment. If you have a financial calculator, it is easy to determine the present value of 48 monthly payments. If not, then a "quick and easy" way to calculate the present value would be to calculate the total dollars, which would be received over a period of time, 48 months for example. Divide the time period – in this case 48 – by two to get an average amount of time, 24 months. In the above example, the $100 per month payment ($2,400 divided by 12) over 48 months totals $9,600. Half that amount would be $4,800, which would be received over an average period of time or 24 months.

These strategies are one step better than purchasing a property with no money down, because you can leave the closing table with cash in your pocket. The greater the amount of equity the seller has in a property, the smaller the debt, the better these strategies work.

While I have purchased millions of dollars' worth of real estate over the course of my investing career, only a small fraction of these were done with myself leaving the closing table with cash. It is important to note that many, if not most of the strategies used in previous examples can be used to take cash out at closing, especially when two or more are combined.

Strategy 27: Seller Rebates at Closing

Let's say you find a $200,000, four-family property with a mortgage balance of $80,000. Go to a lender and request a 55% mortgage, or in this case, $110,000. When mortgages are 50% to 60% of the property's value, they are relatively easy to acquire. They are often called "no-doc" loans. The bank does not verify or document the information you give them. Instead, they rely only on your credit report and your equity in the property. The seller agrees once the underlying mortgage of $80,000 is paid, then the remaining balance of $30,000 will be split 50/50.

The seller pays off the $80,000 mortgage and has pocketed $15,000 in cash. Since the negotiated price for the property was $200,000, you still owe the seller $105,000, which will be received by the seller in the form of a second mortgage. While you have paid $215,000 for the property on paper, you put $15,000 in your pocket at the time of close.

If your credit is insufficient to obtain a "no-doc" loan from a bank, then consider going to a mortgage broker to obtain a privately financed loan on the property you are buying.

Another variation of this strategy would call for the seller to rebate cash at closing to fix up the property. In the example just described, the seller might rebate $15,000 to you at close, and you would still only pay $200,000 for the property.

When seeking to invest in real estate creatively, the bottom line is that you need to know the seller's situation as thoroughly as possible; try to get into the seller's mind, prior to making an offer.

- How will the seller use any cash received?
- Is there really a need for cash or just a want?
- Is the seller security-conscious?
- Why is the seller offering the property for sale?
- What is the seller's attitude toward price vs. terms (would the seller take a higher price for the property in return for zero interest)?

- How desperate is the seller to sell the property quickly?

These are all questions that ideally need to be answered. Additional questions include:

- What is the offering price of the property relative to its value as determined by doing a survey of comparable property sales?
- Are there any "extras" included in the sale, for example, an extra lot, future, appliances or an automobile?
- If the property is rented, how do the rents compare to the true market value rent?
- What credits will you receive at close?
- Is there a broker involved in the sale or is it "F.S.B.O." (For Sale by Owner)?
- What is the condition of the property?
- Are any mortgages assumable?
- What is the interest rate?
- What is the blended interest rate, if applicable?

Lease Options

Here is another great strategy you can use to invest creatively. Most people are familiar with automobile leases, as more than 50% of new car transactions are now leases rather than sales.

At the end of the automobile lease period, typically two or three years, the lessee has an option to buy the car. During the lease, the "tenant" gets to test the car and see if it meets the driver's needs. At the end of the lease, the lessee can either return the car to the "landlord" dealer or exercise the option to buy the car.

Real estate lease options are very similar, except the dollar amounts are larger.

Such realty transactions are a combination rental, sales, and finance for a fixed term, such as one year, three years, five years, or longer.

The longest lease option I have negotiated, as the buyer, was for 15 years. But I have heard of commercial lease options as long as 45 years. However, as a lease option realty seller, I prefer one-year lease options so I can "adjust" the monthly rent and the option purchase price annually.

Several years ago, a local residential real estate broker phoned to ask if I was interested in a lease option on a nice three-bedroom, two-bath house if I could act fast because his client was anxious to return to their home country. We agreed to meet the next morning at a nearby coffee shop.

The broker suggested I prepare a lease option offer, along the guidelines he outlined, so we could discuss it with the owner. As I filled in the blanks on the printed lease option form, the only non-issue was the $125,000 fair market value option price the owner insisted on receiving.

My next issue was the lease option term. Having been cut down on my previous 10-year lease option offers for other houses to five years or less, I was thinking big when I filled in 15 years.

Next, I decided to offer the owner $500 per month net rent. I agreed to pay his monthly mortgage payment, property taxes, insurance, and all necessary repairs. I also agreed to prepay one year's net rent of $6,000. Also, I needed the right to sub-lease to a tenant.

When I got to the line on the lease option form for the rent percent to be credited to my purchase price when I exercise the option, I filled in 50%.

As for the realty broker's commission, I agreed to pay half up-front and the other half if and when I exercised my purchase option.

The meeting went smoothly. The only debate was about the rent credit. Neither the broker nor I recall how we agreed on the odd number of 17%. The owner and I signed the lease option, the broker agreed to arrange title insurance (at my expense), and a few days later my lease option was recorded.

Thirteen years later, I elected to exercise my $125,000 purchase option. By then the owner had died of a heart attack and I acquired the title from his heir in Hong Kong. But that's another story. Yes, the broker then received the remainder of his commission.

When to Use a Lease Option

There are always more lease option buyers than sellers. Buyers understand the benefits. But most sellers don't understand their equal or greater benefits.

Lease option property owners often don't comprehend what their benefits include: continued income tax deductions such as mortgage interest, property taxes, and rental depreciation. If the option purchase price terms annually "adjust" to reflect rising property values, the seller can benefit from increased market-value appreciation, too.

Additional lease option benefits for sellers include an over-supply of eager lease option buyers; lease option tenants will pay higher-than-market rent in return for the rent credit toward the purchase price; tax-free, up-front option money until the option is exercised; lease option tenants will pay top dollar; and the lease option future owner tenant usually treats the house or condo extremely well.

How Buyers View Lease Options

At the closing table a few years ago, a couple who bought their rental house from me on a lease option revealed how they viewed their five-year residency before I practically forced them to exercise their option.

The wife said their $1,500 per month rent seemed high, but she and her husband considered it as $1,000 very reasonable monthly rent, plus a $500 "forced savings account" for their rent credit toward the purchase price.

Lease option buyer advantages include: 1) up-front "option money" is smaller than a typical down payment; 2) lack of mortgage interest and property tax deductions are outweighed by the "forced savings" rent credit (typically 10% to 100% of rent paid); 3) the buyer can try out the home before buying; 4) the option purchase price is locked-in for the specified term; 5) the buyer can move in within a few days after signing the lease option.

How to Sell Homes on Lease Options

Although most local home sales markets are currently quite strong, there are pockets of slow home sales. Whether you are a home seller, builder, or realty agent, a delayed lease option sale is better than no sale. Lease options work in all price ranges, especially when there is little cash buyer demand.

My most effective lease option newspaper classified ad is headlined "$10,000 MOVES YOU IN." Of course, change that amount up or down for your situation. Then describe the house or condo benefits, the monthly rent, and keywords "Rent to Own" or "Lease option."

Saturday and Sunday advertised open houses usually provide quick results. Be prepared with at least 100 information sheet flyers describing the home with an attached rental application form.

It's best to insist on a $500 or $1,000 deposit check from serious prospects. Owners should then run credit checks on all lease option applicants before selecting the best qualified.

How Buyers Can Create Lease Options

Most cities have few or zero lease options advertised. However, prospective lease option buyers can create their own by reading the "homes for rent" classified ads and offering a lease option when you find a house or condo you want to eventually buy, or running your classified ad under "homes wanted," such as "Executive needs 4 BR, 2.5 BA home on five-year lease with option to buy. Excellent references. Call Gary at 123-456-7890."

SUMMARY: Lease options offer major benefits for home sellers, buyers, and realty agents.

Summary of Benefits to Seller

- Price of property is at the top of market value range or based on a formula to include inflation.
- Option money received is tax deferred.
- If rent is not paid on time, the option is forfeited. (Thus, the rent is usually paid on time!)
- The tenant has "pride of ownership" and an incentive to take better care of the property.
- The rent, including option payments, is usually set at or above the fair market rent.

Summary of Benefits to Buyer

- Risk is reduced while financial leverage is increased.
- Option consideration is small compared to the value of the property.
- If the property is not worth more than the option price, the buyer can walk away from the contract.
- Buyer usually receives control and possession of the property.
- Purchaser could even generate profit from the property by leasing it to someone else.
- Consideration paid and any rent credits received.

Sublease Income Property for a Profit

What if you find a single-family home that is offered for sale, far for less than its fair market value. The property is being offered at $50,000 and its value is about $100,000. If rented, its fair market rent would be approximately $500 per month.

You could offer the seller a three-year lease option with payments of $550 to $600 per month. Credit toward the purchase price would be a minimum of $200 to $300 per month. You could sublease the property to a tenant for $600 per month; depending on the terms of your lease option, you could have a break-even cashflow. Even if you have to supplement the rental income with cash out of your pocket, it will probably only be temporary. Over the next three years, you could reasonably expect rents to go up at least 5% per year; by the end of the second year, you will almost certainly have a positive cashflow.

The benefits to the seller in this situation are as follows. Not only would the seller receive the asking price for the property, but all of the tax benefits of owning real estate would be retained, since the property is being leased and is now considered investment property.

The portion of the monthly income that would be credited toward the purchase ($200 to $300) would be exempt from income tax, until the option is exercised or until the option expires.

The benefits for the buyer are obvious. While you may have only a break-even or a very small positive cashflow, you are receiving a $200 to $300 per month credit toward the purchase price; you are, in effect, banking money each month and the tenant is paying for it.

The buyer receives a $200 to $300 per month credit toward the purchase price. The tenant is, in effect, paying for this credit.

The buyer may even have a small monthly cashflow. It is possible that the property value will exceed the option price at the end of the option period. The seller receives the asking price for the property. Tax benefits would be retained on investment property. Non-taxable monthly income would be received until the exercise or expiration of the option.

Protecting Yourself with Lease Options

If you enter into a lease option agreement – without taking care or protecting yourself – then you might find the specific terms of the lease option binding, and it will be almost impossible to exercise. The following precautions are important.

Record the Option:

Anytime you enter into an option agreement with a seller, you should record the option or an affidavit and memorandum of agreement in the public records of the county. This protects you, the purchaser, more than it does a seller. It provides notice to the world that you have an option to buy the property. If the seller should sell the property to anyone during the option period, then the new purchaser will buy the property, knowing you have an option to buy the same property.

To record the option, it should be notarized. If the option agreement is signed before this notarization takes place, then the seller may be reluctant to later sign a second time, in front of a notary public. Make sure it is all done at the same time.

Right to Sublease:

Whether you plan to live in the property or not, you should always make certain that your lease option gives you the right to sublease the property to another tenant. That right is not inherent in a lease, unless specifically spelled out.

Right to Assign:

In some states, the right to assign a contract is protected by law. In other states, it is not. Assignment is the right to transfer the contract and all your rights to someone else. To avoid any misunderstanding or litigation, you should make sure that the right to assign the contract is spelled out in your lease option contract. If you do not exercise the option yourself, then you should have the right to sell it. Your "equity" in that property is valuable. After all, you have been paying rent each month and a portion has been allocated to the option price.

By providing you with the right to assign the contract, the seller also benefits. The seller does not have to find another buyer for the property. As you would expect, the lease option contract provided with your course gives you the right to assign.

Right to Extend:

Some lease option contracts will have a section which spells out the terms under which the option may be extended. Other contracts specifically say that the extension of the lease option is prohibited. Some contracts may be silent on this point. Regardless of what your lease option says or does not say, make certain that you have the right to extend the option period for at least one year. This extension clause could be added to the "lease option" contract or, if there is inadequate room, an "addendum" could be used.

1031 Exchanges

Whenever you sell business or investment property and you have a gain, you generally have to pay tax on the gain at the time of sale. IRC Section 1031 provides an exception and allows you to postpone paying tax on the gain if you reinvest the proceeds in similar property as part of a qualifying like-kind exchange. Gain deferred in a like-kind exchange under IRC Section 1031 is tax-deferred, but it is not tax-free.

The exchange can include like-kind property exclusively or it can include like-kind property along with cash, liabilities, and property that are not like-kind. If you receive cash, relief from debt, or property that is not like-kind however, you may trigger some taxable gain in the year of the exchange. There can be both deferred and recognized gain in the same transaction when a taxpayer exchanges for like-kind property of lesser value.

Who qualifies for the Section 1031 exchange?

Owners of investment and business property may qualify for a Section 1031 deferral. Individuals, C corporations, S corporations, partnerships (general or limited), limited liability companies, trusts and any other taxpaying entity may set up an exchange of business or investment properties for business or investment properties under Section 1031.

What are the different structures of a Section 1031 Exchange?

To accomplish a Section 1031 exchange, there must be an exchange of properties. The simplest type of Section 1031 exchange is a simultaneous swap of one property for another.

Deferred exchanges are more complex but allow flexibility. They allow you to dispose of property and subsequently acquire one or more other like-kind replacement properties.

To qualify as a Section 1031 exchange, a deferred exchange must be distinguished from the case of a taxpayer simply selling one property and using the proceeds to purchase another property (which is a taxable transaction). Rather, in a deferred exchange, the disposition of the relinquished property and acquisition of the replacement property must be mutually dependent parts of an integrated transaction constituting an exchange of property. Taxpayers engaging in deferred exchanges generally use exchange facilitators under exchange agreements pursuant to rules provided in the Income Tax Regulations.

A reverse exchange is somewhat more complex than a deferred exchange. It involves the acquisition of replacement property through an exchange accommodation titleholder, with whom it is parked for no more than 180 days. During this parking period the taxpayer disposes of its relinquished property to close the exchange.

What property qualifies for a Like-Kind Exchange?

Both the relinquished property you sell and the replacement property you buy must meet certain requirements.

Both properties must be held for use in a trade or business or for investment. Property used primarily for personal use, like a primary residence or a second home or vacation home, does not qualify for like-kind exchange treatment.

Both properties must be similar enough to qualify as "like-kind." Like-kind property is property of the same nature, character, or class. Quality or grade does not matter. Most real estate will be like-kind to other real estate. For example, real property that is improved with a residential rental house is like-kind to vacant land. One exception for real estate is that property within the United States is not like-kind to property outside of the United States. Also, improvements that are conveyed without land are not of like-kind to land.

Real property and personal property can both qualify as exchange properties under Section 1031; but real property can never be like-kind to personal property. In personal property exchanges, the rules pertaining to what qualifies as like-kind are more restrictive than the rules pertaining to real property. As an example, cars are not like-kind to trucks.

Finally, certain types of property are specifically excluded from Section 1031 treatment. Section 1031 does not apply to exchanges of:

- Inventory or stock in trade
- Stocks, bonds, or notes
- Other securities or debt
- Partnership interests
- Certificates of trust

What are the time limits to complete a Section 1031 Deferred Like-Kind Exchange?

While a like-kind exchange does not have to be a simultaneous swap of properties, you must meet two time limits or the entire gain will be taxable. These limits cannot be extended for any circumstance or hardship except in the case of presidentially declared disasters.

The first limit is that you have 45 days from the date you sell the relinquished property to identify potential replacement properties. The identification must be in writing, signed by you, and delivered to a person involved in the exchange like the seller of the replacement property or the qualified intermediary. However, notice to your attorney, real estate agent, accountant, or similar persons acting as your agent is not sufficient.

Replacement properties must be clearly described in the written identification. In the case of real estate, this means a legal description, street address, or distinguishable name. Follow the IRS guidelines for the maximum number and value of properties that can be identified.

The second limit is that the replacement property must be received and the exchange completed no later than 180 days after the sale of the exchanged property or the due date (with extensions) of the income tax return for the tax year in which the relinquished property was sold, whichever is earlier. The replacement property received must be substantially the same as property identified within the 45-day limit described above.

Are there restrictions for deferred and reverse exchanges?

It is important to know that taking control of cash or other proceeds before the exchange is complete may disqualify the entire transaction from like-kind exchange treatment and make ALL gain immediately taxable.

If cash or other proceeds that are not like-kind property are received at the conclusion of the exchange, the transaction will still qualify as a like-kind exchange. Gain may be taxable, but only to the extent of the proceeds that are not like-kind property.

One way to avoid premature receipt of cash or other proceeds is to use a qualified intermediary or other exchange facilitator to hold those proceeds until the exchange is complete.

You cannot act as your own facilitator. In addition, your agent (including your real estate agent or broker, investment banker or broker, accountant, attorney, employee or anyone who has worked for you in those capacities within the previous two years) cannot act as your facilitator.

Be careful in your selection of a qualified intermediary as there have been recent incidents of intermediaries declaring bankruptcy or otherwise being unable to meet their contractual obligations to the taxpayer. These situations have resulted in taxpayers not meeting the strict timelines set for a deferred or reverse exchange, thereby disqualifying the transaction from Section 1031 deferral of gain. The gain may be taxable in the current year while any losses the taxpayer suffered would be considered under separate code sections.

How do you compute the basis in the new property?

It is critical that you and your tax representative adjust and track basis correctly to comply with Section 1031 regulations.

Gain is deferred, but not forgiven, in a like-kind exchange. You must calculate and keep track of your basis in the new property you acquired in the exchange.

The basis of property acquired in a Section 1031 exchange is the basis of the property given up with some adjustments. This transfer of basis from the relinquished to the replacement property preserves the deferred gain for later recognition. A collateral effect is that the resulting depreciable basis is generally lower than what would otherwise be available if the replacement property were acquired in a taxable transaction.

When the replacement property is ultimately sold (not as part of another exchange), the original deferred gain, plus any additional gain realized since the purchase of the replacement property, is subject to tax.

How do you report Section 1031 Like-Kind Exchanges to the IRS?

You must report an exchange to the IRS on Form 8824, Like-Kind Exchanges and file it with your tax return for the year in which the exchange occurred.

Form 8824 asks for:

- Descriptions of the properties exchanged
- Dates that properties were identified and transferred
- Any relationship between the parties to the exchange
- Value of the like-kind and other property received
- Gain or loss on sale of other (non-like-kind) property given up
- Cash received or paid; liabilities relieved or assumed

- Adjusted basis of like-kind property given up; realized gain

If you do not specifically follow the rules for like-kind exchanges, you may be held liable for taxes, penalties, and interest on your transactions.

Beware of schemes

Taxpayers should be wary of individuals promoting improper use of like-kind exchanges. Typically they are not tax professionals. Sales pitches may encourage taxpayers to exchange non-qualifying vacation or second homes. Many promoters of like-kind exchanges refer to them as "tax-free" exchanges not "tax-deferred" exchanges. Taxpayers may also be advised to claim an exchange despite the fact that they have taken possession of cash proceeds from the sale.

Consult a tax professional or refer to IRS publications listed below for additional assistance with IRC Section 1031 Like-Kind Exchanges.

References/Related Topics

- Publication 544, Sales and Other Dispositions of Assets
- Form 8824, Like-Kind Exchanges
- Form 4797, Sales of Business Property

Partnerships

Getting started flipping or buying rental properties can be very difficult for aspiring investors. The biggest problem for most investors is finding the money to flip or the down payment for rentals. In some cases an investor has a lot of money, but no time to find deals, renovate houses or perform the other tasks needed to invest in real estate. In other cases an investor may have the knowledge and time to invest, but no money. A partnership can be a mutually beneficial way to invest in real estate if done right.

I used to partner with my colleague Vince. It would have been really tough for me to flip houses or sell real estate without a partner to help with the financing and mentoring. But in some ways I think having a partner also held me back and provided a comfort zone that allowed to me to relax more than I should have. Having a partner in real estate deals can be a great way to get started, but if you don't set things up right it can be a disaster and destroy relationships.

How does a partnership on fix and flips work?

Many people want to flip houses. It appears to them to be a quick way to make a lot of money. I am approached by investors all the time who want to start flipping houses. Flipping is a very difficult business to get into, especially if you have no money. It takes patience to find deals, it takes time to make repairs, it takes expertise and knowledge to learn your market. If it were easy to buy a house with none of your own money, fix it up real quick and sell it a couple of months later for a $30,000 profit, everyone would do it!

Most people who want to flip houses do not take the time needed to learn their market, save money, or research the costs involved when flipping. If you want to flip houses, but need a partner to help fund you, you must bring something to the table. I don't partner with people looking to flip houses, because I stay busy enough with my own deals and flips. If I were looking for a partner though, here is what I would want from them if I was the money source.

- **Local market knowledge:** I would want any investor to know what neighborhoods have potential. What previous deals would have been good flips. What the target purchase price and sales price would be.

- **Know the costs**: Many investors underestimate the costs on a flip. Buying costs, carrying costs, repair costs, selling costs all need to be accounted for. I want details, not that a home "meets the 70% rule."
- **How will you get the deal**: The hardest part of flipping is finding a deal with enough room to make a profit. Are you using the MLS with a Realtor or direct marketing or something else?
- **What is my involvement**: Do I have to do any work in the transaction? Do I have to determine value, find contractors, or find the deal?
- **Who will do the work?** Will you make repairs yourself? Will you hire a contractor or do you already have a contractor? If you do the work yourself, do you have the experience to do it right and quickly?
- **What is the time frame**: Have you planned out how long the process will take and whether it is realistic? It will probably take longer than three months to flip a house.

In a fix and flip partnership, a typical split is the person who provides the money gets 50% of the profits and the person who does all the work gets 50%. Don't expect your money partner on a flip deal to find the deal, find the contractor, or handle the sale. What would they need you for?

If you are splitting up the money and the work portion of the flip, it can get much more difficult. If you decide each partner will pay 50% of the costs and do 50% of the work, it can be tough keeping track of hours and finances. Most people who enter partnerships like this have jobs and try to do the work on the side. One partner ends up doing more work than the other and gets frustrated. Or one partner puts more money in than the other and gets frustrated. The key is to make sure everything is in writing.

How does a partnership work with rental properties?

Rental property partnerships can be even trickier than fix-and-flip partnerships. I have had hundreds of rentals and I don't have partners on those properties either anymore. The tough part is knowing how the partnership will progress through time. One partner may want to cash out in five years while another wants to hold the properties for 30 years.

It is also a little tougher figuring the returns on rental properties. When flipping, you know what the profit is after a flip. With rentals, you have equity pay-down, tax advantages, appreciation, and cashflow. Some of these returns are seen in the form of cash in your pocket like cashflow. Other returns like appreciation and equity pay-down are not seen unless the home is sold or refinanced. Not only do you have to come up with a percentage of the actual profits (cashflow) that will be split, but you have to come up with a percentage of the equity that will be split if the properties are sold or if one partner wants to sell out and the other wants to keep the properties.

Things to consider with a partner on rental properties:

- **Who does the work**: Will both partners work to find properties or will one do all the work? How will repairs and maintenance be handled? Who will screen tenants or will a property manager be used?
- **How much money will each partner put in**: Will one partner put in all the money and the other do all the work? Will it be a mix of money and work?
- **What percentage of the profits will each partner take**: It can be very tough figuring profits with rentals. You will have up and down cashflow months and houses can be depreciated. With depreciation, tax returns will show less profit than you actually make. You also need to have reserves in place for maintenance and vacancies. You have to decide what each partner's role is worth and how profits will be split.
- **What percentage of equity does each partner get**: When you get a mortgage on a property the equity will slowly increase as payments are made and the house might appreciate as well. If you bought the property below market value you also increase equity. That equity does not do good unless you sell or refinance, but you need to figure out what percentage each partner gets if you sell or refinance.
- **What happens if one partner wants out**: The biggest problem with rental properties and partnerships is ending the relationship. How long do you plan to own the property together? What if one partner needs money and wants out? What if the house doesn't make as much money as you thought and a partner wants out? You have to figure out how to end the relationship before the partnership starts, deciding what will happen if one partner wants out.

As you can see it can be very tricky handling a partnership with rental properties. Determining the amount of work each person is responsible for is tough, determining an exit strategy is tough, and determining what percentages each investor gets… and when… is also tough.

If you decide to enter a partnership, everything has to be in writing. I don't care if your partnership is with your brother or your best friend, it should be in writing. There are multiple reasons why everything should be in writing.

- **People forget things**: It would seem you would never forget the details of a partnership that involves thousands of dollars, but it happens. Put everything in writing so there are no mistakes or fall-outs from simply forgetting the terms.
- **Partners need to know roles**: If you are doing a flip with a partner and decide to share the work, how much time will each person put in? One partner may have a family emergency or may have to work overtime. How many hours will each person put in and what are the consequences if they don't pull their weight? One of the biggest problems is one partner thinks he does all the work while the other collects the profit without doing anything.
- **Exit strategies**: With rental properties you have to know what happens if one partner wants to be bought out or has to sell. How is market value determined, how will costs be split, etc.? With a flip, what happens if you decide not to flip the house because the market changed?
- **Use of professional services**: If one partner is a contractor or real estate agent, how will they be paid for their services? Will they get a higher percentage of the profits for their expertise or for saving money on commissions? Will the contractor or agent be paid like they would at any other job?
- **Rates, terms, payoffs**: If you are borrowing money from a partner, all the terms of the loan or agreement need to be in writing. Some agreements are a pure profit split, but others might involve private money lending with interest rates, length of the note, etc.
- **Decision making:** Who has the final say on how much money to spend, how to repair a house, what properties to buy, etc.? What happens if the partners don't agree? This is another big issue that can cause problems if not in writing.

A huge issue with partnerships is when one side either forgets or does not live up to agreed upon obligations. If you have it in writing what the obligations are and what happens if those obligations are not met it will make a partnership much more successful. The partners will have more motivation to work hard and it will be easier to handle problems when they come up.

Many people ask me how to structure a partnership when they collaborate on rental properties. One question was:

"We have the money and knowledge to buy rentals, but we have the opportunity to partner up with another investor, so how do we structure it?"

My answer: Why do you need a partner? Why bring someone in to share the profits on a deal when you have the money and know-how? You will make much more money on real estate deals when you do not have a partner. The purpose of a partner is to provide something that you cannot or do not want to provide. You give up some of the profits to spend less of your own money, use someone's time or their expertise. If you don't need any of those things, don't give up your profits!

I also see many people who are looking for a partner or a mentor to help them start investing. The problem is they want someone to show them how to buy houses, fix them up, find great deals and make a ton of money. But the person looking to be taught how to invest is offering nothing back to the investor, except for a willingness to work hard.

I have this partnership proposed to me over and over and almost every time there are huge problems on my side of the deal.

1. When I ask the person who wants help what they can offer me in return, they say determination, hard work, etc., but they list no specific skills. What can you do better than other people who will help me become more successful or help the deal be more successful? Are you good with computers? Do you have carpentry skills? Are you an expert marketer? Willingness to learn and work hard is not a skill and something everyone says they have. If you want to impress someone, be as specific as possible about how you will help them make more money.

2. Most successful investors do not have time to train someone about the entire process of investing. They also may not want to train someone to compete with themselves! Don't be put off if an investor does not want to mentor you, because it is a very involved process that takes time. Paying for knowledge and experience is also an option and shows you are serious. Most people who want free help and have nothing to offer in return won't even use that help if they get it and it becomes a giant waste of time for everyone.

3. Many aspiring investors looking for a mentor will want someone to tell them how to do everything. I have had people come to me saying, "How do I make money flipping houses?" Well, I could write a book on that and still not answer all of your questions (actually I did write a book on flipping titled "Flipping For Profit Without The Risk"). I point out articles for people to read or point them toward my book but they don't want to take the time to read the articles or pay $20 for a book. They want everything done for them without doing any work. If you want to impress a potential partner or mentor, do your research and learn as much as you possibly can. The more knowledge you have, the better chance you have of impressing someone enough to help you.

If you want to be a partner in a real estate deal you must have something to offer. You need to bring money, expertise, skills, or pay for the opportunity. There are no shortcuts in becoming a successful real estate investor.

CONCLUSION

Partnerships can be a great way to get started if you need help. Partnerships can also be a nightmare if you do not have roles clearly defined or everything in writing. Partnerships also evolve and you may have to be flexible as people's priorities in life change. My partnership with my colleague Vince changed over the years until I ended up buying him out. We had everything in writing when we made changes and that helped things go smoothly.

If you enter a partnership, make sure you take the time to set it up right. If you don't need a partner it sure is nice having complete control… and all the profits.

GETTING YOUR REAL ESTATE LICENSE

Earlier I promised you we were going to talk more about getting your real estate license. The fact is I made more money as a result of using my license than I did in all my investing. That's why I want to share this with you. When I first got my license I didn't want anyone to know. I had no interest in showing houses, working nights or weekends, or driving people around. It turns out I never really had to, though I did at first, because that's what my broker wanted me to do. I was actually good at it. The reason I got my license though was because I thought it would help me with my investing. It did, but not in the way I thought it would.

You see most real estate agents don't invest, nor are they taught how to invest or to even help investors. They're only taught how to help someone else buy and sell a personal home. This created a *huge* opportunity for me. I was invited by a local Real Estate Investing guru to come and speak to his students and share my experiences with them. I liked it! In fact, I started to play a part in teaching the students on a regular basis. They inevitably would ask if I could be their agent. I was really smart so I said, "No" – hundreds of times. Remember, I didn't want to be a regular agent.

I finally consented and told the current class that I would take two of them as clients. At the end of class I had 25 students vying to be the two that I served. I learned one of the most important and profitable lessons in my life's business. Wherever there is demand, there is money to be made. I had demand and I had the valuable combination of the all-important knowledge and skill of investing in real estate… plus I had a real estate license that gave me the right to serve others for profit. That's exactly what I began to do.

I quickly started my own brokerage company and it was the fastest growing real estate brokerage company for three years running. That led to me building other related businesses around this demand, like property management and settlement services.

Would you like for me to show you how? Your life is getting ready to change. You will now be able to be financially free. Not just financially independent, but FREE! I love what's coming next.

Ready for the next level?

Visit www.myinvestmentservices.com/work-with-me

Think you've got what it takes and need just 1 hour
with the Guru to get to the next level?

PLUS you will also get a FREE Blueprint for your business

Investor-Agent, Make More Money Not More Work

The Right Kind of Real Estate Agent

When I first began investing I became agitated at the real estate profession. The agents themselves are, for the most part, decent people. Just like in any walk of life there are good ones and bad ones and a lot in between.

The problem is they are trained by brokerage companies with material focused on the owner-occupant, not the investor.

Real estate agents are inherently driven to succeed and are sincere in their desire to help. The challenge is they often don't know how.

Realtors who don't invest themselves don't understand the rules of engagement for investors. For the most part they do understand the rules of engagement for owner-occupants, though.

Agents who don't work with investors are leaving a substantial amount of money on the table. While the vast majority compete unprofitably for a few really good listings, Investor-Agents are cashing commission checks on a regular basis by working with investors with little or no competition. As a result they also get their investors' owner-occupant business as well, again, with little or no competition.

Likewise, investors who don't get their license are leaving huge piles of money *and* opportunity on the table. Investors are natural born entrepreneurs and getting your real estate license offers powerful opportunities to easily develop multiple streams of income, without having to be a traditional agent. It can grow to provide as much (or more) wealth and income as the investment activities leveraged with your license!

I believe that investing in real estate is the best path to realizing the American Dream. I was fortunate enough to have a great teacher when I first got started at the ripe old age of 23.

I eventually went on to get my real estate license but I only used it for myself. In fact I didn't want other people knowing I had it! When people would ask if could help them buy or sell a home I said, "No."

Ha. I can laugh now.

As I progressed in my investing I was often invited to be a guest speaker at various real estate education seminars. I was even on the radio a few times. That led me down the path of teaching others how to invest.

Students always asked if I could be their real estate agent. Again, I politely said, "No."

I was notoriously stubborn.

After the third class I decided to be a nice guy and help two students from each class by representing them in the field. I wasn't too excited about the money – yet!

When I told twenty-five students I could only help two, I learned one of the fundamental laws of marketing – the law of scarcity.

After I realized how much demand I created by making myself scarce, I decided to command a minimum commission from the investors I taught.

Something very important happened during this process. I created a system to use my license as an income-producing asset.

This system enabled me to keep investing, and at the same time, break all kinds of records in real estate sales.

In 2008, at the height of the great recession – when half of all real estate agents had to get out of the business – I single-handedly serviced 110 clients with no team or any assistant of any kind. In the middle of the worst economy in 80 years, my real estate business grew while most others were dying.

By following the suggestions in this book, you too can become an Investor/Agent. And *make more money… not more work!*

A Tale of Two Roles

Originally, I thought I was the only investor who went on to get a real estate license.

Over the years, I have met folks – investors like me – who also obtained their real estate license out of frustration. And just like me, they didn't want other people to know.

In fact, in almost every investor course I've taken and each investor book I've read, we are given the impression that it's not necessary for an investor to get a real estate license.

Many real estate gurus are anti-real estate agent.

In their eyes, real estate agents are expendable. Simply another tool, and not even really necessary. Essentially real estate agents could be used and not thought of once the investor got out of them what they wanted. No wonder so many investors struggle!

Ironically, I discovered many of these gurus actually had their real estate license! The bottom line is that investors rarely figure out how to find a great real estate agent who knows how to recommend investments, and investors rarely make an effort to understand real estate agents and the role they can play as valuable team members.

The primary role of the investor is to invest profitably. In order to do that he needs to run his investment empire as a business. And in order to do that successfully he needs highly valuable players on his investing team.

Real estate agents almost never invest. I have only found a few who started out as real estate agents and then got into real estate investing – I mean in a meaningful way.

I have observed in almost every instance that agents who went on to invest invariably apply the rules of the owner-occupied world of real estate to the investor world of real estate.

It doesn't work that way. Never has and never will. The two worlds have two completely different sets of rules. I call these the rules of engagement.

I have also observed that most real estate agents really don't want to work with investors. Real estate agents are taught to work primarily with owner-occupants who want to buy or sell their own homes. They are rarely, if ever, taught how to work with investors.

In fact, a lot of real estate brokers and experienced agents tell other agents not to work with investors because they waste your time. That's because they simply don't understand investors and the world of investing. They are trying to treat investors the same as they would treat an owner-occupant. That doesn't work. Everybody gets frustrated and everybody gives up because they think the other person stinks, or doesn't listen, or doesn't know what they're doing.

I can tell you from firsthand experience that it can work and it does work. I have been doing it for a long time. I actually prefer working with Investors because unlike most owner-occupants they usually know what they're doing. They are efficient and I get tons of repeat business from them. I don't have to keep looking for more and more new customers. I have all the customers I can handle.

There were times when I was actively practicing with my real estate license that I would have more than twenty contracts going at the same time. And remember, I had no help. And I was still investing myself and even managing several dozen of my own properties! I did it by understanding both roles of investing and real estate agency and I developed a system to make the most money with least amount of work!

The Chicken or the Egg?

I am often asked, "Should I get my real estate license first before I start investing?" or "Should I start investing first before I get my real estate license?" I'm not a lawyer but I have learned to appreciate the stock lawyer answer to almost every question – it depends!

If you are young and just starting out or you are more experienced in life (i.e. older) and starting over, you may need to generate cashflow like yesterday! If that is the case you likely don't have cash saved away anywhere either. In this situation I suggest getting your license first. It's quick and easy. You can then service the people you already know (your circle of friends, family, neighbors, etc.), other Investors, and you can also participate in wholesaling.

With wholesaling you control and profit from property without actually owning it. Wholesaling is also a great way to grow your database of investors and future partners in larger real estate investment deals like apartment complexes, shopping centers, and office buildings.

So, if you need cashflow and you don't have cash saved, you need to generate sales *ASAP* and save some of those commissions.

If you have some savings and need cashflow then perhaps you should invest first in a few rental properties to generate passive income. This will give you a more solid base from which to operate. You could also get your license at the same time to generate commission income as well. At the very least you will earn commissions on your own deals!

If you are already investing, I suggest getting your license as soon as possible. You are leaving income on the table with each transaction. As mentioned above, you can earn commissions on your own deals and if you locate more investment opportunities that you can't take on at the moment, you can present them to your clients and at least earn commissions.

And, like me, you can further leverage your license as an income-producing asset. Just like a duplex! You can develop additional lines of business like a brokerage company or property management company. These businesses will build substantial wealth and income for you and you're already engaged in the very activities you need to make this happen!

Of course you could wholesale them too, by either doing a net listing (in some states) or a straight wholesale through an LLC – where another agent does the work – and you can earn a referral fee. These are a few opportunities that we will explore more later.

If you are already a real estate agent I suggest you get in the investing game immediately. I'm not suggesting that every real estate agent should invest, but if you are a real estate agent the rest of the world looks at you and asks, "If you are an agent then why don't you own a lot of investment property since you know so much?" How's that for applying pressure? A much better reason is that you will be able to leverage your real estate license and use it more as an income-producing asset. Moreover, there is no other investment in the history of the human race that has had more impact on more people's lives.

If you are a fully engaged real estate professional then you are by nature an entrepreneur. As an entrepreneur you should naturally gravitate toward real estate investing. If this does not describe you then I assume you view your real estate license as a job. Why not instead think of your license more fully as an income-producing asset for your business?

The difference is that with the former, if you go away on an extended vacation and don't work on your vacation, then your production will suffer. I know it will suffer because in addition to not being able to effectively service your clients you will probably not be generating leads either.

Furthermore, by working with Investors you can land million dollar deals, both investment and owner-occupant, that never would have been available while working with owner-occupants alone. After all, Investors represent a cross-section of society. A fair percentage live in million dollar homes they also want to buy and sell from time to time. Can you guess who they call to do this? You'll have almost no competition.

When operating like a business, you will likely have someone executing your lead generating activities for you and you will likely have team members who can continue to take listings and work with buyers. The bottom line is that if you are a true real estate professional then you really ought to be thinking like an entrepreneur and operating like a business.

Remember the facts surrounding World War II. If Winston Churchill and Franklin Roosevelt hadn't cooperated, in spite of our storied past, Europe, and in fact our world would not be what it is today. Imagine what you can do for yourself and your family –

whether you're an agent or an investor with a real estate license – by choosing to work with investors.

Real Estate Agent = A Living

Real Estate Investor = A Great Living

Investor/Agent = An Incredible Living

Getting Your License

Before you can practice real estate you need to obtain a real estate practitioner's license for the state in which you wish to represent others in real estate transactions.

There are typically two classes you need to take, one is national and one is state. They are usually 30 hours each. You can now either take these completely online, or in a physical classroom with other students, or a combination of the two.

There are multiple class providers. Many real estate firms offer them for prospective agents. They may even offer to pay for you to attend if you sign up with them for one year.

I do not normally recommend this latter approach. I recommend you take the classes and pay for them out of your own pocket.

In order to practice, real estate licensees do need to place their license with a real estate firm. If you have paid for the courses yourself, after you pass the licensing exams you will have a choice of companies to practice real estate with.

Once you have taken the classes, you will be required to take two exams: state and national. I highly encourage you to take several practice exams, and even take a class that prepares you specifically for these tests. When I prepared for the broker's exam I took thirty practice exams.

Once you have taken the classes, passed the exams, and placed your license with a real estate brokerage firm, you now have the right to practice real estate.

This does not mean that you are prepared to practice real estate, rather you simply have earned the right to practice because you now supposedly have a fundamental understanding of real estate law.

That is all the classes are designed to do – educate you on the very basic legal rules and regulations you need to be familiar with so consumers you represent will get fair representation.

Now you need to learn how to use your license in the business sense. This book is not intended to educate you on all of the skills necessary to become a successful real estate agent. This requires continuous education on your part for as long as you practice.

The world of marketing and advertising is constantly changing. You will learn a lot of what you need to know from your broker, other agents in your office, and your own blood, sweat, and tears. I will go over, in simple terms what is expected of you in the roles of agency.

Different Kinds of Representation

Seller Representation

Real estate agents could be involved in representing users and Investors who are interested in disposing of their properties. This is a traditional activity in a commercial and investment brokerage, just as it is in a residential brokerage. When acting as a selling broker, an agent has an agency relationship with the seller and owes him or her fiduciary duty.

Buyer Representation

Another activity in which real estate agents might be involved is representing users and investors who are potential buyers of properties in selecting and acquiring these properties. When acting as a buyer's broker, the agent has an agency relationship with the buyer and owes a fiduciary duty to him or her. This activity is more common in commercial and investment brokerage than in residential brokerage. For example, an agent could represent several fast food chains in their search for locations to purchase as sites for their restaurants. By becoming familiar with the specific requirements of a few users, the broker can provide a service to his or her clients.

Landlord Representation

Further activity in which investment real estate agents might be involved is the exclusive representation of landlords in their attempts to locate tenants who would be users of their vacant spaces, negotiating the leases for the use of those spaces.

As *leasing agents*, brokers would be involved in many more transactions than brokers involved in the investor or development part of the business. In fact, many commercial investment managers agree that the best way to transition from residential real estate to non-residential real estate is through leasing commercial space. This activity allows agents to interact with many tenants and property owners, all of whom have specific needs that agents can try to fulfill. In addition, brokers can become familiar with a variety of properties present in their marketplaces.

By showing potential users several properties, agents get to see a variety of spaces and have an opportunity to become familiar with the available inventory in the market.

By showing several properties to potential users, agents get to talk to and meet many property owners who have spaces to rent.

By showing multiple spaces, agents interact with other tenants who anticipate moving from their spaces and will need to find new spaces to occupy in the future.

Tenant Representation

Still another user brokerage activity in which investment real estate agents could be involved is the exclusive representation of users looking to relocate and negotiating leases for space in landlords' properties. By representing specific users, agents become aware of the users' needs and the requirements properties must meet for the users' businesses.

Of course you can use your license to help owner-occupants buy and sell their own homes. Even though I was supposed to do this at first, I later warmed up to the idea and made a lot of money doing it. Let's face it, all the Investors you service at one time or another will want to buy or sell their own home. You will also meet many tenants who will one day buy their own home. You already have a database full of these folks. You might as well service them and further leverage the use of your real estate license and earn more commissions!

What's more, these folks all have friends, relatives, neighbors, co-workers, and fellow church members who want to buy and sell homes from time to time. I highly encourage you to remind your clients that you can service them too, and encourage them to refer these people to you. When that happens you should reward them for their good behavior!

Speaking of referrals, the more you grow and prosper with your license, the greater your reputation will spread. One way you can benefit is by sending referrals to agents in other areas.

Surely, your clients have friends and relatives in other areas who either want to buy or sell their own home or they may want to invest in real estate. A referral from you will carry a lot of weight and it will earn you a referral fee. Do not overlook this very valuable income stream. I have built an entire line of business around this very concept.

Building a Team

Ah yes, building a business. First of all I remind you to treat this entire venture as a business and run it as such. One of the best ways to manifest this is to build a team around yourself and your business.

When I first got really busy, I had developed systems, processes, and procedures for me to follow every day so that I could handle all of the business. When building my brokerage company, Win Realty Advisors, I actually built a team first. The first person I hired was an admin person. She was from another brokerage company and had an awesome reputation for being able to manage multiple tasks simultaneously and get a lot done – a lot more than 99% of other people.

My recommendation to you is, when you get really busy, hire a superstar admin. Be picky, don't settle. Remember the old saying – hire slow and fire fast. Your definition of busy may be different than that of the next person. I was juggling more than twenty transactions, teaching classes, investing in property, and managing property all at the same time. I was pretty busy.

Whenever you find yourself heading down the road of unhappiness – from relationships that need more of your time, you needing more of your time, and God needing more of your time – then it is time to make your first hire.

After that you will figure out what to do next. It may include delegating the execution of your marketing plan, or delegating buyer showings. You will know when the time comes.

One of the best things about building a team is that it will position you to build your own brokerage firm in the future if you choose to do so.

There's more! All of your investor clients are accumulating a lot of rental properties and they need help managing them. I think it is a really good idea for you to offer to manage these properties for them!

As a real estate licensee with your license in a brokerage firm you can do this. Some firms are more accommodating than others. I have found Keller Williams is the best for entrepreneurial real estate agents who want to grow their own businesses. In fact I know personally several KW agents who manage several hundred units each as an agent with KW.

You can learn more about this by reading my book "Build a Property Management Business for Profit and Build Wealth for Life." Not only do you earn management fee income but all of these folks can bring in additional sales for you, too!

As you can see, there are a number of opportunities for you to build wealth and income by working with investors. You simply leverage what you are already doing. You can leverage your systems and operations, including bookkeeping and marketing, in many directions.

Even at the most basic level, you can't buy every property and neither can your clients. When you identify more great investment properties than you or your clients can handle, refer the deal to another agent or investor and earn commission anyway from your efforts. Remember, your real estate license is an income-producing asset. Treat it like that and you will profit.

As you grow you will need systems, processes, and procedures to allow for successful growth. These systems are not just for bookkeeping, marketing and advertising, and transaction flow but also for client support and representation.

Client Support and Representation

One of the first things you need to do when working with investors is to become familiar with the instructions I give to investors who work with me. You will find them in the *Flip* and *Rental Rules of Engagement* sections earlier in this book. Please remember that there are major differences between working with owner-occupants and working with investors.

When working with owner-occupants you generally do most if not all of the work. You do a lot more hand holding. They don't usually know a lot and so you have to explain everything to them. They also tend to be more emotional in their selling and buying behavior. They also only need you once every several years.

Investors, on the other hand, get easier to work with over time. They continue to learn. They are hands-on. In fact, if you follow my instruction sheets, you will see that I delegate a lot of the work to them. You give them the data and let them do the financial analysis. They do drive-bys. They do the physical analysis.

Anytime an investor approaches and wants me to do all the work for them I take it upon myself to educate them first. If they don't want to do things my way then I send them down the highway to some poor sucker of an agent who doesn't know any better and has time to waste. Not me and not you.

I also command a minimum commission. This protects me when working with investors who want to buy cheap foreclosures.

With investors I get to dictate the work on my schedule. They may not know it but that is what is happening. I always schedule my showing days and times a week in advance. I send an email to my active clients on Wednesday and give them the day and time blocks I have available the following week. Then it's first come, first serve.

They must give me the MLS numbers of the properties they want to see at least two days in advance of our scheduled date and time to meet and view properties. Oh, I occasionally get the knucklehead who can't follow simple instructions. You know, the ones who never could get to school on time and when they did they turned in their homework with food stains. If they even had their homework.

I give them a chance or two to correct their behavior, and I help them do that, but if it appears habitual I draw the line and they get the message.

I love working with investors because it's repeat business. It's the gift that keeps on giving. Many of my students have gone on to buy large apartment buildings earning me large commissions and large property management contracts. I am able to leverage all of my activities working with Investors into additional lines of business, providing additional income streams and wealth-building opportunities.

Perhaps one of the best benefits of working with Investors is how many friendships are developed with people while doing something we both love – building wealth and income with real estate!

BEING THE RIGHT KIND OF REALTOR

If you are not a licensed real estate agent then read this. If you are a licensed real estate agent then you need to read this too, so you will know what all of my students expect from you! Please re-read the section titled "The Right Kind of Realtor."

This is what I teach investors to look for when selecting a real estate agent. This should be an eye opener for you. Also, I do not intend to insult you. I am one of you! I am merely enlightening you to what is expected of you as an Investor-Agent.

Marketing

How do you market yourself as an Investor-Agent?

Join Local Investor Clubs – I have belonged to multiple investor clubs. I highly recommend REIA (Real Estate Investor Association) clubs. There are some with hundreds and thousands of members. Every time I go to a meeting I get multiple deals – listings, buyers and property management. Warning: don't join unless you are an investor or you have gone through our training. If you don't walk the talk they will simply ignore you or worse.

Write Articles – I have written articles for several years now – at least three times a week. This really helps you establish credibility. The investor clubs will reward you also. They will publish articles in their newsletters.

Create a Monthly Community Workshop – This is one of my favorites. I started in a local library with maybe a handful of people. The word spread and I grew to 12, 24, 48 then 70+ and the library said I had to go! Then I went to a hotel and grew to over 200 people. Even when I had only a small group in the beginning I got a deal out of every single meeting. When it grew to over 200 people I always had a line 20+ deep waiting to talk to me at the end of the session. I always got multiple deals out of these events. Amazing!

Write a Monthly Newsletter – OK, I have to admit I started and stopped this multiple times. It is time consuming. However, when structured and titled properly, it does bring in business. BIG HINTS: Don't call it "John's newsletter." No one will open it and the pros will make fun of you. Call it something relevant like Jacksonville Investors Press. Also, don't just put real estate related info in there. Include information on other subjects like local events, personal development, health, money, cars, children, shopping – you get the picture. Make it interesting. It is work but it does work.

Craigslist – Bar none, this is one of the best ways to reach your marketplace. It's free and has a wide audience. They even have a tutorial for you.

Facebook, Twitter, LinkedIn – Use your social media networks to get the word out. Be careful how you use social media, though. There are rules of etiquette you must first learn for each one. The number one taboo is spamming your network. Never abuse the privilege of social media. If you do you will be shunned, un-friended, un-liked, un-connected and unsuccessful!

Church – Churches usually have weekly bulletins in which you can advertise your vacancies. This works well for large congregations but I would use it in small churches as well. Look in your church's current bulletin and there should be instructions or at least contact information that you can use to get started.

Grocery store – They usually have a bulletin board where you can pin a flyer with tear-off phone number tabs. You need to check this regularly. Sometimes they disappear. Sometimes other people will post their notice right over top of yours. If you're really lucky all of your number tabs will be gone!

Restaurants – They often will let you put a stack of flyers or business cards near the checkout. The next time you're dining at one of your local favorite restaurants speak to the owner or manager. Someone with the authority to act is always on duty at a restaurant. Please note that there are some other great marketing and advertising opportunities here. For example, ask the proprietor if he/she will offer a discount or free meal coupon (get several) for you to use as a reward to give to your good tenants who refer other good tenants to you. Use your imagination!

Local publications – Penny Saver, Green Sheet, they're in every community and are very inexpensive. Unlike the large publications like your big city paper, I have had a lot of success with these types of publications. Call and ask for their rules and regulations. Learn the rules of their advertising game and you will master the game. Some ads you will place for one to two weeks. Some you will place for a year. You will also learn where in the publication to place your ads, how big, how small, special features, etc. Hint – Any time you can have your ad placed in a box you will get better results!

Join Local Investor Clubs

Create a Monthly Mastermind Group

Direct Mail – This by far brings in the best leads. You can identify your target prospects by accessing your local tax records – usually free and online – and locate the owners of multi-unit properties. Then send them something that they will see perceived value in. Remember the old saying in advertising "WIIFM"… What's in it for me?

Your Own Website

Blogging

AdWords

Joint Ventures

Affiliates

YouTube

The possibilities are endless. I believe God wants us to be happy not sad, wealthy not poor, healthy not sick. I believe it is our duty to fulfill the purpose He has intended for our lives, which is to bring others closer to Him. What better way to do this than to be our highest and best selves, living examples of how joyful life can be when we make the absolute most of the precious gift of life He has given us.

When you own investment real estate you are providing a good service to your fellow man. You are helping yourself by helping others first.

And herein lies one of the greatest truths of success and that is that if you help enough other people get what they want then you will get plenty of what you want. You can thank Zig Ziglar for that pearl of wisdom which is actually scriptural in its origin.

There are three basic ways of investing in real estate as a beginner.

1) You can invest in rental properties.
2) You can invest in flipping properties.
3) You can wholesale properties.

Demographics

This data is objective, comprised of facts and statistics about the local population. Most of this data is collected by the U.S. Census Bureau. It describes the age, sex, income, home value, and whether the household owns or rents. This information is very important as, it deals with the facts gathered during the census.

I also suggest using your Multi List System to its fullest extent.

What's Next?

Buy and Sell Large Apartment Complexes.

Start Your Own Real Estate Brokerage Business.

Start Your Own Property Management Business.

Start Another Business Related to Real Estate and Investing like a Painting, Plumbing, or Electrical Contracting Business.

The bottom line is this. In order to not just survive but thrive you will have to feel, think, speak and act like a business because you are a business. As a business, use the following statement as an affirmation to say to yourself every day: "I am a business and I leverage my real estate license as an income-producing asset to generate multiple streams of income." You will leverage what you are already doing.

Please review the following diagram. Now you can see how to maximize your time and effort to generate the most income in the least amount of time and with less expense.

Path to Prosperity

What Else Is Next?

In addition to building other businesses you could start investing in larger properties. That's what I did. My next move was to buy a 78-unit apartment building. I learned more about real estate that way, particularly in the world of commercial real estate. I have been involved in the purchase and sale of other commercial properties as a result and I want to share with you what I learned.

The following will help you gain more understanding of what lies ahead for you if you choose. This information will be a little more technical in nature than what you've read so far. You're ready for it now and I'm anxious to share it with you!

For more information visit:

https://bit.ly/2WEonGH

For a limited time, get 1 month FREE membership
to our Silver community where you have access to
free tools, contracts, Real Estate Statistics, and
Expert Insider Information including personal interviews,
and other books for FREE!

Commercial Properties

Investing In Commercial Properties

If you are dead serious about growing and expanding your real estate business as a real estate investor, real estate broker/agent or both, then please keep reading. If you struggle with making decisions in your life, particularly when it comes to business and/or finance, then stop now.

The following is a general but thorough explanation of real estate investing in the commercial world. When you operate in the commercial world you have to be able to be decisive. Otherwise you will waste your time… and other people's time and effort… and they will not give you a second chance.

Generally speaking, commercial agents/brokers are not going to roll out the red carpet for you if you are also a broker/agent. In other words you better know what you're doing.

This next section is a great way to familiarize yourself with some of the terminology and methods used in the commercial world. Then you and I can work together to take some meaningful effective action and get some results under your belt so you can really build your empire based on financial and intellectual strength.

This is the level that most real estate investors aspire to. It is where very large fortunes can be made. Are you with me? Are your ready to play with the big boys? Good. Let's get started.

Much of the following material is courtesy of classes I have taken in commercial real estate over the years with my own experiences provided to lend context.

Generally, the commercial investment brokerage business is divided into activities, which deal with either users or investors. If one considers that real estate is only a square foot of space that must be used by someone, there are two uses for the property.

This first one is looking at the business of the users, on the property. Example, fast food franchises look at the spaces which they are occupying as places where business is conducted. Whether the franchisees are tenants or owners of the space, they look at the space as a place to sell food. The cost of occupying the space is a cost of doing business as providers of food products. All things being equal, tenants prefer properties with the lowest cost of occupancy.

While the income source to the users above is the sale of food, investors have a different view in the use of a square foot of real estate. Investors are in the business of selling; they're looking for the use of that square foot to others who can use the square feet in their businesses. Investors are interested in the income the properties can produce; they use the rental of the square feet as a base, calculating the possible income stream of the property. Essentially, investors prefer properties with the highest income streams.

Whether agents are working in the user or the investor part of the industry, there are specific activities in which they might become involved. Let's have a look at them.

Agent Activities

　　　　User Brokerage

- Leasing
  - Landlord Representation
  - Tenant Representation

　　　　Investor Brokerage

- Sales
  - Seller Representation
  - Buyer Representation
- Development
  - Site Selection
  - Construction
- Financing
  - Loan Brokerage
    - Mortgage Banking

User brokerage

The most common activity in which agents might participate is bringing together tenants and landlords in transactions. Most users choose to control and occupy property through a lease. At the same time, brokers or agents must be mindful of the motivations and needs of the investor and the motivations and needs of tenants, too, such as what their intent is for the property.

Over the years I have managed thousands of tenants in hundreds of units for dozens of owners. And I made a ton of money in the process! I made money at least a dozen different ways. Of course I also collected a management fee every month, and a leasing fee every time I leased a vacant unit. I collected lease application fees, lease renewal fees, late fees, and nuisance call fees. I collected extra fees for pets and smokers. I charged a 10% override for maintenance and repairs to the owners *and* to the contractors performing the work. I also collected sales commissions every time an owner bought or sold a property.

Property management provides one of the best lead sources you will ever have. Every time a prospective tenant applies to rent one of your units you get current and prior landlord information. Once you screen the prospective tenant you can then offer your services to the current and prior landlords! And you get paid an application fee to get this contact information! On top of that you have contact information for attorneys, insurance company reps, contractors like roofers, electricians, plumbers, carpenters, flooring installers, locksmiths, municipality employees (including zoning and occupancy officers), utility companies, appraisers, title reps. The list goes on and on and you can reach out to all of these people and offer your services! Hallelujah! Come to Papa!

Let's break this down into the major roles.

LEASING

Landlord Representation and Tenant Representation were both covered under the "Investor-Agent, Make More Money Not More Work" section of this book.

Investor Brokerage

This is another area where I have made a ton of money. It started out small. When I first got my license I used it only for myself in my own investing activities. I slowly started using my license to generate commissions by representing other investors in their investing activities. Then I built an independent brokerage company named Win Realty Advisors. I was able to leverage these investor relationships to generate additional income by offering property management services, title services, and appraisal services. In the meantime however, I generated a lot of commissions from the inherent repeat business I got from investors.

Duties of an Agent in an Investor Brokerage

The most common brokerage activity is bringing together buyers and sellers in a transaction. Stockbrokers, food brokers, and commodity brokers provide all the same functions as real estate brokers. Although brokers do not have any ownership in the properties, they are generally compensated on a commission basis and collect a fee based on a percentage of the transactions.

SALES

Seller Representation and Buyer Representation were both covered under the "Investor-Agent, Make More Money Not More Work" section of this book.

Development of Commercial and Investment Brokerage

Many commercial investment real estate agents become involved with creating a product through the development process. There are many different activities in the development part of commercial and investment brokerage.

Construction

Commercial investment real estate agents may be involved in the construction phase of a property under development.

Financing

Commercial investment real estate agents could arrange the financing for a property to be built.

Site Selection

Commercial investment real estate agents may be involved with users and investors of properties in selecting sites. This helps a property owner to determine the best location for the next development.

REQUIREMENTS RELATING TO ACTIVITIES IN MORTGAGE BROKERAGE

Each state's individual real estate laws have specific requirements relating to activities in mortgage brokerage. Generally, mortgage brokerage activities can be conducted by real estate licensees who also have a mortgage brokerage license. Certain federal laws, such as the Secure and Fair Enforcement for Mortgage Licensing Act (SAFE Act), regulate the activities of brokers, when involved with loans made on residential properties.

Brokerage

This allows commercial investment real estate agents to concentrate on brokering mortgage financing by representing borrowers who are looking for financing.

Mortgage Banking

This allows commercial investment real estate agents to be involved in mortgage financing by representing institutional lenders who have funds to place in real estate.

In either activity, agents should have knowledge of the financial characteristics of the properties, because a property's ability to be financed depends on the income the property produces.

Real Estate Agents Could Also Be Investors

From this section, you should understand right now we are talking about commercial investment real estate agents. As an Investor-Agent you could (and I think should) become involved in owning commercial and investment real estate, through investment in direct ownership of real estate.

As an Investor-Agent you should be aware of the financial characteristics of the real estate. Cashflow is the main reason we invest. The cashflow depends on the effects of the law of supply and demand, the availability of financing, and the effects of income tax laws.

Many investors progress from an entry-level investment, into small residential properties, and finally to the most risky – raw land speculation. While continuing to advance in risk, some investors decide to invest in money, not property; this allows them to become involved in real estate as hard money lenders.

Each step in the progression includes more risk. As investors move up, there are fewer properties, tenants, lenders, buyers, and sellers. But the belief is, as the risk increases, the expected returns must be larger. Most investors get to a level where they are comfortable and continue to do all their investing at that level.

The four major property types encountered by investors and real estate agents increase in complexity, while rising in risk. *Residential* properties are usually the least complicated. *Office* properties are the next most favored property. *Retail* and *industrial* properties are more complicated, with industrial properties being the most complicated – and purchased by fewer investors. However, there are cycles in the marketplace; at any time, real estate agents may notice one of the property types is more favored than the other property types.

Market Analysis

Regardless of the property type, the agent or investor will typically use two types of data to complete their market analysis. There is information on the property's location, and then there is information regarding the specific property.

Market data

Market data deals with people. Economic, demographic, and lifestyle data is used to help determine the demand for a property. Never thought that economics class would come in handy, did you? As a refresher course, the breakdown works like this:

Economic data refers to data regarding employment by industry. Employment is an important economic indicator, as changes in employment changes demand for real estate.

In other words, more people, more buying. Simple, right?

Macroeconomics pertains to the study of the overall economy. The conditions of the national economy can have a direct effect on the local economy. The study of the local economy would be called microeconomics. When industries and services experience a change in demand for their products and services, the area in which the industry is located will be affected.

In simpler terms, supply and demand of people is not enough; there are other factors you must consider. If you are an agent in Florida, then what would you take into consideration? The weather – hurricane season. This could affect where you purchase real estate, or if a buyer will decide to… well, buy.

Employment data

Employment data is usually described in one of these ways:

- **Workforce characteristics**. This overlooks the workforce. It will take into account the percentage of employment, education levels, and skills of those employed.

- **Type of employment**. This is going to look at what type of employment is readily available, through the available data.
- **Lifestyle Characteristics.** Employment will obviously trickle down into the lifestyle. It will dictate the community identity, trends and values, and recreational opportunity. Why? Because employment dictates the amount of money for each person; if you have an abundant community of welders, then you will want to use provided data to configure their possible budget. If not, you may find little success.

Recreational opportunities

The abundance, or lack, of recreational opportunities can affect the population size of a community and therefore the demand for real estate. For example, Aspen, Colorado, attracts many people for its recreational opportunities. Certainly, there are other areas of Colorado that have the same climate as Aspen, but it is the recreational opportunities that started, and still drive, the growth of the city and surrounding area.

Intellectual and educational opportunity

Areas with colleges and universities promoting higher education may draw a more highly educated population, which may attract a certain population that attracts certain employers.

Cultural trends and values

Certain communities become popular and attract people, following a particular trend. Laguna Beach, California, and Santa Fe, New Mexico, are known as artist communities, and they attract a population that has similar interests, and those people will pay higher prices to live in such a community.

Community identity

Some communities have a distinct identity. Certain college towns attract people to live there, even after completing their education. Certain communities have developed an ethnic identity, and attract certain groups of people to live there.

Psychographics

The study of lifestyle characteristics is called psychographics. These studies help businesses identify emerging trends, niche markets, and new opportunities. For example, the trend toward specialty coffees has caused the growth of several specialty coffee shops, such as Starbuck's and Seattle's Best. Even McDonald's and Dunkin Donut, have started selling specialized coffees.

Demographics

This objective data is comprised of facts and statistics about the local population. Most is collected by the U.S. Census Bureau. It describes the age, sex, income, home value, and whether the household owns or rents. This information is important, since it deals with the facts gathered during the census.

Comparables

The study of individual properties within a market usually breaks down into studying comparable properties in four general ways:

- **Building data.** Each specific property type has a unique way of categorizing and communicating property details.
- **Rental data.** Investors are interested in the cashflow that properties produce through rents received. Each property can be looked at as a unique stream of rental income.
- **Building services.** Not all buildings of the same type offer the same services, such as parking, janitorial, air conditioning, technology, and heat and air conditioning.
- **Community services.** Each building is located in a community that has its own individual amenities such as nearby transportation, restaurants, shopping, and recreational opportunities.

COMMON CLASSIFICATIONS OF RESIDENTIAL INVESTMENT PROPERTIES

1. Garden
2. Mid-Rise
3. High-Rise
4. Others

Garden Apartments

Located in suburban or rural areas, garden apartments are generally one- and two-story properties. Most units can be accessed from the outside of the property, using an exterior stairway to gain access to the second-story apartments. Rarely do garden apartments have elevators. Most units have individual utility meters and individual air-conditioning units. The property usually has a central laundry facility, and it may have one or more swimming pools. With this information, who do you know that would be an ideal buyer for garden apartments?

Mid-Rise Apartments

Located in the suburbs, mid-rise properties generally run from four to nine stories, consisting of studio, one-bedroom, two-bedroom, and three-bedroom units. Most units are accessed from a central hallway, which might be serviced by an elevator. Elevators are a blessing, aren't they? Although the units have individual utility meters, the building might have central air conditioning. These properties often have parking structures, a central lobby area, and recreation facilities. With this knowledge, who do you know that would be an ideal buyer for this apartment?

High-Rise Apartments

In the major urban areas, where land is scarce and expensive, high-rise properties are built. They are usually studios, one-bedroom, two-bedroom, and three-bedroom units; all are accessed from the central hallway, which is serviced by an elevator.

Located in urban neighborhoods, these properties often take advantage of city skyline views, and offer their tenants proximity to employment, security, recreation, and other amenities. Knowing all this, who do you know that would be an ideal buyer for a high-rise apartment?

Other Types of Residential Properties

Lastly, there are other types of properties… the red-headed step-children of residential properties. Joking, just joking. There are many other types of residential properties though, including single-family, duplexes, triplexes, and four-units. These properties do not have professional management, often being managed directly by the owner of the property.

LENDER CLASSIFICATIONS OF APARTMENT BUILDINGS

1. Class A: Newer, Institutional Grade
2. Class B: Older, Institutional Grade
3. Class C: Older, Declining Area
4. Class D: Older, Declining Area

Lenders have developed general classifications of apartment buildings, so they can communicate among themselves and other members of the industry, with some level of uniformity. The classifications are Class A, Class B, Class C, and Class D.

IREM®

There is no sugarcoating this next part, so let's just jump right in. The Institute of Real Estate Management of the National Association of Realtors (IREM) prints an annual publication titled *Income/Expense Analysis: Conventional Apartments*. For this publication, IREM® gathers actual income and expense records of apartment owners throughout the country. Afterwards, they print summary information, which is used by property managers and owners; the property managers and owners can then measure the financial results of their properties against the IREM® data. Information about IREM® can be found at www.irem.org.

Property and Ownership Characteristics

Office properties are those properties which typically provide space for service industries. These spaces can then be used for the manufacturing or retail functions of the economy.

Investors often move from residential income property ownership to ownership of office properties, because they want to reduce the amount of management activity. Office buildings have some characteristics of an apartment building, such as many tenants; but office tenants go home at night and on the weekends. In addition, the landlord-tenant relationship can be more businesslike than the relationship between apartment building owners and their tenants.

Office suites are relatively interchangeable. Generally tenants of office buildings choose properties based on location. Since much of America's business is being done by smaller private firms, the location requirements of the owners of the businesses are the most important factor. Owners of the businesses make their decisions based on the following:

- Their perceptions of the images of the buildings in comparison with their perceptions of their businesses. Appearance is everything, right?
- The ease of the commute to and from the business owners' homes.
- The location of the office buildings in relation to the geographic area where the business's clients are located. Once again, appearance is everything, right?
- Smaller office properties with one tenant, or a small number of tenants, are owned and managed by individual investors. Larger, multi-tenant properties are often owned by investment groups.

High-Rise Office Buildings

First built in Chicago in the 1800s, for all you history-buffs, these buildings have multiple stories, and are primarily made of steel and concrete construction. The exteriors are likely to be of pre-cast concrete or glass. Most are located in the central business districts of major cities. Tenants are often large national or multinational firms (big-wigs), who need large amounts of space (to count money). They are concerned with the brand and image perceived by their employees and clients.

Mid-Rise Office Buildings

These buildings may also have elevators, since they are often more than two stories high, and they are primarily of concrete construction. The height of the buildings, marketplace, and zoning restrictions limit the number of stories. These buildings can be found in central business districts and also in suburban areas. Tenants are often smaller national or regional firms (little-wigs), who occupy smaller amounts of space (still to count money) and do not demand the image of a high-rise building (hence, the little-wig).

Low-Rise Office Buildings

Most of these buildings are made of wood, and are not more than two stories. They are designed to fit in with the neighborhood. They are almost always located in the suburbs, and these buildings offer tenants the opportunity to have an exterior entrance to their units. These are also in demand by tenants who do not want to get "lost" in the larger properties (I say, "Buy a GPS"). Tenants are often regional or local businesses (who, sadly, have no-wigs); owners usually want to be located close to their homes and the businesses of their clients.

CLASS A, B, OR C BUILDINGS

In addition to the classifications of high-rise, mid-rise, or garden buildings, office properties are classified as A, B, or C buildings. Class A buildings are generally less than 20 years old, built of high quality, have modern functions, and are maintained very well. Class B or C buildings are often older and less functional. This classification is highly subjective and market specific. A Class A building in downtown St. Louis, Missouri, will probably be different from a Class A building in Duluth, Minnesota.

Office Building Measurement Guidelines

Office building efficiency is important to tenants. The term efficiency relates to the amount of space tenants must pay in relation to the space they occupy. Highly efficient buildings limit the amount of common area tenants pay for, and inefficient buildings force tenants to pay for common area.

Tenants talk about usable area in describing the space they occupy. Landlords talk about the rentable area, for which tenants must pay rent. When the usable square footage equals the rentable, buildings are highly efficient and landlords and tenants do not argue about this issue.

Common Questions

Office tenants and landlords often argue over the amount of square footage the lease covers. Common questions regarding a specific lease are the following:

- Does the tenant pay rent on common areas such as hallways, bathrooms, and lobbies?

    Answer: Yes, the landlord collects rent from the tenant based on the total area of the floor the tenant actually uses, which includes hallways and bathrooms.

- Does the space stop at the inside surface of the office wall, the middle of the office wall, or the outside surface of the office wall?

    Answer: Generally, the office area is measured from the inside of permanent walls and the center core of temporary walls.

- Does the space stop at the inside surface of the windows, on the exterior wall of the office space, or the outside edge of the windows on the exterior wall?

    Answer: Generally, the office area is measured from the inside of the permanent exterior wall.

How Office Space Is Measured

As previously said, landlords and tenants have a built-in conflict when determining how much space tenants must pay rent upon. The common terms used by investors and tenants are *usable square feet* and *rentable square feet*.

To establish acceptable answers to the questions raised above, the Building Owners and Managers Association International (BOMA®) developed the *Standard Method of Floor Measurement for Office Buildings (Standards)*. Information about BOMA® can be found at www.boma.org.

The BOMA® website has this description of the *Standards*:

Standard Method for Measuring Floor Area in Office Buildings

Order# 133-FMS96-489

Since 1915, the BOMA *Standard* has been the only floor measurement method for commercial real estate, which is approved by the American National Standards Institute (ANSI). This approval is a must for building owners, managers, facilities managers, tenants, appraisers, architects, leasing professionals, lending institutions, and others.

The revised *Standard* includes how to measure new tenant amenities and building features, such as spacious entrance lobbies, conference centers, health clubs, and daycare facilities. Generously illustrated with clear, easy-to-read diagrams, the *Standard* defines approaches to measure the following:

- Gross Building Area
- Gross Measured Area
- Building Rentable Area
- Floor Rentable Area
- Floor Usable Area
- Usable Area
- Floor Common Area
- Basic Rentable Area
- Building Common Area

- Rentable Area
- Office Area
- Store Area
- Overview and Global Summary sections help you apply the *Standard* quickly and easily. Start measuring your building a better way. Order the *BOMA Standard* today. BOMA International, 1996.
- Prior to the 1980s, common areas were generally restricted to the floor on which the tenants occupied their space.
- In the 1980s, office buildings started to be constructed with common areas, which served tenants of the entire building regardless of the floor, or floors, the tenants occupied.
- While a complete discussion of the *Standards* is beyond the scope of this book, knowledge of some common definitions needed by real estate agents is useful.

BOMA® Definitions:

Office Area: The area where a tenant normally houses personnel or furniture.

Usable Area: The measured office area.

Rentable Area: The usable area of an office area with its share of floor common area and building common area. Rentable area = usable area x R/U ratio.

Floor Common Area: The areas on a floor, such as washrooms, janitor closets, electrical rooms, elevator lobbies and public corridors, which are available primarily for the use of tenants on that floor.

Building Common Area: These are the areas of the building that provide services to the building tenants, but are not included in the office area of any specific tenant.

Dominant Portion: Refers to the permanent outer wall of the building. Generally, if more than 50% of the surface of the outer wall is glass, then the glass becomes the dominant portion.

R/U Ratio: The conversion factor that, when applied to usable area, gives the amount of rentable area.

Usable Area: Generally the usable area is measured using the following:

- The finished surface of the office side of the wall that creates the hallway corridor and any other permanent building interior walls
- The center of the temporary partition that separates this office area from the office area of another tenant

- The inside surface of the dominant portion of the exterior wall

An Example of Area Measurement

Looking at the office building in its entirety:

- The entire office building is 20,000 square feet.
- The square footage of the common areas is 3,333 square feet.
- Usable square feet: 20,000 total square feet - 3,333 square feet common area = 16,667 usable square footage.

R/U Factor = 20,000 rentable square feet ÷ 16,667 usable square feet = 1.2

Looking at the rentable square footage of one office in this building:

- Distance A to C = 40 feet, measured from the inside of Wall A, which abuts the hallway and the inside of the glass wall (dominant portion).
- Distance B to D = 44 feet, measured from the center of the walls that separate this office from other offices.
- R/U Factor = 20,000 rentable square feet ÷ 16,667 usable square feet = 1.2
- Calculation of rentable square feet:

STEP 1:

40 feet
X 44 feet
1760 square feet of *usable office area.*

STEP 2:

1760 usable square feet
X 1.2; R/U Factor
2112 *rentable* square feet

When dealing with rentable and usable square footage, two terms which are used interchangeably, are *efficiency factor* and *load factor*. The use of these terms can cause confusion among office building owners, tenants, and agents.

Efficiency Factor

Efficiency factor measures how efficient the building is from the tenant's point of view. A building that is 100% efficient has no common area allocated to the tenant. In a building that has an efficiency factor of 100%, the usable square footage is equal to the rentable square footage. From the tenant's point of view, the higher the efficiency rating of a building, the less common area the tenant will have to have included in his rentable area.

In the previous example, the building has an efficiency factor of 83.33%.

1/RU = Efficiency Factor 1/1.2 = 83.33

If the usable space is 1,760 square feet and the building has an efficiency factor of 83.33%, tenants will pay rent based on 2,112 rentable square feet: 1760/83.33 = 2122

Load factor measures the amount of common area that is added to the usable area. A building that has a 0% load factor has no common area allocated to the tenants. In a building with a load factor of 0%, the usable square footage is equal to the rentable square footage. From the tenants' point of view, the lower the load factor in a building, the less common area tenants will have to include in their rentable area.

In the previous example, the building has a load factor of 16.67%.

1-R/U = Load Factor   1-83.33% = 16.67%

If the usable space is 1,760 square feet and the building has a load factor of 16.67%, then tenants will pay rent based on 2,112 rentable square feet.

Whether you use the efficiency factor or load factor in your calculations, you must be able to accurately measure the usable square feet.

While the office tenant uses 1,760 square feet, the rent will be based on 2,112 square feet.

An investment agent or broker working with office properties will need to be familiar with the BOMA® Standards. Keep in mind though, these measurement standards are not used for the measurement of retail or industrial properties.

PROPERTY AND OWNERSHIP CHARACTERISTICS OF RETAIL PROPERTIES

A retail property might be a single building or a super regional mall. The purpose is still the same: *to display and sell goods* or *provide services* to the public. That is the point of any business; it is the only way to be a successful business.

Investors are attracted to retail properties, because retail properties demand even less direct management than an office building. Retail tenants are generally in their space longer hours than office building tenants. Retail tenants have grown accustomed to performing the traditional landlord responsibilities related to repairs, maintenance, and operating expenses. While the property owners have less management responsibility, they might take on more risk.

The first reason retail properties are considered more risky is that more than 50% of retail properties are single-tenant. In fact, there might be more single-tenant retail buildings than any other property type in the United States. While several of these properties might be located in one area, each property is a success only if the single tenant is successful. Generally, multi-tenant properties are considered less risky than single-tenant properties.

The second reason retail properties are considered more risky is because retail spending is the first area of discretionary spending. Remember what was said earlier? Employment and area play a role into buyers; if lay-offs occur or paychecks are small, then people will cut out spending needless money first. With the reduction of retail spending on the part of consumers, retail businesses might fail.

HOW RETAILERS DETERMINE MARKET AREA OR TRADE AREA

Before investing in retail space, you or your Investor-Agent will need to know what is important to the retailers renting the investment space.

One of the most important characteristics is the market area itself. How many customers can they reasonably expect to see and will it be enough for the retailer to be profitable?

Retailers use one of four methods for determining Market Area:

1. In-the-door approach
2. Population/Expenditure approach
3. Customer Spotting approach
4. Drive-Time approach

The geographic area in which retail stores receive their continuous sales is called the market area, or trade area. Commercial and investment agents, working in retail, will have to learn how their clients define their market areas. Market area will be a prime determinant of the location of a retailer. Ideally, retailers would like to be located in the center of their market areas.

Methods Retailers Use in Determining Market Areas or Trade Areas and Examples

In-the-Door Approach (Drive-By): This method of determining market, or trade area, deals with the question of how much vehicle traffic is required to support a location. According to industry research, retailers know that based on traffic count information, a certain percentage of the traffic will stop and come "in the door." Retailers want to know the traffic count that goes by their locations each day. This measure – of determining potential sales volume – would be important for strip centers and free-standing properties. The retailers in enclosed malls are interested in a different type of traffic – *foot traffic* – that goes in front of their store entrances.

EXAMPLE:

Facts:

- A store needs $6,000 per day in sales volume.
- The average sale, based on customers who enter the store, is $150.
- Of the customers who enter the store, 50% actually make a purchase.
- Of the drivers who pass the store, 0.2% enter the store.

Then:

- $6,000 sales volume per day ÷ $150 average sale = 40 sales needed each day to meet the sales volume required.
- Assuming half of the customers entering the store make a purchase, 80 customers must enter the store so that 40 sales are made.
- Assuming two-tenths of one percent (0.2%) of drivers enter the store, 25,000 cars must pass by the store each day.
- As a result of this information, the retailer will look for a location where at least 25,000 cars drive by each day.

Population/Expenditure Approach: This method of determining a market, or trade area, is based on the population in the market area. Retailers would need to know how many dollars of sales per square foot are needed to support their stores. Once that figure is known, retailers will study industry averages to determine how many dollars are spent per capita. With these two factors, retailers will estimate how many people must be in their market area.

EXAMPLE:

Facts:

- A store needs $2,500,000 annual gross sales to be supported.
- On the products offered in this store, $75 is the average annual amount spent per person.

Then:

- $2,500,000 annual gross sales ÷ $75 annual amount spent per person means 33,5000 people need to live in the market area or trade area of the store.
- As a result of this information, the store must be at a location where it can service 33,500 people.

Customer-Spotting Approach: This method of determining a market or trade area is based on the location of existing customers. Retailers get this information in two ways. First, the sales clerk obtains your address or zip code information when you buy a product; and second is in-store surveys, which obtain the same information as the first way.

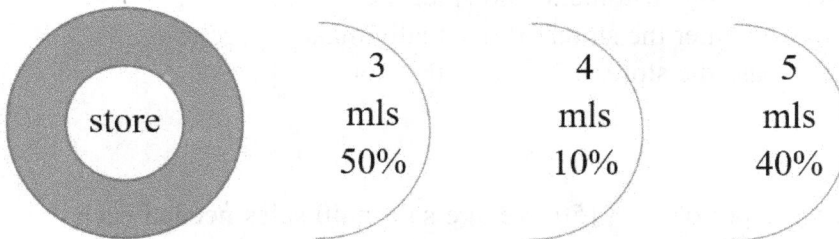

Once this information is obtained, it is mapped. The retailer might determine whether the existing location is best, whether they should relocate, or add a second location. This information helps determine which would be advisable.

EXAMPLE:

Fact:

- The industry average is that people drive five miles or less to shop at similar stores.

Then:

- After using point-of-sale information and survey results, a retailer finds that 50% of the customers in the store come from within a three-mile radius; 10% come from between three and five miles away; and 40% come from more than five miles away.
- Perhaps the storeowner should research adding a second store four to five miles from the existing store before someone else does.

Drive-Time Approach: This method of determining market area is based on the theory that people will travel only so far to obtain a product. By studying the addresses of past customers, retailers can determine how far in miles or how long in minutes people are traveling to get to their location.

EXAMPLE:

Fact:

- Studies indicate that people will drive only five minutes to pick up a pizza or wait only 10 minutes for a delivery pizza.

Then:

- If the industry says that it takes 10,000 people in a market to support a pizza store, then a representative of the pizza company is actually driving the streets to determine the market area. How far can a delivery driver get in 10 minutes going north, east, west, and south? After plotting those points on a census tract map, the pizza company can determine how many people live within that driving-time area. If there are more than 10,000 people, the location should work.

If you have ever been to Waikiki, you probably noticed an ABC store and McDonald's on every block. Since most people in Waikiki travel by foot, the location of the same retail outlet is likely a result of the retailers knowing that people will walk only so far to buy products.

The International Council of Shopping Centers (ICSC) publishes material about the development, ownership, and management of shopping centers. Their information can be found at http://www.icsc.org/.

In their publication titled *ICSC Keys to Shopping Centers Fundamentals Series*: *Overview,* the three major classifications of retail properties based on the ICSC descriptions are Malls, Strip Centers, and Free Standing.

Malls are usually enclosed with a common area running between groups of stores. A feature of a mall is that there is a common parking lot, and customers enter the majority of stores from the enclosed common area.

A *Strip Center* is a row of stores attached to each other either in a straight line, an L-shape, or U-shape configuration. The stores may be attached with a canopy or common façade, but they do not generally have enclosed areas. A feature of a strip center is the parking, which allows customers to park close to the entrance of a specific store.

Freestanding retail buildings are numerous. A retailer simply has a building that sits by itself; it is not connected physically to any other building, and has its own parking area from which customers can enter the store directly. Fast food restaurants are common examples of freestanding buildings.

Eight Shopping Center Types:

1. Neighborhood Center
2. Community Center
3. Regional Center
4. Super Regional Center
5. Fashion/Specialty Center
6. Power Center
7. Theme/Festival Center
8. Outlet Center

Malls and strip centers are considered shopping centers. Whether a shopping center is configured as a mall or as a strip center, there are eight major classifications of shopping centers, which real estate agents should recognize.

1. Neighborhood Center: A neighborhood center serves a market area, and it provides day-to-day shopping convenience for consumers. Many of these centers have one anchor tenant, either a supermarket or drugstore. The anchor tenant(s) generally occupy 30% to 50% of the total size of the center. Smaller stores offering products or services needed by this market area's consumers are also found in a neighborhood center.

The size of neighborhood centers runs from 30,000 to 150,000 square feet, and the centers require 3 to 15 acres for the stores and parking.

2. Community Center: A community center serves a market area of approximately three to six miles; it provides the consumers in its market area with a wider range of retail and service stores. Many of these centers have two or more anchor tenants; they may be supermarkets, super drugstores, or discount stores. The anchors generally occupy 40% to 60% of the total size of the center. Smaller stores offering apparel, or other soft goods, make up the rest of the center. These centers are built in a strip-center configuration in a straight line, an L-shape, or U-shape. Some community centers are referred to as discount centers.

The size of community centers runs from 100,000 to 300,000 square feet, and the centers require 10 to 40 acres for the stores and parking.

3. Regional Center: A regional center serves a market area of approximately 5 to 15 miles, and it provides the consumers in its market area with general merchandise and primarily apparel. Many of these centers have two or more anchor tenants, which might be full-line or junior department stores, mass merchandisers, and discount department stores. The anchors generally occupy 50% to 70% of the total size of the center. These centers are built in a mall configuration with inward orientation of stores connected, which can be accessed by a common walkway and with parking surrounding the center.

The size of regional centers runs from 400,000 to 800,000 square feet, and the centers require 40 to 100 acres for the stores and parking.

4. Super Regional Center: A super regional center serves a market area of approximately 5 to 25 miles, and it provides the consumers in its market area with a deeper selection of merchandise through multiple anchors. Just as regional centers, the anchors generally occupy 50% to 70% of the total size of the center; these centers are built in a mall configuration, which are connected by a common walkway. Many super regional centers need to be multilevel.

A super regional center is generally larger than 800,000 square feet and requires 60 to 120 acres for the stores and parking.

5. Fashion/Specialty Center: A fashion/specialty center serves a market area of approximately 5 to 15 miles, and it provides the consumers in its market area with the following: upscale apparel shops, boutiques, and craft shops. Many of these centers do not actually have anchor tenants, but have restaurant or entertainment tenants. These centers can be built in a mall configuration or a strip configuration, but the landscaping is always high quality.

The size of a fashion/specialty center runs from 80,000 to 250,000 square feet, and the center requires 5 to 25 acres for the stores and parking.

6. Power Center: A power center services a market area of approximately 5 to 10 miles, and it provides the consumers in its market area with home improvement stores, discount department stores, warehouse club stores, or off-price stores. There are usually three or more anchors, and these anchors are often referred to as "category killers." There are few additional retailers in a power center, and the anchors might comprise up to 90% of the square footage of the center.

The size of power centers runs from 250,000 to 600,000 square feet, and the center requires 25 to 80 acres for the stores and parking

7. Theme/Festival Center: A theme/festival center does not generally serve a defined geographic market area. The concept behind a theme/festival center is to provide leisure and tourist-oriented retail and services. The biggest appeal of this type of center is to tourists. Restaurant or entertainment facilities serve as the anchor tenants. Generally located in an urban area, this kind of center is often found in an older, sometimes historic building. Configuration of theme/ festival centers can be either mall or strip centers.

The size of a theme/festival center runs from 80,000 to 250,000 square feet, and the center requires 5 to 20 acres for the stores and parking.

8. Outlet Center: An outlet center is usually located in a rural or tourist location. The market area might range from 25 to 75 miles. The biggest appeal of this type of center is to consumers, who want to buy products from manufacturers' outlet stores, where name-brand merchandise can be purchased at a discount. Generally not anchored, the configuration of outlet centers resembles that of strip centers, but some are arranged in a "village" cluster.

The size of an outlet center runs from 50,000 to 400,000 square feet, and the center requires 10 to 50 acres for the stores and parking.

Commercial or investment agents and their investors, choosing to work in retail, must understand the differences between the shopping center types and will need to include these terms in their vocabulary.

Industrial Properties

The Urban Land Institute defines industry as the following: "The gainful activity involved in producing, distributing, and changing the form of raw materials; or assembling components and parts, packaging, warehousing, and transporting finished products." Urban Land Institute information can be found at http://www.uli.org/.

Industrial properties house the process of manufacturing, warehousing, and distributing the products. Industrial properties are primarily devoted to these activities, but may have some minor part of the building devoted to office space.

The National Association of Industrial and Office Properties, NAIOP®, is a very good source regarding information for industrial properties. Its website is www.naiop.org.

Investors who want to minimize their involvement with property management and contact with tenants invest in industrial properties. Tenants often pay all of the expenses and do all the maintenance of the property. While many tenants in industrial properties are national firms, there is risk associated with investments in industrial buildings, because there is usually only one tenant. When that tenant moves out, the building may need substantial renovation to be attractive to a new tenant, and there may be a lengthy period of time during which the building sits empty. Investors accept this extra risk in return for the elimination of management involvement.

Determining the Basic Needs of a Successful Industrial Investment Property

One of my earliest experiences in industrial space had to do with a Volkswagen plant in Western Pennsylvania. Years ago they packed up and left the region in a bit of a funk! Rumor was that management discovered that factory workers were drinking beer on the job and hid the empty cans in the rocker panels of the cars coming off the assembly line. Consumers complained of a mysterious rattling noise and upon inspection discovered the empty beer cans! This is part of what presumably led to Volkswagen leaving the area. In any case, as you might imagine, the facility was empty for years. How'd you like to have a large industrial plant that you owned empty for years? Well, this is why I suggest that industrial space is perhaps the most risky of the four major types of investment spaces. On the other hand, as you might imagine, tenants of industrial space usually stay a very long time. The facility was eventually occupied by SONY! So, let's dig into some facts to help you determine whether or not you want to participate in the world of industrial space investing.

In general, an industrial property needs four main items to be successful:

1. Access to transportation
2. Available labor pools
3. Availability of heavy duty utility services
4. Proper zoning and use permits

Access to Transportation

Transportation of industrial properties include heavy-duty local roads, metropolitan freeway systems, regional railroad systems, national airway systems, or a combination of all four. Large warehouses also need large amounts of land to accommodate bulky goods being transported.

Available Appropriate Labor Pool

Data about the labor pool would include: the number of workers available, how close the labor pool is to the facility, and the current wage and benefit packages being paid to these workers.

Availability of Heavy-Utility Services

Industrial properties need heavy-duty utilities, such as sanitary sewer and treatment facilities, water supply, treatment and distribution facilities, natural gas, heavy electricity service, telecommunications services, and possibly fiber-optic cables.

Proper Zoning and Use Permits

Over the years, the zoning restrictions placed on industrial properties have become more restrictive.

Along with general zoning restrictions, new concepts, such as Planned Unit Developments (PUDs) and floating zones, have been developed to allow innovative approaches to the use of land.

Zoning regulations for industrial properties are designed to create planned employment centers, which benefit the employees and the neighbors of the industrial properties.

Industrial businesses need skilled workers. Businesses study what the trends are in employment, as they relate to the availability of workers.

THE VARIOUS WAYS TO CLASSIFY INDUSTRIAL BUILDINGS

Industrial properties are often classified by *the way they are used.* Common classifications are:

1. General Purpose
2. Special Purpose
3. Single Purpose

General Purpose Industrial

General-purpose buildings are those with a wide range of alternative uses. This is the most common type of industrial property. They can be adapted to light manufacturing, assembly, storage, or distribution. These buildings are often built on spec, meaning that developers build the building before they have a specific tenant.

Special Purpose Industrial: Refrigerated Storage

Special-purpose buildings have physical characteristics or facilities suitable to a smaller range of uses. An example is a refrigerated storage facility or airplane maintenance hangar.

Single-purpose buildings are adaptable to only one particular process or one particular firm. Examples would be grain silo or petroleum refinery. The more specific a building is designed, the less convertible the building is to other uses.

Single Purpose

Many times industrial usage requires mostly vacant land, as in this electrical distribution yard.

LOCATIONS OF INDUSTRIAL PROPERTIES

Industrial properties are located in a variety of ways. *Freestanding* buildings are those that stand by themselves. They are usually the largest of the properties. *Multi-tenant* properties are home to the smallest tenants who need industrial properties. *Industrial parks* are single properties managed by one entity, and they may be home to both freestanding properties and multi-tenant properties.

COMMON CLASSIFICATIONS OF INDUSTRIAL INVESTMENT PROPERTIES BY TYPE INCLUDE:

1. Bulk
2. Manufacturing
3. Office/Warehouse
4. Research and Development

Bulk

Think of industrial places that utilize sand or stone; most of the time, these enclosures are semi-circular with a roof, allowing transportation easy access. These buildings are large, many times 50,000 square feet or more. There is little need for office space. Loading docks, parking surfaces, and ingress and egress roads must be heavy duty, to accommodate the transportation methods of getting the inventory to and from the building. Many properties need rail service.

Manufacturing

Manufacturing plants are large buildings, often more than one million square feet, and are quite specialized to meet the specific needs. The properties must accommodate receiving, production, and shipping activities. These properties are prone to obsolescence, because production methods are constantly changing, and the configuration of the building must change, or it is no longer useful.

Office/Warehouse

Office/warehouse properties are used for the storage and distribution of products, where some portion of the building is developed into office space. Although many of these properties are constructed of concrete or metal, the newer trend is to use brick.

Research and Development

Research and development properties are popular with investors, because they are generally located near universities and white-collar labor forces. These buildings are standard in construction, but are highly improved through specific tenant improvements. Rent is higher than it is for industrial-type properties, because these properties are often seen as a hybrid between an office building and a manufacturing building.

Industrial Parks

Industrial buildings are often grouped by use or type, in a development called an industrial park. The National Association of Industrial and Office Parks (NAIOP) has issued Industrial Park Criteria and Standards. Information regarding NAIOP can be found at their website www.naiop.org

The NAIOP's definition of an industrial park is the following:

The assembly of land provides facilities for business and industry consistent, with a master plan and restrictions. This results in the creation of a physical environment that achieves the following objectives:

- Consistency with community goals
- Efficient business and industrial operations
- Human scale and values
- Compatibility with natural environments
- Achieving and sustaining highest land values

Some characteristics NAIOP looks for in an industrial park are:

- Paved streets
- Adequate utility system for multiple tenants
- Adequate landscaping
- Architectural control of site, buildings, and signage
- Supervision of environmental issues
- One management plan

Finance

USE SUPPLY AND DEMAND TO DETERMINE VALUE

Economists have wrestled (MMA style) for hundreds of years with the question of what determines value. The so-called *classical economists* (probably geeks, I mean Greeks) believed it was the labor that gave a product its value. Others focused on its rarity – the rarer, the greater its value (e.g., diamonds, spices, or gold). It was not until around the turn of the 20th century that they zeroed in on the interaction of supply and demand. A paraphrase of the great analogy penned by Alfred Marshall in 1890 sums up the interaction: "You can no more tell which determines price, supply or demand, than you can tell which blade of the scissors does the cutting. It is the interaction of the two that does the work."

Supply

The supply of real property is the amount of space that will be offered for sale or rent at a given time at a given price. It is influenced by the following:

- Costs of producing the space
- Sellers' needs and intent
- Perceptions of market condition
- Zoning practices

Demand

The demand for real estate is the amount of space that will be bought or rented at a given time and price. Demand is influenced by the following:

- Alternative space available
- Market conditions for the buyer's or tenant's products
- Perceptions of market conditions

Supply - Demand Curves

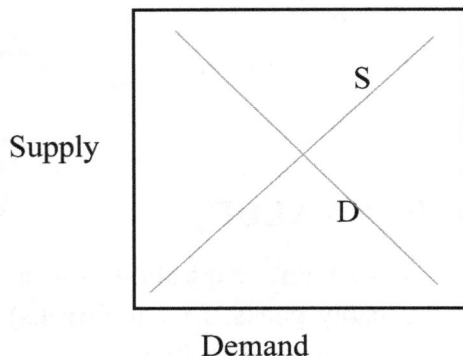

Supply

Demand

The supply curve (S) tilts upward and to the right – as the price for space *increases,* more and more will be offered for sale or lease as landlords, builders and sellers look for increased profits.

The demand curve (D) tilts downward and to the right – as the price for space *decreases* more and more will be bought or leased, because more users will be able to buy or lease.

Equilibrium Point: The price at which both buyers, sellers, landlords and tenants come together is the *equilibrium point* (or sweet spot), for that transaction. Each is satisfied, since this is the best price available for a specific real estate product. The equilibrium point is shown as the intersection of the supply and demand curve.

Small changes occur all the time to move the equilibrium point up or down each curve. These are small changes of relatively short duration, after which the market returns to normal and is stable again. But what happens when there is a major change in the market? For example, what happens to a market for retail space and hotel space when Disneyland opens a new theme park? This dramatic change is certainly not temporary, and therefore the old supply and demand curves are modified.

Major changes such as this create what is called a shift in the supply-demand curves. A whole new set of curves becomes relevant, and a considerable disruption in the market can be expected:

Supply

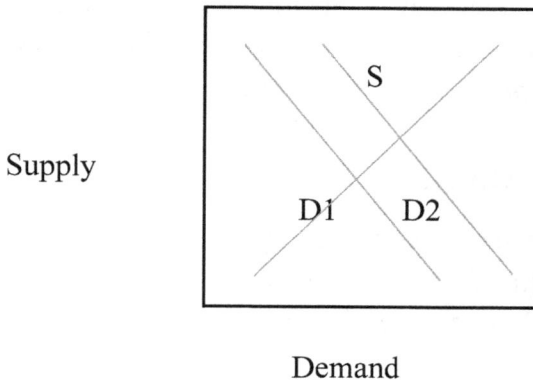

Demand

We have not traveled up or down the demand curve. We have seen a complete shift in demand from one demand curve (D1) to a new demand curve (D2). More tenants are demanding space from a fixed supply of space. A new equilibrium will be found, and this market situation would be called a *seller's market*.

Simplistically, it could be said that the real estate market can be described as a marketplace made up of people, property, and money.

The Real Estate Marketplace

- People Looking for Property
- Money Looking for Property
- Property Looking for Money
- Property Looking for People

- People look for property.
- Property looks for people – vacant properties look for tenants by owners.
- Money looks for property – lenders look to place money into loans backed by real estate and investors look to place money into real estate ownership.
- Property looks for money – properties look for lenders.
- In a perfect world of supply and demand, there is a balance of people, properties, and money. If the supply of properties available gets out of balance, then there will be a change in the pricing of the properties.
- While the dot-com businesses were forming, the number of people looking for space increased, but the supply of space remained constant. The price of the space went up, and builders entered the market to build new spaces because of the higher potential rents. This situation is called a seller's market. When that market contracted, the number of tenants decreased, the supply stayed constant, and the price for properties decreased. This situation is called a buyer's market.

If the supply of money gets out of balance with the demand for properties, then there will be a change in cost of money. When the supply of money available from lenders decreases, interest rates increase. When the supply of money increases, lenders must lower interest rates to give borrowers an incentive to buy new properties or refinance.

UNDERSTANDING POSITIVE LEVERAGE

Generally, the term *leverage* refers to using financing to acquire a property. The statement: "The property was acquired using 75% leverage" means that an investor obtained financing in the amount of 75% of the total purchase price of the property. The remaining equity of 25% was invested in cash.

Positive leverage occurs when the yield on a property purchased on an unleveraged basis (i.e., free and clear) is greater than the interest charged by the lender. Then the yield to the investor using leverage will be higher if they use financing to purchase the property.

Let's look at an investment and break it into three parts: the property, the lender, and the investor.

EXAMPLE:

- A property can be purchased for $500,000 by paying all cash.
- The first year, net operating income (NOI) of the property is $50,000 and is expected to remain the same for two years.
- It is expected that the property can be sold at the end of the second year to net $500,000 after selling costs.

A) Property Free and Clear

- Purchase Price ($500,000)
- Year 1 NOI $50,000
- Year 2 NOI $50,000
- Sale Price $500,000
- **Unleveraged Yield = 10%**

In this case, the yield to the investor on an unleveraged, or free-and-clear, purchase is 10%. The investor pays $500,000 cash to purchase the property and gets $50,000 back each year in net operating income (NOI). Because there are no loan payments to be made, the investor keeps the $50,000 each year. The yield is 10% based on the $500,000 the investor has invested. The investor gets a full return of the investment at the sale because there is no loan to pay off.

$50,000 NOI ÷ $500,000 Purchase Price = 10% yield

The property produces a 10% return based on operations and the projected sales price if purchased without financing.

B) Lender

We will add the lender's position in this transaction.

Instead of buying the property for cash, the investor can obtain a 70% loan to value (LTV) loan from a lender. To make the calculations easy, the terms are 8%, interest only, with annual payments.

- $500,000 Property Price X 70% Loan to Value (LTV) = $350,000 loan.
- $350,000 loan X 8% interest rate = $28,000 in annual debt service.

In this case, the yield to the lender is 8%. The lender gets $28,000 back each year, based on the $350,000 it has invested. Because this is an interest-only loan, the lender gets a full return of its investment when the loan is paid off at the sale of the property.

C) Investor Using Leverage

As we will see, this is an example of positive leverage, because the yield on a purchase of the property – on a free-and-clear basis – is higher than the interest rate charged on the loan.

By adding the investor's position to this transaction, you will see the effect of using positive leverage.

- The investor will have to put $150,000 down to purchase the property.
- The investor will receive $22,000 in cashflow, after making the loan payments.
- The investor will receive $150,000 on the sale of the property, as a result of receiving the Sale Price and paying off the loan.

What Is Really Happening?

What is really happening here is that the property produces a 10% yield. The lender actually buys 70% of the property but takes only 8% on the part it buys, leaving 2% for the investors.

The investors buy 30% of the property, receive 10% on the part they purchase, and 2% on the part of the property the lender purchases.

The effect of positive leverage is that investors will achieve a higher yield. This only happens if they purchase the property using the available financing, rather than if they purchased the property on a free-and-clear basis.

UNDERSTANDING NEGATIVE LEVERAGE

Negative leverage occurs when the yield on a property purchased on an unleveraged basis is lower than the interest charged by the lender. If we look at the same investment but change the interest rate on the loan to 12%, we will see the effect of negative leverage.

Assume in the last example – where the yield on the property remains at 10% – the interest rate is 12%. This would be negative leverage.

What is happening here is that the property still produces a 10% yield. The lender actually buys 70% of the property but takes a 12% yield on the part it buys. The property produces only 10%, so it must take its additional 2% from the investor.

The investor buys 30% of a property, yielding 10%, but must give 2% to the lender. As a result, the investor's yield will be less than 10%.

The effect of negative leverage is that investors will achieve a lower yield if they purchase the property using the available financing than they would if they purchased the property on a free-and-clear basis.

NEUTRAL LEVERAGE

Neutral leverage occurs when the yield on a property purchased, on an unleveraged basis, is the same as the interest charged by the lender. If we look at the same investment but change the interest rate on the loan to 10%, then we will see the effect of neutral leverage.

What is happening here is that the property produces a 10% yield. The lender actually buys 70% of the property and takes a 10% yield on the part it buys.

The investors buy 30% of a property yielding 10% and get the 10% on the part they buy.

In neutral leverage the investor and the lender get their share of the yield on the property, and neither party has to give any share to the other party.

The effect of neutral leverage is that investors will achieve the same yield. This works if they purchase the property using the available financing, as they would if they purchased the property on a free-and-clear basis.

Agents who want to become involved in investment real estate will need to understand financing.

If agents decide to become involved with investment real estate, they will have to become familiar with the types of financing used by investors – how investors and the properties qualify for loans, and the reasons investors use financing to purchase properties.

UNDERSTANDING PRICE VERSUS VALUE

A comment heard frequently on the street is: "I bought it below market." In fact, there is no such thing. A property may be purchased at a price lower than it had been previously offered or lower than the price of a similar property. But at the moment a sale takes place, that is the market price for that property. The stock market is an excellent analogy, because transactions in a particular stock occur daily in a range of prices. Each transaction is at the market price at that time.

Are price and value the same thing? Not really. Price is simply what the buyer had to give up in order to acquire the property. The value to the buyer might be much greater. We will discuss the sources of value in the next section, but for now let's identify the types of value to get a perspective on this elusive term.

Types of Value in Commercial Investment Real Estate:

- Assessed Value
- Insurance Value
- Loan Value
- Investment Value
- Appraised Value
- Liquidation Value

Assessed Value

The assessed value must be determined by the tax assessor to set the level of taxes on a property. Each state and county has its own rules the assessor must follow.

Appraised Value

A qualified appraiser establishes an appraised value using the cost, income, and comparative approaches to value. An appraiser is usually asked to estimate the *market value* for the property. Market value can be defined as: the price a typical investor will pay for a property based on its highest and best use. Each investor has their own opinion of the market value. Lenders rely on appraisal values as a way to estimate the selling price a property will command.

Insurance Value

The insurance value is the value of that portion of a property, which can be damaged or destroyed in a catastrophe but can be replaced with insurance proceeds.

Investment Value

The investment value is the value an individual investor assigns to a property. Generally, investment value is determined by some discounted cashflow strategy, based on the investor's opportunity cost or cost of capital.

Investors care about the market value, because they do not want to pay more for the property than a typical buyer would pay. However, there are always exceptions. An example would be the office building owner, who wants to buy the adjacent single-family houses around the office building; this could allow a parking increase.

Three approaches are used in determining investment value in investment or commercial real estate.

1. Income approach
2. Cost approach
3. Comparable approach

The **income approach** requires the projection of cashflows from acquisition, operations, and disposition of the property. These cashflows are discounted to determine their present value. Sometimes the capitalization rate is used to determine the value of the property by the income approach to value.

The **cost approach** is basically looking at how much it would cost to replace the property. If the property being considered is not new, consider depreciation of the improvements. Depreciation is used to deal with the property, because it may be in poor repair or it may be outdated functionally.

The **sales comparison approach** uses a survey of recent sales of similar properties, to estimate the value of the property being considered. The total sales prices are usually divided by some measurement of unit; this helps to give a comparable value based on a standardized unit.

Additionally, adjustments to the value per unit calculated, are made to adjust among the comparable for items: age, condition, and location. There is usually a range of values estimated by the comparable approach, or there is a value established by using the average of the comparable properties being studied.

Liquidation Value

The liquidation value is the value a property would bring if it sold through a distressed sale, such as a foreclosure.

Loan Value

The lender assigns a loan value to a property that is used as security for a loan. This amount represents the lender's desire for yield and appetite for risk. It is a value specific to the lender, not the borrower.

Value in Use

Value in use is the value of a particular piece of real estate. Some users of real estate actually own the real estate; some users are tenants in real estate owned by others. Generally, value deals with how the real estate being used will contribute to the profitability of the business. Not all users of real estate want to own their real estate.

THE IMPORTANCE OF APPRAISALS AND DETERMINING VALUE

Appraisals in residential real estate are different from those found in commercial and investment real estate. The most common method of determining an appraised value – in a residential property – is the sales comparable approach. In this approach, sales of similar houses in similar neighborhoods are tracked to determine a value.

In commercial and investment property, the appraiser is concerned with comparable sales data, but is also concerned with the income the property is expected to produce on investor properties. This is because the income is what supports the ability to make the loan payments, and it also pays the reproduction cost of the property.

Describe the concept of values in commercial and investment real estate

We might think that price, cost, and value mean the same thing; but for appraisal purposes, each term might have a different meaning. It is possible that the price, cost, and value might be the same, but very likely they are different.

Price

Price refers to the asking price or the selling price of the property. This is the amount that is being offered for a property today or paid in the past. This value approach reflects the price one person has determined, which is what he or she will pay for a specific property.

Cost

Cost is either the actual amount paid for property in the past, or the dollar amount needed to build the property. This value approach reflects either a historic number or a number in the future, and it is difficult to apply to the entire market.

Value

Usually, value is defined as the power of goods or services to command other goods or services in the marketplace.

A real estate example is the agreement of tenants to sign leases. The tenants have agreed to exchange their money, in return for the use of the property. Both the tenants and the landlords have agreed to exchange goods and services, and that exchange establishes a value for the use of the property.

Market Value

Market value is a term defined in the appraisal profession. The Uniform Standards of Professional Appraisal Practice (USAP) has defined value as follows:

> *"The most probable price a property would bring in a competitive and open market under all conditions requisite to a fair sale, the buyer and seller each acting prudently and knowledgeably and assuming the price is not affected by undue stimulus."*

Assumptions in this definition are the following:

- Buyer and seller are typically motivated
- Buyer and seller are well informed or can obtain competent advise
- Buyer and seller are acting for their best interest
- The property has been exposed to the market for a reasonable time
- Payment is in cash or in comparable financing terms
- Price represents normal terms unaffected by special or creative financing or unusual sales concessions

Highest and Best Use (HABU)

The Highest and Best Use of a property is the legal use of a property that will yield the highest present value.

A commercial or investment property may have several values, depending on how the property can be used. For example, a vacant lot might be the site for an apartment building or a retail store. An old warehouse in the downtown district may have more value as loft apartments than it would as a warehouse.

The definition of highest and best use is:

...the most probable use of land or improved property that is legally possible, physically possible, financially feasible (and appropriately supportable) from the market, and which results in maximum profitability.

Remember, creativity is the key!

The four criteria the appraiser will consider in a highest and best use analysis are the following:

- The use is physically possible.
- The use is legally possible.
- The use is financially feasible.
- The use offers the maximum productivity.

The analysis of the highest and best use of a property involves two considerations: 1) the most likely and profitable use of the site; 2) if a property is "already improved," what use could help maximize the property's value.

Basic highest and best use assumptions include:

- The competitive level will dictate whether an area is best used for commercial, residential, or multi-family. Zoning could present a problem though. If market preference conflicts with zoning – and consequently violates the legal permissibility test – a developer will consider: if there is enough profit incentive to justify the added costs before obtaining a zoning change and developing the site.
- As long as the value of the property "as improved" is greater than the value of the site as "if vacant," the best use is usually the "improved" property.

- Once the value of the vacant land exceeds the value of the improved property (including demolition costs), the highest and best approach will usually dictate that improvements be demolished.

Sometime the highest and best use is not always determined by the economic benefits, but some other element important to the community. An example would be turning vacant land into a park on a beach front.

APPRAISAL APPROACHES TO MARKET VALUE

In an appraisal of a commercial or investment piece of real estate, the appraisal will contain three approaches to value.

1. Sales comparison
2. Cost
3. Income

The appraiser's opinion of value will blend all three approaches, or will state that one approach outweighs the others to such an extent that maximum weight will be given to that approach.

Sales Comparison Approach

In the sales comparison approach, the appraiser is trying to establish value based on the prices buyers have paid for similar properties in the past.

The steps the appraiser takes in the sales comparable approach are the following:

- Find the comparable sales that have occurred recently.
- Adjust the comparable property values for variances with the property under consideration.
- Net the adjustments.
- Select the value of the property under consideration, giving greater weight to the properties that are most similar.

If there are many sale comparables, then this method of determining value can be effective. It can be less effective when there are few sale comparables.

This method is given weight in the sale of similar properties. The best method of determining the value of four-unit apartment buildings in a neighborhood, might be to look at the recent sales of similar properties.

For example, an appraiser might find four recent sales of four-unit apartment buildings all built by the same builder in the same year, in the same neighborhood. No adjustments need to be made. The sales prices are as follows:

- Sale #1 $ 475,000
- Sale #2 $ 500,000
- Sale #3 $ 525,000
- Sale #4 $ 500,000

Total $2,000,000 ÷ 4 Sales = $500,000 Value

The sales comparison approach would set the value at $500,000.

Cost Approach

The cost approach to value considers the cost of reproducing the property, minus any depreciation that has taken place.

The steps the appraiser uses in the cost approach are the following:

- Estimate the cost to reproduce the existing building, and make any required improvements.
- Estimate the amount of depreciation that has taken place.
- Subtract the amount of depreciation from the cost to reproduce the building.
- Estimate the value of the land.
- Add the value of the land to the depreciated value of the building.

The cost approach is often the most important for users of commercial and investment real estate. Users always consider whether they should buy an existing building or build a new building.

For example, an existing building appraises for $1,550,000.

The cost to build a new building and the site improvements	$1,000,000
Less: The amount of depreciation in the existing building	350,000
Plus: The cost of the land	700,000
Total per the cost approach	$1,550,000

Income Approach

I = Net Operating Income (NOI)
R = Cap Rate
V = Value

Therefore:

R = I/V
And
V = I / R
And
I = R x V

The income approach is used when the property being appraised is being rented or could be rented to tenants. Investors like this approach, because the appraiser determines the value based on the income the property produces.

The income approach is effective because it looks at the property and determines value as an investor does. The investor is essentially buying the cashflows the building produces. The income approach is rarely used in the appraisal of residential properties occupied by the owner.

Capitalization Method Based on Comparables

The capitalization method determines value by applying a market yield rate to a market net operating income (NOI). The capitalization method uses the IRV formula. The appraiser will use the following steps:

- Select comparable properties that have sold.
- Determine the selling prices and NOIs for each sale.
- Calculate the cap rate for each sale.
- Calculate an average cap rate for the market.
- Convert the terms in the IRV formula to terms used in real estate so we can calculate value, cap rate, or NOI.

This method is effective when there are adequate sales in the market, allowing the appraiser to develop the comparable cap rate.

EXAMPLE:

	Sale Price	NOI	Cap Rate
Sale #1	$200,000	$20,000	10.0%
Sale #2	$225,000	$20,250	9.0%
Sale #3	$250,000	$24,000	9.6%
Sale #4	$200,000	$18,000	9.0%
Average Cap Rate			9.4%

The Cap Rate the appraiser would use is 9.4%.

Application: If the NOI of the property being appraised is $20,000, then the value would be $212,800 (20000/9.4% = 212,766, rounded to 212,800).

Deriving a Cap Rate When There Are No Comparables

There are times when a property is too specialized, or there is a lack of comparable sales, so the appraiser must use a mathematical approach to build or derive a cap rate. (Hopefully, you paid attention in all your math classes!)

This can be a very complicated process, but here is a simple example. In the market, lenders are making 75% loans and want a 10% interest rate. Investors, who must make a 25% down payment, want a 15% yield. The cap rate needed to meet both the lenders' and investors' goals would be determined by the following calculation:

	Amount Invested	X	Desired Yield	=	
Lender	75%	X	10%	=	.0750
Investor	25%	X	15%	=	.0375
Total	100%				.1100

The Cap Rate needed must be 11%. If the NOI is $20,000 and the derived Cap Rate is 11% the value of the property is $181,800 (20000/11%=181818, rounded to 181800).

This mathematical formula is sometimes called the weighted average or band of investment.

Let's see if this approach meets the needs of the investor and the lender if the price is $181,800.

Lender's Position:

- $181,800 Price X 75% Loan to Value (LTV) = $136,350 Loan
- $136,350 Loan X 10% Desired Yield = $13,635 Annual Debt Service (ADS)

Investor's Position:

- $181,800 Price X 25% Equity = $45,450 Down payment
- $45,450 Down payment X 15% Desired Yield = $6,818 Cash Flow

Total Property Position:

$20,000	NOI
-13,635	Annual Debt Service (ADS)
$ 6,363	Cashflow (slight difference in rounding)

Let's see whether this approach meets the needs of the investor and the lender if the price is $200,000, which represents a 10% cap rate.

Lender's Position:

- $200,000 Price X 75% Loan to Value (LTV) = $150,000 Loan
- $150,000 Loan X 10% Desired Yield = $15,000 Annual Debt Service (ADS)

Investor's Position:

- $200,000 Price X 25% Equity = $50,000 Down payment
- $50,000 Down payment X 15% Desired Yield = $7,500 Cashflow

Total Property Position:

$20,000	NOI
-15,000	Annual Debt Service (ADS)
$ 5,000	Cashflow

The $5,000 cashflow available for the investor is less than the $7,500 needed to achieve a 15% yield. The investor would be willing to pay only $35,700 (rounded) for a $5,000 annual cashflow based on a 15% desired yield. Therefore, the property would be worth only $185,700 ($150,000 + $35,700).

Discounted Cashflow Method

The capitalization method considers only the income from the first year of the property operations. To look at all the cashflows, the appraiser would use the discounted cashflow method of determining the present value of the cashflows discounted at a required yield. This method of appraisal takes into account the time value of money strategy, and is beyond the scope of this book. (Once again, I hope you paid attention in math class!)

Common Investor Rules of Thumb
Found in the Marketplace

As in any business, there are rules of thumb that evolve in everyday use. Most of them are not grounded in solid analytical theory, but they have a long, useful life. Investment real estate is no exception.

Agents working in residential real estate should be familiar with these rules of thumb. All of them have major flaws in their concept. This chapter will only briefly outline what the rules of thumb are, how to calculate them, and what their shortcomings are.

Cost Per Square Foot

Cost Per Square Foot = Total Cost of Property / Total # of Square Feet

This rule of thumb is a tool for making cost comparisons. It is used by breaking a building down into its smallest part, and then comparing the cost of a square foot in the building, to the cost of a square foot in a comparable building. Owners of real estate are interested in the cost per square foot, because the building will not produce any rental income when occupied by the owner user.

To calculate the cost per square foot, divide the asking price of the building by the number of square feet in the building.

$900,000 asking price/10,000 sq. ft. = $90/sq. ft.

Once you know the number of square feet in the building being considered, you could multiply the number of square feet by some standard value to determine the value.

10,000 sq. ft. X $90/sq. ft. = $900,000 value

One obvious problem is *there is no valid standard value.* No two buildings are alike, even if built at the same time by the same builder.

Another problem is that this measure *does not take into consideration the income generated by the building or the expenses of operating the property.* Is a vacant building worth more or less than an occupied building?

314

Users of real estate use this rule of thumb primarily to compare different locations for their businesses. If one vacant office building can be purchased at $80 per square foot, and another building is available at $65, we have a difference in cost and must ask why there is a difference.

CASHFLOW MODEL

The remaining rules of thumb deal with the cashflow generated from a property. The Cashflow Model is a standard approach to looking at the cashflow of an investment piece of real estate.

> Potential Rental Income
> <u>- Vacancy</u>
> = Effective Rental Income
> <u>+ Other Income</u>
> = Gross Operating Income
> <u>- Operating Expenses</u>
> = Net Operating Income (NOI)
> <u>- Annual Debt Service (ADS)</u>
> = Cashflow Before Tax (CFBT)

Gross Rent Multiplier (GRM)

GRM = Total Cost of Property / Potential Rental Income

The gross rent multiplier (GRM) is a comparison tool used by investors to see how many years it will take to earn back the purchase price of property through rent. It is often used by investors of smaller, similar multi-family properties because income and expenses are similar.

The gross rent multiplier (GRM) is calculated by dividing the value of the property by the potential rental income for the first year.

$900,000 Value ÷ $100,000 Potential Rental Income = 9 GRM

A nine gross rent multiplier (GRM) would be expressed as a "GRM of 9," or "9 times gross."

This means that it would take nine years to collect enough rents to earn back the price of the property. As a comparison tool, we can now look at payback periods to value investment real estate. Similar properties should have similar payback periods.

Assume that the last six transactions on four-unit residential properties resulted in a gross rent multiplier (GRM) of eight. Two new listings have come on the market, one with a 9 GRM and one with a 7 GRM. Can you begin to make some value comparisons?

If you know a standard value for gross rent multipliers (GRMs) and the potential rental income, then you can determine the value of a property by multiplying the potential rental income by the GRM.

$100,000 Potential Rental Income x 8 GRM = $800,000 Value

$800,000 Value/8 GRM = $100,000 Potential Rental Income

The weakness of the gross rent multiplier (GRM) – as a value comparison tool – is found in the fact that this rule of thumb depends on first-year potential rental income only. It does not take into consideration items in the cashflow model below potential rental income, such as vacancies, operating expenses, or financing.

Calculating Cap Rate

Potential Rental Income
- Vacancy
= Effective Rental Income
+ Other Income
= Gross Operating Income
- Operating Expenses
= Net Operating Income (NOI)
- Annual Debt Service (ADS)
= Cashflow Before Tax (CFBT)

Which of these apartments do you think has more value? Apartment building A has tenants pay $100,000 rent, and they pay all of their own utilities; apartment building B has tenants pay $100,000, but the owner pays all the utilities. Both properties are priced at $800,000, too. The answer: both, because they both have a GRM of 10!

Capitalization Rate (Cap Rate)

Net Operating Income (NOI)

Cap Rate = NOI / Purchase Price

In economics, the term "to capitalize" means to convert an income stream to a value.

With the capitalization rate tool, if you know the net operating income (NOI) of a property, then you can calculate a value by dividing the income stream by the rate of return desired.

EXAMPLE:

If you have an opportunity to buy real estate that produces $90,000 of Net Operating Income (NOI) each year, and you want a 10% rate of return, then you would pay no more than $900,000 for the real estate.

$90,000 Net Operating Income (NOI) ÷ 10% Rate of Return = $900,000 Value

If you paid more than $900,000, then the rate of return would be less than 10%; and if you paid less than $900,000, the rate of return would be more than 10%.

If you know a property value and know its net operating income (NOI), then you can calculate the rate of return by dividing the income by the value.

EXAMPLE:

If you have an opportunity to buy real estate, which is priced at $800,000 and has a net operating income (NOI) of $90,000, then your rate of return is 10%.

$90,000 Net Operating Income (NOI) ÷ $900,000 Value = 10% Rate of Return

To achieve a rate of return higher than 10%, either the price would have to decrease or the Net Operating Income (NOI) would have to increase.

If you know the value and the rate of return desired, you can calculate how much Net Operating Income (NOI) should be produced, by multiplying the value by the desired rate of return.

$900,000 Value X 10% Rate of Return = $90,000 Income

In investment real estate, a capitalization rate is used to estimate a value of a property for a buyer or a seller. Assuming there is a standard value for capitalization rates, a property with a known income would have a market value.

> Potential Rental Income
> - Vacancy
> = Effective Rental Income
> + Other Income
> = Gross Operating Income
> - Operating Expenses
> = Net Operating Income (NOI)
> - Annual Debt Service (ADS)
> = Cashflow Before Tax (CFBT)

As you can see, net operating income takes into consideration more parts of the cashflow model than potential rental income. The comparison of investment real estate is easier, if we consider all these elements and deal with net operating income. Many appraisers use this measure of income when determining the value of a property.

One weakness in using the capitalization approach is it assumes that the property is purchased on an all-cash basis, meaning there is no debt service. Most investment real estate is purchased using financing. This changes our calculations, because we are not only concerned with the total price of the property and net operating income, but we are also concerned with our down payment, and the mortgage payments we must make.

Cash on Cash Return

Cash on Cash Return = Cashflow Before Tax / Initial Investment

The real issue might be how much cashflow is retained by the investor

This rule of thumb takes into consideration all of the elements of our cashflow model, because it deducts the annual debt service from the net operating income. It includes all the elements of our cashflow model.

> Potential Rental Income
> - Vacancy
> = Effective Rental Income
> + Other Income
> = Gross Operating Income
> - Operating Expenses
> = Net Operating Income (NOI)
> - Annual Debt Service (ADS)
> = Cashflow Before Tax (CFBT)

We can then compare the CFBT to the down payment needed to buy the property to calculate a yield.

Assume that the $800,000 property with $80,000 NOI can be purchased with a $600,000 loan (75% LTV). Further, assume that the payments on the loan are $66,000 per year. The cashflow the investor receives after all payments are made is $14,000.

$80,000 Net Operating Income

Less $66,000 Annual Debt Service

Equals $14,000 Cashflow Before Tax

$14,000 Cashflow Before Tax ÷ $200,000 Down payment = 7% cash on cash

One weakness is that it is dependent on the specific person or entity that purchases the property.

Using the rules of thumb that have been discussed, these are four ways to determine whether this is the correct property to purchase. Which rule of thumb depends on the particular situation in which you find yourself.

In addition to the shortcomings previously discussed, the most glaring deficiency of all of these rules of thumb is that *they ignore the holding period of the investment past the first year.* They all help the investor come to some initial valuation based on first-year results of ownership. They make no differentiation as to when the investor will receive the benefit included in the calculation.

Basic Cashflow Analysis

The value to an investor of any investment is based on *the future income stream that investment will produce.* Real estate is no exception. The cashflow model is the basis for valuing real estate.

Potential Rental Income
- Vacancy
= Effective Rental Income
+ Other Income
= Gross Operating Income
- Operating Expenses
= Net Operating Income (NOI)

Central to this model is an estimation of the net operating income (NOI). From the NOI, we only have to subtract the annual debt service (ADS) to get the cashflow before tax (CFBT).

Net Operating Income (NOI)
- Annual Debt Service (ADS)
= Cashflow Before Tax (CFBT)

In forecasting NOI, we are faced with two separate tasks, which are of equal importance.

First we must project the gross operating income (GOI). To do so, we must project the rental income the property will generate.

Then we estimate the level of vacancy and credit losses the property will experience. Finally, we estimate the amount of any other income the property might receive. When we have done all that, we can calculate the GOI.

Our second task is to project the level of operating expenses we will incur to operate the property. These expenses refer only to the cash outflow necessary to operate the property. They do not include non-cash items such as cost recovery.

Using the Property Acquisition Form

The Property Acquisition Form is used to determine how much cash an investor needs; this number will configure the purchase of the property and pay the closing costs required. The Cash Required at Acquisition is the initial amount of cash the investor makes.

Property Acquisition Form			
Cost of Property Acquired			
Price of Property			
+ Closing Costs (0%)			
Total Cost of Property Acquired			
Property Financing			
Bank Loan Principal			
Bank Loan Proceeds			
Total Net Loan Proceeds			
Cash Required at Acquisition			

Using the Annual Property Income Form

At the end of this section, you will find a form, just as above, and you will want to use it as a guideline to help you. Note: There are many versions of this form available to commercial and investment agents, in both hard copy and computer-generated formats. What is important is not which form is used, but rather that the use of this format leads to the correct calculation of the numbers provided.

CASH FLOW ANALYSIS

Gross Income:

Est. Annual Gross Income	_____
Other Income	_____
Total Gross Income	_____
Less Vacancy Allowance	_____
Effective Gross Income	_____

Expenses:

Taxes	_____
Insurance	_____
Water/Sewer	_____
Garbage	_____
Electricity	_____
Licenses	_____
Advertising	_____
Supplies	_____
Maintenance	_____
Lawn	_____
Snow Removal	_____
Pest Control	_____
Management (offsite)	_____
Management (onsite)	_____
Accounting/Legal	_____
Miscellaneous	_____
Gas	_____
Telephone	_____
Pool	_____
Elevator	_____
Replacement Budget	_____
Total Expenses	_____
Net Operating Income	_____

Debt Service:

1st Mortgage	_____
2nd Mortgage	_____
3rd Mortgage	_____
Total Debt Service	_____

CASH FLOW: _____

Gross Operating Income

Here is a summary of the first part of a forecast of Net Operating Income:

Potential Rental Income
- Vacancy and Credit Losses
= Effective Rental Income
+ Other Income
= Gross Operating Income

To project potential rental income, you would do the following:

1. Analyze the existing leases that cover the occupied space in the property.
2. Research market comparables of vacant spaces similar to the current spaces vacant in the property.
3. Survey the current tenants to find out whether they have plans to downsize, expand, or relocate in the near future.
4. Determine whether the current rents in the building are above or below the market rents for available similar vacant space to determine whether the rents being paid are in line with the market.

To estimate vacancy and credit losses, you would do the following:

1. Assemble the vacancy histories for the past several years for similar properties.
2. Analyze the impact of changes in rental rates (up and down) on the vacancy rates.
3. Determine the current supply vs. demand condition for this kind of space.
4. Research the current market trends.
5. Estimate what amount of similar space is projected to become available in the next two years (both under construction and on the drawing boards).

To project sources of other income, you would do the following:

1. Determine whether there is any income that is not associated with the primary purpose of the building, such as freeway billboard signs, which can be rented to advertisers on mini-storage properties, or satellite dishes on the rooftops of office buildings.
2. Look for other opportunities for income that have not been used by the owner.

Real Estate Taxes

1. Use the assessed valuation of the property and the mill levy.
2. What is the trend in this county?

3. Can the assessor's office give you any idea of future changes affecting your property?

Operating Expenses

In the course of operating any type of rental real estate, a number of costs are incurred. Some of these are called *fixed* costs. You still have to pay property taxes and insure the building against fire and liability. Other expenses are called *variable* costs, because the owner has some control over them. For example, you would not be advertising, buying supplies, or paying a manager if the building were shut down.

Estimating these expenses in advance is a mixed task. You can be very precise in your estimate of property taxes and insurance. Other costs, such as maintenance, are harder to predict with any kind of certainty.

Other owners will try to be more market specific in their forecasts. They will talk to other owners, brokers, property managers, and others, who have current experience at managing properties similar to their own.

Another approach is to obtain estimates from the actual providers of the services, who are going to generate these costs. All of these approaches have validity. Whatever strategy owners use, they must make every effort to be as accurate and objective as possible. You are reminded of the old analysis rule: GIGO – *garbage in, garbage out.* It is easy to make the bottom line of your projections look good by subjectively understating your operating expense.

Listed below are most of the expense categories that will be relevant to the operation of a property. They are listed in the order in which they occur on the annual property income form.

Accounting and Legal

1. These costs will be incurred and should be forecast, even if performed by the owner.
2. Check with your attorney for the cost of an eviction because you are certain to have some.

Advertising, Licenses, Permits

1. Check with the local government for any required licenses.
2. Plan the advertising campaign in advance. Check on rates, cost of signs, and so forth.

Property Insurance

1. Get proposals from specific providers, being very careful to compare similar coverage.
2. Decide on special coverage such as business interruption insurance.
3. Share the risk by carefully evaluating deductibles against their incremental premiums.

Property Management

1. Will a professional manager be hired, or will the owner do it?
2. A cost should be projected here even if the owner does the managing. Otherwise, the cashflow projections that result from this forecast will overstate the return generated by the property.
3. If a percentage of the revenue is used as the basis of compensation, be sure it is based on gross operating income. If you base the fee on the potential rental income, then you are not giving the manager any incentive to avoid vacancies and credit losses.

Repairs and Maintenance

1. Age of the building and amount of deferred maintenance is the key here.
2. It is advisable to get an expert's assessment of the condition of the roof, plumbing, wiring, water heaters, furnaces, air conditioners, and so forth. Most tradesmen will provide this service to become the source for any repairs.
3. Management firms and IREM publications are also good sources of information.

Supplies

1. Maintenance supplies will be needed no matter who does the work.

Utilities

1. Get utility company records for the two previous years.
2. Base all projections on a full year's basis. There are wide variations between months depending on the location of the property.
3. Check leases for pass-through provisions or expense stops.

Miscellaneous

1. All projected expenses not previously allocated.
2. Includes such things as snow removal, pest control, janitorial, and the like.

There are other operating expenses that might become part of your analysis. Examples of these expenses are personal property taxes, payroll, and associated taxes and benefits.

After calculating the operating expenses we are ready to calculate net operating income.

NET OPERATING INCOME AND CASH ON CASH

Subtracting the total operating expenses from the GOI gives the NOI.

This is the operating result of the property.

As can be seen from a review of the operating expenses, the net operating income (NOI) includes only the results of operating the property. That is why appraisers use this number for their income approach to value.

> Gross Operating Income
> - Operating Expenses
> = Net Operating Income
> - Annual Debt Service
> = Cashflow Before Taxes

The final objective of our analysis is to determine the Cashflow Before Taxes.

> Net Operating Income
> - Annual Debt Service
> = Cashflow Before Taxes

The CFBT derived on the Annual Property Income Form will become the input data for the Multiyear Cashflow Form.

We have now completed the entire analysis of the first year of ownership of the property, ending with the calculation of cashflow before taxes (CFBT).

While the annual property income form is a snapshot of one year, a multi-year cashflow view shows a moving picture of the operations of the property. This can be for a five-year analysis, for example.

Determining Sales Proceeds

The sales proceeds form is used to determine the expected sales proceeds from a property. It is similar to the seller's net sheet.

Gross Sale Proceeds
- Costs of sale (commissions, taxes, prorations, etc.)
- Loan balances
- Prepayment penalties
= Net Sales Proceeds

This gives you the sales proceeds before taxes. The sales proceeds before taxes refer to the return of investment dollars, which come back to the investor at the sale of the property.

Conclusion

Upon the conclusion of the analysis, the investor or Investor-Agent can determine the cashflows from the acquisition, operations, and disposition of a commercial or investment property. The agent and the investor will then look at these numbers and compare this property with other properties available, making a more informed decision.

Group Ownership of Commercial and Investment Real Estate

When a residential agent becomes involved with commercial and investment real estate, it is likely that the ownership of the property will be something other than joint or community property. Agents will encounter partnerships, corporations, limited liability companies, and real estate investment trusts. Group investing is a popular alternative way for the ownership of real estate to be held. Groups own a substantial portion of the commercial and investment real estate in the United States. It is important for a real estate agent or broker to be aware of the many facets of group ownership, in order to protect the investors.

In addition, many agents or brokers actually want to be in charge of pooling money from their clients, to form their own groups.

Group investing is often referred to as syndication. The words *group investing* and *syndication* are often used interchangeably. A syndicate is defined as a group of people who form an association to undertake a business transaction.

LEARN HOW GROUP INVESTMENTS OFTEN MEET THE NEED FOR POOLING OF RESOURCES

Formation

The main reason for forming a group of investors is generally the need to pool the resources of many investors (mostly money) to facilitate the acquisition of equity. Many groups purchase the property for all cash.

Lack of Available Financing

During the real estate cycle, there is always a time when it is difficult to obtain financing for projects. If the investing world is made up of investors who have 20% equity but the banks are requiring 40% equity, then it will take two investors to complete a purchase of commercial or investment real estate. Forming a group will facilitate the acquisition process.

Diversification

Another important reason for the forming of groups to buy commercial real estate, is the desire of investors to diversify their investments to minimize risks. Instead of an investor purchasing just one property, a group of investors might purchase more than one property, thereby spreading the risk among multiple properties.

The Three Areas of Activity in Group Investing

1) Acquisition

Real estate brokers or salespeople can become involved in the acquisition of commercial or investment real estate for the group they are forming.

In addition, real estate brokers or salespeople might be involved in working with groups formed by others. Many groups are looking for property to purchase and count on real estate agents to introduce them to properties.

2) Management

Real estate brokers or salespeople can become involved in the management of commercial or investment real estate for the group they have formed. In addition, they might work with groups formed by others in the management phase. Many groups are looking for property managers to handle the day-to-day operations of the property they own. The Institute of Real Estate Management (IREM) teaches practical educational courses emphasizing the management skills needed to properly manage commercial or investment real estate for others.

3) Disposition

Real estate brokers or salespeople can become involved in the sale of commercial or investment real estate, for the group they have formed.

In addition, real estate brokers or salespeople can be involved in working with groups formed by others. Many groups are looking for real estate professionals to handle the sale of properties their group owns.

When working with properties owned by groups, it is important that brokers or salespeople be certain that the people have the authority to bind the groups into contractual relationships. In residential transactions, it is often taken for granted that the people signing the contracts have the authority, but this is not the case in commercial or investment real estate. The best way to be certain of the authority of the people is to see copies of the documents, which detail the people and the authority to bind the groups to contracts.

THREE TYPES OF GROUP INVESTMENT OFFERINGS THAT AGENTS MIGHT ENCOUNTER

Fully Specified

A fully specified syndication is one which is identified prior to any money being raised from the members of the group. Often a fully specified offering is limited to one property. This is the most common type of syndication found in the marketplace. For example, a group formed to raise money to buy a specific apartment building or industrial building, would be considered a fully specified offering.

Semi-specified

A semi-specified offering is one in which some of the properties are specifically identified, but additional money might be raised from the group members, and the group might buy other properties that become available.

Generally, a semi-specified offering has a specific acquisition strategy to be followed within one property type. For example, a group might have an acquisition strategy to buy a specific office building from a lender. While this is occurring, they simultaneously raise extra money, so the group can buy a second office building from that lender, should another building become available.

A semi-specified offering is usually a larger offering than a specified offering.

Blind Pool

In a blind pool, there are no properties identified at the time the money is raised from the members of the group. Here, the strategy of the group is to raise all the capital first, and then acquire properties as they become available. Generally, the group will have a strategy, such as buying triple-net-leased industrial buildings in the Silicon Valley, with tenants who have good credit ratings.

Blind pools might be very large in terms of the money raised from the members of the group. Generally these offerings involve many investors, and the offering will not be a private offering.

DETERMINE OTHER CONSIDERATIONS

1. Legal and Security Considerations

When brokers or salespeople become involved with group investing, they enter a new world of additional considerations. You do not need to be afraid of unfamiliar legal and security aspects of group investing, but you do need to know how and when these considerations will affect you.

2. The Need for a CPA and Lawyer

Having a CPA who understands real estate and an attorney who understands security laws is mandatory.

3. Lending Considerations

Regardless of whether you have a group entity as a buyer, lenders will have specific requirements as to who signs on the loan. This consideration is outside the scope of the group investment discussion, but is an area of which you should be aware.

4. IRS Considerations

Many of the side questions regarding group investment might actually deal with the IRS, concerning its rules and regulations. Be certain of which area you are concerned with during your outside questions and research.

5. A long-term relationship

Becoming involved in group investments requires a commitment to a long-term relationship with investors.

Investments last several years, and real estate brokers or salespeople must be prepared to be involved with the members. Many groups remain together long after the properties are sold, especially in the case of a group selling the property on an installment sale and holding paper.

Most investment groups' legal documents require two things: 1) to keep financial statements for the six most recent fiscal years; 2) keep the entire books and records for the groups for the current and past three years.

Investors give up direct control of their investment and the properties in which their money is invested. They do not have the same day-to-day involvement they would have if they made a direct investment. As a result, they do not have the same amount of information regarding their investments. Sponsors must communicate with the investors frequently. Some projects – such as construction projects – will demand monthly reports, whereas other projects – such as a single-tenant – net-leased building, might need only semi-annual reports.

In addition to the reporting of the operations of the project, the sponsors must provide annual operational reports and income tax information to the investors.

LEGAL ENTITIES USED TO FORM GROUP INVESTMENTS

Well, we're almost done and we find ourselves nearly back where we started from! I want to revisit legal entities and perhaps provide a little more insight into the various forms of property and business ownership and their uses.

GENERAL PARTNERSHIPS OF TWO OR MORE PEOPLE

General partnerships can be formed by as few as two people, with each person being a general partner.

All general partners share equally in management

As a general partner, each person has the ability to take part in the day-to-day management of the properties owned by the partnership. This characteristic is ideal for a partnership between a lender and a developer formed to develop a particular piece of property. This could be called a joint venture. Each party has a particular expertise and brings a different value to the partnership. It makes sense that each partner would be interested in taking part in making the day-to-day management decisions.

Joint and Several Liability

As general partners, each partner is totally liable for all the debts of the partnership regardless of the amount of money each partner invests in the partnership.

For example, assume that in a general partnership, one partner invests $500,000 in cash and the other partner invests only $5,000 cash. But, as an additional contribution, the partner who invests only $5,000 agrees to oversee the construction of the project and build the property for cost. Each general partner would be totally liable for any and all judgments levied against the property if the project fails. Of course, insurance might be available to protect the partners against various losses, but on any uninsured loss, each partner would be fully liable.

Title to property is held in the name of the partnership

In a general partnership, the title to the property is held by the partnership, not the individual partners. For example A&B Partnership might consist of investor A and B, but the title is held by A&B Partnership. The partnership owns the real estate, and the individual partners have a personal property interest in the partnership.

This becomes an important consideration in certain situations, such as with death or divorce. The asset owned by the investor is really not real estate but an interest in the group. While the real estate has a marketable value, the interest in the group investment might not have the same value. It is possible that the estate of the person who died or the divorced spouse might not be able sell the property to free up his or her ownership interest. This is another area in which the lack of liquidity in a group investment might be a disadvantage.

Partnership is a tax-reporting entity only; investors get K-1s and pay taxes

The partnership will file a tax return at the end of the year reporting the results of the property operations using federal income tax Form 1065. However, no tax is paid by the partnership.

The partnership will allocate to each partner his or her share of taxable income or loss depending on the formula contained in the partnership agreement. Most formulas call for a pro rata distribution of profits or losses among partners, but there are provisions in the tax code that allow for a *disproportionate allocation*. Such an allocation might give one partner all of the cashflow and the other partner all of the tax losses. A tax attorney or accountant would be needed to draft such disproportionate allocations.

The individual partners will receive a Schedule K-1 from the partnership reporting their allocation of taxable profit or loss for the year. The information from the Schedule K-1 is then reported on the individual partner's federal tax Form 1040 and might result in an increased or decreased tax liability for the individual partner.

Because of the allocation of income or loss to the individual partner and the resulting reporting of that allocation on the individual's tax return, a general partnership is called a pass-through entity.

CHARACTERISTICS OF LIMITED PARTNERSHIPS

Two or more investors

A limited partnership must have two or more partners. One partner must be a general partner who manages the partnership and has the authority to bind the partnership. The general partner is willing to assume unlimited liability. The remaining partners are classified as limited partners.

General partner performs all management functions

By definition, a limited partner has limited involvement in the partnership, including limited involvement in property management, leaving all of the management to the general partner. To protect his or her status as a limited partner, the partner must not take any actions that would cause the partner to be reclassified as a general partner.

Limited partners have limited liability

A limited partner is liable only for the money he has at risk. This means that if a limited partner has invested $5,000, he would lose only that amount in the investment. His liability is limited to his investment.

Some partnerships have provisions for additional investments over and above the original investment. This provision is sometimes called a capital call or an assessment provision. If a provision such as this were in the partnership agreement, limited partners would also be liable for that amount over and above the initial capital investment.

Even with a capital call or assessment provision, limited partners know at the outset the total extent of their liability.

To maintain the limited liability feature, limited partners must be limited in their involvement in management. They must be passive with regard to their management of the partnership's business. If investors begin to take part in management, they suddenly look like general partners to the IRS and face the potential of losing their protection of limited liability.

Ownership interests are illiquid

Ownership interests in limited partnerships are personal property and not real property, and there is seldom a market for limited partnership interests. Investors in limited partnerships must be prepared to stay in the investment groups until the property investment cycle is completed.

Partnerships file tax reports, but partners get K-1s and pay taxes

Just as in general partnerships, partnerships file an informational return with the IRS and distribute Schedule K-1s to individual limited partners, who then report their share of income or expense on their own tax returns. Limited partnerships are pass-through entities.

Partnerships have limited lives

Limited partnerships have finite lives, meaning that the partnership agreements call for a date on which the partnerships will end. This is different from the lives of corporations, which are infinite.

Limited partners should be certain that the lives of the partnerships are long enough to allow the partnerships to hold the properties a sufficient time and to have sufficient life to allow the partnerships to sell the properties and carry back seller financing for a reasonable number of years.

The partnership holds the title

In limited partnerships, as in general partnerships, titles to the properties are held by the partnerships, not the individual partners. The partnership owns the real estate, and the individual partners have a personal property interest in the partnership.

LIMITED LIABILITY COMPANY (LLC)

History

The first limited liability company law was passed in Wyoming in 1978. In 1988, the IRS formally approved this structure, and in 1996, all 50 states had approved legislation that enabled the formation and operation of limited liability companies. The LLC might be formed by only one member. The owners are its members who can manage the entity directly or appoint managers to operate the entity or supervise officers hired to run the day-to-day activities of the entity. The key documents for an LLC are the articles of organization and the operating agreement.

An LLC created under the laws of one state might do business in other states by registering the LLC in each state in which it desires to do business.

Limited liability is available for all members of the group

In a limited liability company, investors are called members, not shareholders or partners. All members can have limited liability whether they are active or passive with regard to their role in management.

This is a major difference between limited partnerships and limited liability companies and allows the members of an LLC to take an active role in the management of the business of the group.

An LLC is a pass-through entity

In a Limited Liability Company, income or losses from the operation of the business are passed directly through to the members of the group without being taxed at the organization level.

There are no restrictions as to members

In limited partnerships and corporations, specifically S corporations, there are restrictions as to who can be a partner or a shareholder. Many of these restrictions are eliminated in LLCs. For example LLCs have no restrictions against foreign investors being members of the group or against a corporation being a member of a group.

In addition, there are no restrictions as to the number of members in a group or whether a lender to the group could also be a group member.

Special Allocations

In LLCs, the possibility exists for providing disproportionate allocations, as discussed in the General Partnership section.

Multiple classes are allowed

In an LLC, there can be multiple classes of investors. One class of investors might be lenders, another class might be equity investors who want a preferred return, and another class might be equity investors who want the tax shelter and appreciation.

For example, a doctor with a small pension fund could invest the pension fund money in a group and take a secured position as a lender. She could then invest her own money and take a fixed portion of the cashflow as a return. She could also bring in other doctors to invest and give them the tax shelter and the remaining cashflow and appreciation.

Fewer corporate formalities are required to protect the limited liability of group members

The limited liability available to shareholders in a corporation might be lost if the corporation fails to hold regular meetings or keep an updated set of corporate books. When the corporate formalities are not adhered to, creditors are able to pierce the corporate veil of protection for the shareholders.

In LLCs, the lack of corporate formalities itself will not allow creditors to proceed directly against a group member, bypassing the protection of limited liability.

Laws differ by state

Many states allow the formation of an LLC with only one member.

Each state has its own rules as to who the members of a group can be and whether there can be multiple classes of members in an LLC.

Miscellaneous

It is possible that groups such as limited partnerships, general partnerships, and sole proprietors who wish to convert their current entity structure to an LLC might be able to contribute their properties to an LLC on a tax-free basis. However, corporate conversion to an LLC is most likely a taxable event.

In a real estate venture, as well as in any other business venture, seldom is one of the investors willing to assume general liability for all obligations of the business as is required of the general partner in either a general partnership or limited partnership. Of these three pass-through entities, the LLC offers the best protection from liability for the operation of the business.

CORPORATIONS

This is the typical form of entity used by larger business organizations. A corporation is formed according to the laws of an individual state and might then be registered to do business in any other state.

The shareholders own the corporation. The shareholders elect the directors, who in turn hire the officers of the corporation. The officers run the business on a day-to-day basis.

Generally, the corporate entity is not favored for the ownership of real estate because of the double taxation that exists by virtue of the fact that the corporation must pay taxes on the taxable income generated by the property and the individual shareholder pays taxes on the cashflow distributed as dividends. This double taxation is avoided by the use of a pass-through entity, such as a partnership or an LLC.

In addition, the strict requirements of maintaining corporate formalities or being faced with the loss of limited liability make the corporate structure a difficult one in which to own and operate real estate group ownership.

REAL ESTATE INVESTMENT TRUSTS (REIT)

This form of group ownership is favored on Wall Street and used in the largest capital formation transactions. It is a specialized area in which special legal and financial consultation must be sought out and obtained. A REIT is actually a corporation to which special rules are applied so that it can avoid taxation at the corporate level. Two of the special rules are that each year the corporation must distribute 95% of the cashflow to its shareholders and that there must be at least 100 investors in the REIT within one year of its date of formation.

Security Regulations

This section is perhaps the most important in terms of keeping you out of trouble and in compliance with the law. Since you've made it this far then you perhaps have been or will be involved in syndication or public offering memorandums. I have been myself and it is a fascinating way to learn, grow, and prosper at a whole new level involving big players in the world of investing.

Consider this. If you could pool funds together from multiple people, use these funds to purchase a lot of real estate, then manage that real estate for a fee and profit as well from commissions earned on the buy side and eventual sell side, would you be a happy camper? Well, that's exactly what I did several years ago. We created a closed end mutual fund involving some sophisticated folks from Wall Street. We sold shares of the fund to investors. We used the capital to acquire a few portfolios of real estate. We sold some of the individual properties to repay some of the investors. And we earned a property management fee for managing the properties in the portfolio. Not a bad day at the office and I learned a ton in the process. Here is some of what you need to know before proceeding.

Many agents or brokers who are interested in forming their own groups to buy investment or commercial real estate will be surprised to know that what they are getting involved in is the sale of a security, not the sale of real estate. The area of securities laws is vast, and the material presented here is only to alert you to this new area of business and to warn you to get professional advice from a securities lawyer. Be certain to understand that the securities laws may apply even when you are pooling money from family and friends to purchase a single family house as a rental.

In a historic court case in the 1930s, the courts identified four characteristics of an investment in real estate that determine whether the investment is considered a security and therefore comes under the rules and regulations of the security industry.

In this case, it was determined that a citrus grove owner in Florida who was selling ownership in the land of his citrus grove was not selling real estate but was actually selling a security because his investors invested with the expectation of earning a return on their investment based on the profitable operation of the citrus grove.

In this case, the investors actually bought parcels of land, as small as a quarter of an acre, in a very large citrus farm in Florida. When they were presented with a chance to buy a parcel of land they were told that the operator of the farms would handle all the production of the citrus products developed from the farm and split the profits with the land owners.

The citrus grove ran into bad times and failed. The individual property owners stopped paying on their land purchase contracts. They were foreclosed upon, but the property owners sued the owners of the citrus grove saying that they really had not been sold land, but sold a security. The case went to court and was finally settled by the Supreme Court, when it set a four-prong test for the definition of a security.

ELEMENTS OF THE DEFINITION OF A SECURITY

To be considered a security, an investment must be deemed to have all four of the following characteristics: Investment of Money, In a Common Enterprise, With Expectation of Profit, and Solely from the Efforts of a Third-Party Promoter.

Investment of money

The investor must invest money into the investment or contribute property that has a monetary value. This characteristic does not include the contribution of labor to a group.

In a common enterprise

The investment of money must be made into an enterprise that owns the property. The entity must be some sort of group investment with more than one investor. There is no requirement as to which ownership entity must be used because the grouping of investors together makes it an enterprise for the purpose of this definition. The enterprise might be a partnership, an LLC, a corporation, or a REIT.

With expectation of profit

The investment must have been made with the expectation that a profit would be made on the investment. If there is no expectation of a profit, the money invested in the group could be considered either a gift or a loan because the loan repayment would be made of principal and interest. In securities law, interest is not considered profit. Of course, a gift need not be paid back at all.

Solely from the efforts of a third-party promoter

This characteristic refers to whether there is someone whose actions will determine the financial outcome of the investment and the financial return to the members of the group.

In the citrus farm case, the Court determined that, even though the investment was land, the land owners invested their money in the common enterprise of the citrus farm where they expected to make a profit, but the profit they expected had to come as a result of the owner of the citrus farm, not through their own efforts.

Is There an Exception When Dealing with Family and Friends?

Many times agents ask if there is an exception to the securities laws when they are only dealing with family and very close friends. The answer is that there is not any such exception for family and friends.

Is a loan a security?

Actually a note is a security, but most states have their own law relating to making loans that take the loan out of the definition of a security. However, the agent must be careful when putting multiple investors into one loan. Legal council must be consulted as both the federal and state laws have something to say about this type of pooling of investors' money

Is a timeshare a security?

When an investor buys an individual unit in a timeshare or vacation condo, the investment might be considered more than a real estate investment in the situation where the unit must be part of a rental pool, managed by a management firm. If the buyer was induced to invest their money and buy the property based on the income to be generated by the management company's renting out the owner's unit along with the other units, the investment might actually be a security. Most states have recognized this problem and have taken control of the timeshare industry in state specific legislation.

PURPOSE OF FEDERAL SECURITY REGULATIONS

Regulate the Security

Based on the amounts of money lost in the financial industry crash in the 1930s, the federal government passed legislation to protect investors. This legislation is the basis for the security laws we have today.

The federal laws that regulate the security (The Securities Act of 1933) regulate the paper, or the security itself. The laws state exactly what the security can be and require registration of the security with the federal government. The basic premise of this regulation is that investors are given all the information they need to make informed decisions before they invest.

Consult Your Broker and a Securities Attorney

As many real estate brokers do not want their agent working in the securities area, the agent should consult with their broker before pooling money from investors. Because a person must follow the laws dealing with offering a security, you should also consult a securities lawyer.

Just as you must have a real estate license to sell someone else's real estate, you must have a securities license to sell someone else's securities. You may be able to sell your own securities without a securities license, but you should consult a securities attorney before starting.

Need more advanced help?

Visit www.myinvestmentservices.com/work-with-me

and get a FREE 1-on-1 private coaching session.

Think you've got what it takes and need just 1 hour
with the Guru to get to the next level?

PLUS you will also get a FREE Blueprint for your business

Conclusion

I've always loved working with entrepreneurs – often business owners who have a passion for what they do. Real estate investors and Investor-Agents are in fact entrepreneurs. They possess naturally, or develop through education, information, and taking action the character traits of persistence, dogged determination, passion, perseverance, ambition, courage, discipline, a positive outlook, a positive attitude, thick skin, and many other traits but most of all the desire to be free. I mean really FREE. Did you ever dream of flying when you were a kid? That's your spirit calling out to be FREE. That spirit is still within you today. It will never die. In spite of life's circumstances and the efforts of society to make you conform remember this: you are still that little kid and you are going to be FREE. I'm going to help you achieve this.

When I was a little boy I used to get strep throat so bad my trachea would close up and I couldn't breathe. At first I didn't panic because I would knock on the wall next to my bed and Mom would come in and get me breathing again. When I was 10 years old, I contracted strep again but Mom had to go to school for a parent teacher conference with my sister's teachers. She told me that if I couldn't breathe to not panic… and go to the bathroom and use the medicine I had to help me breathe again.

While she was gone my trachea closed up and I panicked. I collapsed in the hall trying to get to the bathroom. I know what it's like to want to breathe and not be able to. I don't know if I can describe in words what that feels like. Thankfully, I eventually grew up and never had strep again.

Later in life I broke my back in two places and couldn't walk. I remembered what it felt like as a child to not be able to breathe. As an adult I had to summon the courage to take action, to learn all I could, and do everything I could to be able to walk again.

I also learned one of the most valuable lessons of my life. After I surrendered to God my challenges *and* my ambitions, to live by faith and be grateful for everything (and I do mean everything, good and bad), I did everything in my power to do my part to be whole again.

It occurred to me that I was capable of tremendous effort beyond what I had previously known and if I could summon the will to act in times of crisis, why couldn't I summon the will to do this on any given day?

Well I can, and so can you. I live life this way every day. Some people think I am a super human because of all I do. I'm not. I'm Gary Wilson. I have the same number of bones and muscles as you. My brain is the same size as yours. I pray you don't have to experience the same trials that I've had but I know you will experience trials in your own life. I also know you will be tested. Let me ask you, if you can rise to the occasion in times of need… can you, will you, rise to the occasion every single day of your life?

Before we both continue with our life's journey I want to revisit the Wheel of Fortune I put at the end of the "Investor-Agent: Make More Money Not More Work" section.

Let's make sure you have a plan in place now that you are finished reading this book and preparing to turn the last page. When you look at this wheel, you can see that you can enter and begin profiting from a number of starting positions. Let's say you are, or want to start, flipping homes. That section of the wheel is your starting point. But your Path to Profit doesn't end there. It begins there.

At this point you may want to get your real estate license and begin listing and selling your own flips. This way you can start to generate more income in the form of commissions through the use of your license, thereby leveraging what you're already doing to generate multiple streams of income.

Let's say you're buying rentals and managing them yourself. Again, you could begin managing your own properties through an LLC and while you're at it, get your real estate license and manage other people's properties too, generating all that extra income. Starting to get the picture?

Let's say you don't have a dime to your name. You could start wholesaling and generate income that you could then use to do your own investing in rentals or flips.

Let's say you are a real estate agent and you want to start your own investing. Decide what type of investing you want to do first. If you want to flip homes, then work with investors who are flipping homes. You will earn extra commissions (read the section "Investor-Agent: Make More Money Not More Work") and apply those proceeds to doing your own flipping, plus you'll learn more just by being in the flipping game with other investors.

Maybe you want to own rentals. Well then, start working with investors who invest in rentals. You will earn those commissions, learn a ton *and* not only start buying your own rentals but start managing them too… for even more income.

Is this making sense? Here again is the wheel. Have a look and start to imagine where you are now and where you want to go on your Path to Profit. Then call me. Email me. Come to one of the Massive Passive Cashflow Method 3-day events. Come see me teach in person at one of the daily classes.

Visit MyInvestmentServices.com/events to see where I'll be teaching. Take one of the training programs associated with any of the five major disciplines in Investment Real Estate. Don't just sit there. DO IT!

Real Estate With Gary Wilson — **Path to Prosperity**

INVESTOR AGENT

01 You invsest
02 Wholesalers
03 Rental Investor
04 Build Team
05 Referrals
06 Owner Occupied
07 Property Manager
08 Flippers

Start Now

What are you waiting for? What are you still doing here reading this book?

Right now: Create a "To Do List."

Get a round "To-It."

Get an index card out and write on it "I Promise…." and fill in the blank with the promise to yourself to take the first step. Then follow the link below and get a FREE 1-on-1 private coaching session! That will get you started!

Need more advanced help?

Visit www.myinvestmentservices.com/work-with-me

and get a FREE 1-on-1 private coaching session.

Think you've got what it takes and need just 1 hour
with the Guru to get to the next level?

PLUS you will also get a FREE Blueprint for your business

Suggested Reading:

James Allen, *As a Man Thinketh*, Tribeca Books, 2011.

Robert G. Allen, *Creating Wealth: Retire in Ten Years Using Allen's Seven Principles*, Free Press, 2011.

Robert G. Allen, *Nothing Down for the 2000s: Dynamic New Wealth Strategies in Real Estate*, Free Press, 2004.

Rhonda Byrne, *The Secret*, Atria Books, 2006.

Michael Corbett, *Find It, Fix It, Flip It: Make Millions in Real Estate – One House at a Time*, Plume, 2006.

Jack Cummings, *Real Estate Finance and Investment Manual*, Wiley, 2008.

Napoleon Hill and Arthur R. Pell, *Think and Grow Rich*, Tarcher, 2005.

Anthony Hoffman, *How to Negotiate Successfully in Real Estate*, Simon & Schuster, 1984.

Robert Kiyosaki, *Rich Dad Poor Dad: What the Rich Teach Their Kids About Money That the Poor and Middle Class Do Not!* Warner Business Books, 1997.

Robert Kiyosaki, *You Can Choose to be Rich,* 12-CD audio series with three books, 2003.

Ron LeGrand, *How to Be a Quick Turn Real Estate Millionaire: Make Fast Cash With No Money, Credit, or Previous Experience*, Kaplan, 2004.

Ron LeGrand, *Ron LeGrand's Cash Flow Systems Course: For Sale By Owner.* www.ronlegrand.com

Martin J. Miles, *Vest-Pocket Real Estate Advisor*, Prentice Hall, 1990.

Frank McKinney, *Burst This!: Frank McKinney's Bubble Proof Real Estate Strategies*, HCI, 2009.

Frank McKinney, *Frank McKinney's Maverick Approach to Real Estate Success: How You Can Go From a $50,000 Fixer Upper to a $100 Million Mansion*, Wiley, 2005.

Anthony Robbins, http://www.tonyrobbins.com/products/

Carleton Sheets, *No Down Payment*, Home Study Course, http://www.carletonsheets.com

Robert Shemin, *Secrets of a Millionaire Real Estate Investor*, Kaplan Business, 2000.

Robert Shemin, *Secrets of a Millionaire Landlord*, Kaplan Business, 2001.

Russ Whitney, *Building Wealth: Achieving Personal and Financial Success in Real Estate and Business Without Money, Credit, or Luck*, Touchstone, 2006.

Loan Formulas

FULLY AMORTIZED LOAN

- In a fully amortized loan, the calculated loan payments will return exactly the lenders' principal over the term of the loan, while simultaneously giving lenders a yield on their investment (the loan) equal to the stated interest rate.
- At the end of a fully amortized loan, the outstanding balance has been reduced to zero.
- In a fixed-rate, fully amortized loan, the amount of the monthly payment will not change during the life of the loan.

EXAMPLE:

- A $10,000 loan, with 10% annual interest and a three-year amortization period, will have three equal annual payments of $4,021.15. The payments, which include interest and principal, are called debt service.

Debt Service
Amortized Mortgage

Year	1	2	3
Debt Service	$4,021	$4,021	$4,021

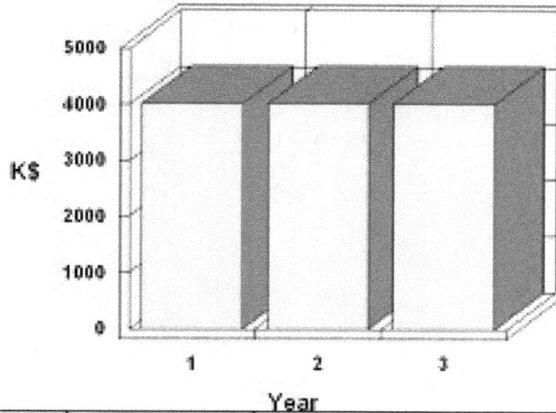

Year	Loan Balance	Interest Payment	Principal Payment	Ending Balance
1	10,000.00	1,000.00	3,021.15	6,978.85
2	6,978.85	697.89	3,323.26	3,655.59
3	3,655.59	365.56	3,655.59	0

Year 1

- $10,000 loan balance X 10% interest = $1,000.00 interest due
- $4,021.15 payment - $1,000 interest = $3,021.15 principal
- $10,000 loan balance - $3,021.15 principal = $ 6,978.85 balance

Year 2

- $6,978.85 loan balance X 10% interest = $ 697.89 interest due
- $4,021.15 payment - $697.89 interest = $3,323.26 principal
- $6,978.85 loan balance - $3,323.26 principal = $ 3,655.59 balance

Year 3

- $3,655.59 loan balance X 10% interest = $ 365.56 interest due
- $4,021.15 payment - $365.56 interest = $3,655.59 principal
- $3,655.59 loan balance - $3,655.59 principal = $ 0 balance

As you can see below, the interest portion of each payment goes down as the principal gets paid off with each payment. The portion of payment will increase as less of the fixed payment amount is required to pay lenders the interest.

Loan Interest
Amortized Mortgage

Year	1	2	3
Interest	$1,000	$1,000	$1,000

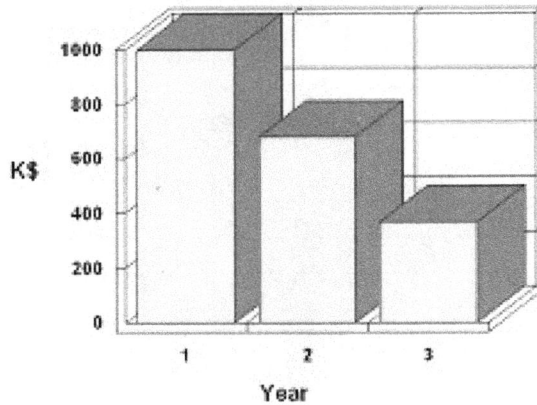

Loan Principal
Amortized Mortgage

Year	1	2	3
Principal Pay Off	$1,000	$679	$366

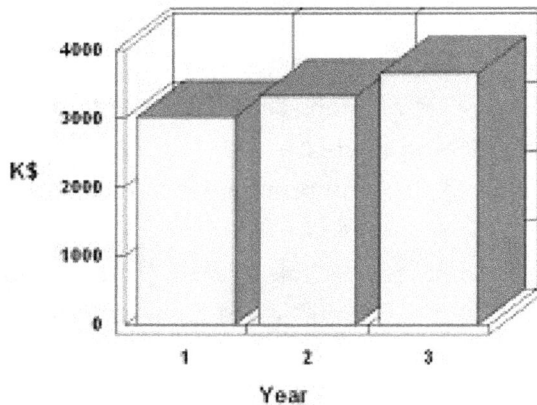

INTEREST-ONLY LOAN

- In an interest-only loan, the periodic payments are just enough to pay the interest, but they are not enough to repay any of the principal.
- As each payment is made, lenders receive a return on the outstanding balance of the loan. The outstanding balance of the loan remains constant. The payment remains the same and as a result, the amount paid toward principal remains at zero.
- At any time, the outstanding balance is equal to the original loan amount.

EXAMPLE:

- A $10,000 loan, with annual payments of $1,000, a three-year term, and a 10% annual interest rate, will not amortize any principal during its term.

**Loan Interest
Interest Only Loan**

Year	1	2	3
Interest	$1,000	$679	$366

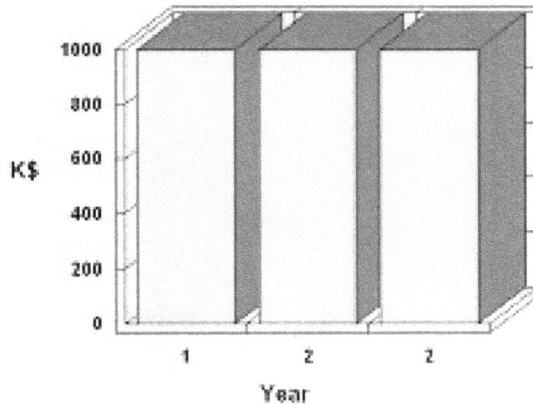

Year	Loan Balance	Interest Payment	Principal Payment	Ending Balance
1	10,000.00	1,000.00	0	10,000.00
2	10,000.00	1,000.00	0	10,000.00
3	10,000.00	1,000.00	0	10,000.00

WORKING WITH PARTIALLY AMORTIZED AND NEGATIVELY AMORTIZED LOANS

Partially Amortized Loan

- In a partially amortized loan, the periodic payments are enough to pay the interest, but not enough to completely repay the loan within its term. The term is usually less than the amortization period.
- As each payment is made, lenders receive a return on the outstanding balance of the loan. As the outstanding balance of the loan decreases, the amount paid in interest is reduced. The total payment remains the same, and the amount paid toward the principal increases with each payment.
- Over time, the outstanding balance decreases, but the loan does not last long enough for the entire loan amount to be amortized.
- The amortization period describes the time it would take to repay the entire loan amount. The term is the amount of time the borrower actually has the money. For example "30 years, due in 15" is a term describing a loan with payment amounts set to pay it off in 30 years but that the borrower must pay off at the end of 15 years.

EXAMPLE:

- A $10,000 loan, with annual payments of $4,021.15 and a 10% annual interest rate, will only partially amortize in two years, typically stated as a three-year loan that is due in two years.

Year	Loan Balance	Interest Payment	Principal Payment	Ending Balance
1	10,000.00	1,000.00	3,021.15	6,978.85
2	6,978.85	697.89	6978.85	0
3				

Year 1

- $10,000 loan balance X 10% interest = $1,000.00 interest due
- $4,021.15 payment - $1,000 interest = $3,021.15 principal
- $10,000 loan balance - $3,021.15 principal = $6,978.85 balance

Year 2

- $6,978.85 loan balance X 10% interest = $697.89 interest due

- $7,675.89 payment - $697.89 interest = $6,978.85 principal
- $6,978.85 loan balance - $6,978.85 principal = $ 0 balance

Interest Detail

Partially Amortized Loan

Year	1	2
Interest	$1,000	$698

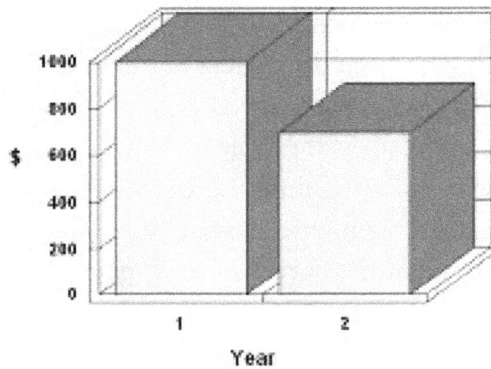

Loan Principal Detail
Partially Amortized Loan

Year	1	2
Principal Pay Off	$3,012	$6,978

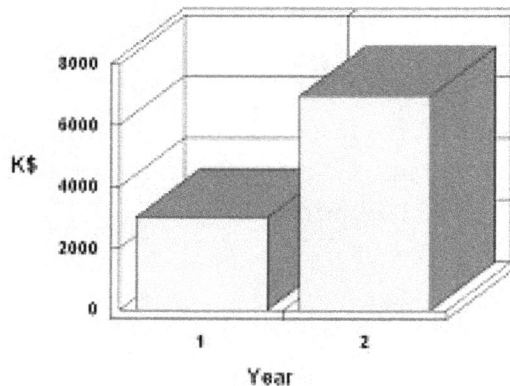

Negatively Amortized Loan

- In a negatively amortized loan, the payment made is not enough to pay the stated interest rate. In effect, the unpaid interest is an extra new loan each time a payment is made.
- The unpaid interest is added to the loan balance at each payment period.

EXAMPLE:

- A $10,000 loan, with no payments required and a 10% annual interest rate.

Year	Loan Balance	Interest Payment	Principal Payment	Ending Balance
1	10,000.00	0	0	11,000.00
2	11,000.00	0	0	12,100.00
3	12,100.00	0	0	13,310.00

Year 1

- $10,000 loan balance X 10% interest = $1,000 interest due
- $0 payment
- $10,000 loan balance + 1,000.00 interest not paid = $11,000.00 balance

Year 2

- $11,000 loan balance X 10% interest = $1,100 interest due
- $0 payment
- $11,000 loan balance + $1,100 interest not paid = $12,100.00 balance

Year 3

- $12,100 loan balance X 10% interest = $1,210 interest due
- $ 0 payment
- $12,100 loan balance + $1,210 interest not paid = $13,310.00 balance
- When this loan pays off, the $13,310 balance reflects the repayment of $10,000 of original loan principal and the $3,310 of interest added to that original amount.

Lenders are interested in the amount of risk they take when they make a loan. There are several ways lenders attempt to minimize the risk. One way is by making sure the original amount of the loan is less than the value of the property. A second way is to be certain that the amount of income is more than the amount the borrower is required to pay each year.

LOAN-TO-VALUE RATIO

Loan to value (LTV) ratio is the ratio of the loan amount to the value of the property. In investment real estate, it is used the same way as in residential real estate. The use of this ratio allows lenders to determine how much equity there is in the property over and above the amount of financing.

EXAMPLE:

- A lender has appraised a small office building to have a value of $1,000,000 and has agreed to make a $750,000 loan. The loan to value (LTV) ratio has been set at 75%.
- Or, if the lender quotes a loan-to-value (LTV) ratio of 75% and the property has a value of $1,000,000, the investor can calculate that the maximum loan from this lender will be $750,000.
- $1,000,000 Property Value X 75% Loan to Value (LTV) = $750,000 Loan

Adjusting the LTV up or down is an approach, which lenders use to adjust for risk in a mortgage investment.

In specific lending marketplaces, lenders' perceptions may be that one product type is riskier than another; lenders may then place an LTV ratio on a new loan, requiring the owner to contribute a larger portion of equity to the acquisition.

Loan to Value Ratio (LTV)
versus
Loan Amount

Assumption on LTV	Loan Amount
50% of Property Price	500,000
55% of Property Price	550,000
60% of Property Price	600,000
65% of Property Price	650,000
70% of Property Price	700,000
75% of Property Price	750,000
80% of Property Price	800,000

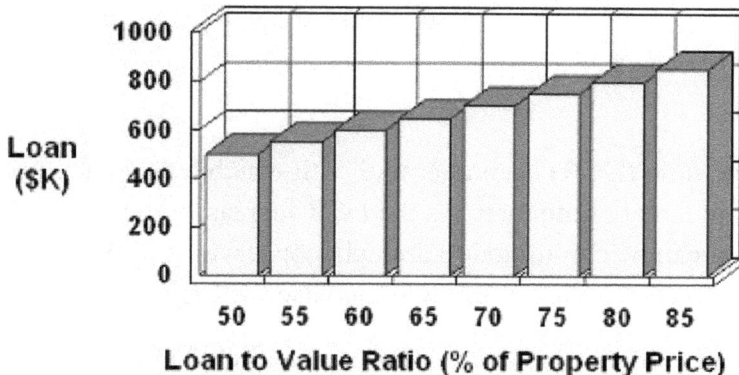

Loan to Value Ratio (% of Property Price)

DEBT COVERAGE RATIO (DCR)

The debt coverage ratio (DCR) is the ratio of net operating income (NOI) to the annual debt service (ADS) on the loan. This is the calculation lenders make, when determining whether the property produces enough income to allow the borrower to make the mortgage payments.

$$\text{Debt Coverage Ratio (DCR)} = \frac{\text{Net Operating Income (NOI)}}{\text{Annual Debt Service (ADS)}}$$

EXAMPLE:

- If the net operating income (NOI) of the property is $100,000, and the lender states that the annual debt service (ADS) allowed is $80,000, the debt coverage ratio (DCR) would be stated as 1.25.

$$\frac{\$100,000 \text{ Net Operating Income (NOI)}}{\$80,000 \text{ Annual Debt Service (ADS)}} = 1.25 \text{ Debt Coverage Ratio (DCR)}$$

Or, if the lender tells the investor that the DCR will be 1.25 and the investor knows that the NOI is $100,000, the investor can calculate that the ADS available for mortgage payments would be $80,000.

$$\frac{\$100{,}000 \text{ Net Operating income (NOI)}}{1.25 \text{ Debt Coverage Ratio (DCR)}} = \$80{,}000 \text{ Annual Debt Service (ADS)}$$

The debt coverage ratio (DCR) is another tool with which lenders attempt to manage risk in an investment in a real estate loan. As the DCR increases, the amount of net operating income (NOI) that can be committed to annual debt service (ADS) decreases. If a lender views the risk in a certain loan, lenders will increase the DCR.

Once the amount of NOI that can be used for payment of ADS is determined, lenders will state the terms of the loan. Of course, the lower the amount allowed for annual debt service, the lower the amount of loan the borrower can acquire.

Debt Coverage Ratio (DCR)
versus
Loan Amount

Assumption on DCR	Loan Amount
1.1 Times Debt Coverage	863,264
1.15 Times Debt Coverage	825,731
1.2 Times Debt Coverage	791,325
1.25 Times Debt Coverage	759,672
1.3 Times Debt Coverage	730,454
1.35 Times Debt Coverage	703,400
1.4 Times Debt Coverage	678,279

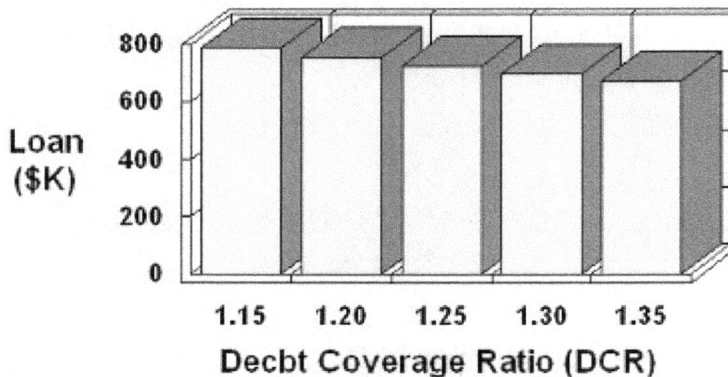

In this chart and graph, it is assumed the loan is 10% interest with monthly payments, amortized over 30 years.

INTERACTION BETWEEN THE RULES OF THUMB

Lenders use a combination of two rules of thumb discussed above, which determines the loan that will be made on investment real estate. By applying the loan-to-value ratio and the debt coverage ratio, lenders will calculate two maximum loan amounts; then they will make the smaller loan allowed.

EXAMPLE 1:

- A retail building is expected to produce $100,000 of net operating income (NOI) during the first year of ownership and has been appraised at $1,000,000.
- A lender states that it will make a loan for this property based on lending criteria of a loan-to-value (LTV) ratio of 70% or a debt coverage ratio (DCR) of 1.25, whichever is less.
- The loan is being made at 10%, amortized over 30 years, monthly payments.

1. Calculating the loan amount using the Loan to Value (LTV) approach:

- $1,000,000 Appraised Value X 70% Loan to Value (LTV) = $700,000 loan.

2. Calculating the loan amount using the Debt Coverage Ratio (DCR) approach:

- $100,000 Net Operating income (NOI)
- _____ = $80,000 Annual Debt Service (ADS)
- 1.25 Debt Coverage Ratio (DCR)
- $80,000 Annual Debt Service / 12 months = $6,667 in monthly payments
- $6,667 in monthly payments, with 10% interest, amortized over 30 years will result in a mortgage of $759,672.

Solution:

1. The Loan to Value Ratio (LTV) approach results in a $700,000 loan amount.

2. The Debt Coverage Ratio (DCR) approach results in a $759,672 loan amount.

What will the lender do?

The lender will loan on the *smaller* of the two loan amounts. In this case, the maximum loan will be $700,000, determined by the loan to value (LTV) ratio. While the $6,667 monthly payment can support a loan of $759,672, the lender's loan requirement is that the loan it makes will not exceed a 70% loan to value. Therefore, the maximum loan is $700,000.

EXAMPLE 2:

Assume all of the above information stays the same, but the term is now only 20 years. Does the loan amount the lender will give to the investor change?

1. Using the Loan to Value (LTV) approach:

- Using the Loan to Value (LTV) approach the maximum loan will be $700,000. This remains unchanged.

2. Using the Debt Coverage Ratio (DCR) approach:

- Using the Debt Coverage Ratio (DCR) the maximum loan payments remain at $6,667. But with a 10% interest rate and a 20-year amortization period, the maximum loan would be $690,831.

Solution:

1. The loan to value (LTV) ratio approach results in a $700,000 loan amount.

2. The Debt Coverage Ratio (DCR) approach results in a $690,831 loan amount.

What will the lender do?

The lender will loan on the smaller of the two loan amounts. In this case, the maximum loan will be $690,831, which is determined by the debt coverage ratio (DCR) approach. While the lender might make a loan based on a 70% loan to value ratio, the lender has determined that the borrower cannot commit enough of the net operating income (NOI) to make the payments on a loan of $700,000.

Loan Debt Coverage Ratio
versus
Loan Amount

Assumption Value	20 Year Loan	30 Year Loan
1.1 Times Debt Coverage	785,035	821,821
1.15 Times Debt Coverage	750,903	786,090
1.2 Times Debt Coverage	719,615	753,336
1.25 Times Debt Coverage	**690,831**	**723,203**
1.3 Times Debt Coverage	664,260	695,387
1.35 Times Debt Coverage	639,658	669,632
1.4 Times Debt Coverage	616,813	645,717

As you can see, the loan amounts available for the loan with a shorter term will be lower. With a shorter term, payments will increase to reduce the principal at a faster rate. As the amount of that debt service dedicated to principal increases, the amount of the available loan decreases.

Definition of Terms

Abstract of Title: A summarized history of the title of real property listing rights and liabilities such as easements, mortgages, liens, and transfers of title. The abstract gives evidence of the chain of title and whether or not the title is clear.

Acceleration Clause: A clause in a mortgage that provides, at the option of the lender, the entire unpaid balance of the note would be due immediately upon failure to make a required payment or upon the sale of the property. In the latter case it is known as a due-on-sale acceleration clause. Usually it is found in paragraph 17 of a mortgage.

Accretion: The gradual buildup of soil by water.

Accrued Interest: Accumulated interest earned or due but not yet paid.

Acknowledgment: Legal declaration before a notary or duly authorized officer of a jurisdiction that the one signing an instrument is who he or she claims to be.

Acre: A quantity of land equal to 43,560 square feet (for example, a square 208.7' x 208.7' or a rectangle 100' x 436.5').

Adjusted Cost Basis: For accounting purposes, the original cost plus improvements minus depreciation or cost recovery taken.

Ad Valorum: A measure of worth based on the value of something. For example, real property taxes calculated on the market value of the property.

After Tax Cashflow: Effective gross income minus operating expenses and debt service plus or minus any tax savings or tax liability. (Also known as net spendable income.)

Agency: A relationship of trust whereby one party, the principal, entrusts another party, the agent, to act in his or her behalf and to represent him or her in doing business with other parties.

All Inclusive Trust Deed: The borrower obtains a new mortgage which is structured to include the old mortgage. The borrower makes payments on the new mortgage directly to the lender, who makes payments on the old first mortgage. (Also known as a Wrap-Around Mortgage.)

Amortization: The reduction of debt over a fixed term on an installment basis.

Amortized Loan: A loan in which the principal as well as the interest is payable in monthly or other periodic installments over the term of the loan.

Annuity: A payment of equal installments paid periodically for a given number of periods.

Appraisal: An estimation of value of real property as of the present or past date (not future). Any of three methods are used where applicable: cost approach, income approach, and market data approach.

Appraiser: A disinterested party who evaluates a property and determines a value for it.

Appreciation: Growth in value.

Appurtenance: Anything attached to the land which becomes a part of the property. A fence would be an example.

Arrears: The payment of money after the fact. Interest or taxes paid in arrears would represent money paid for a period of time gone by.

Asking Price: The price an appraiser has determined for a property and the price for which it is on the market.

Assessed Value: The value placed on the property by the taxing body of a county. This value is then used as a basis for computing taxes.

Assessments: A tax charge against real property by the taxing body of a county.

Asset: Any possession of value that an individual owns which may be used for payment of a debt.

Assign: To transfer one's rights in a bond, mortgage, lease, or other legal instrument to another person.

Assumption of Mortgage: To expressly take responsibility for the payment of a note secured by an existing mortgage on real property, thereby becoming a co-guarantor of that note.

Attorney at Law: A person licensed to practice law.

Balance Sheet: A financial statement showing assets, liabilities, and net worth.

Balloon Payment: A large final payment due on a note, usually after partial amortization of the debt, through installment payments.

Bankruptcy: Proceedings against a debtor, who has been declared legally insolvent, to distribute the debtor's property among the creditors.

Bill of Sale: A document used to transfer title to personal property (chattel).

Bird-Dog: People who are on the lookout for properties that are for sale. Sometimes they earn a referral fee, if the property is purchased by an investor through their referrals.

Blanket Mortgage: One mortgage that covers several different parcels of real property.

Blended Interest Rate: The interest rate resulting from half the difference of the interest rate originally written for the mortgage and the current market rate of interest. Generally, when loans are not assumable, asking the bank to rewrite the mortgage at a blended interest rate is the next best thing.

Boiler Plate: Preprinted sections of a contract.

Bounds: Boundaries that are natural (lakes, trees, rocks, etc.) or artificial (roads, railroads, etc.).

Buyer's Broker: A broker who represents the *buyer* when entering a real estate transaction. Generally, the *seller* pays the broker's commission at the closing.

Capital: Money used for investing purposes.

Capital Gains: The profits realized above adjusted cost basis on the sale of property.

Cashflow: Effective gross income minus operating expenses and debt service. (Also known as cash throw-off.)

Caveat Emptor: "Let the buyer beware." This statement does not apply where the buyer and seller are using an agent (broker).

Chattel: Personal property.

Chattel Mortgage: A mortgage on personal property.

Closing Date: A predetermined day that the transaction of buying/selling property will take place.

Collateral: Real or personal property pledged as security for repayment of a loan or debt.

Commission: Usually a percentage of the purchase price paid to the broker or agent for services rendered.

Common Law: Law that is not codified, developed from common usage and custom.

Competent Party: A person legally able to contract; being of legal age and sound mind.

Concessions: During negotiations, these are the items that each party is willing to give up in order to get the items each party really wants.

Condemnation: The process by which property of a private owner is taken, with or without consent, for the public use. Fair compensation must be paid.

Consideration: Something of value exchanged by a party to influence another party to enter in a contract.

Contingency: A possible event based on the happening of an uncertain future event.

Contract: A legal agreement entered by two or more parties which created an agreement to do or not to do something.

Contract for Deed: A contract for the sale of real property wherein the seller is obligated to provide a merchantable title after the buyer has paid for the property, usually in installments. (Also known as an Agreement for Deed or Land Contract.)

Contract for Purchase and Sale: An agreement between buyer and seller of real property to transfer title to that property at a future time for a specific sum of money. (Also called a sales contract).

Conveyance: An instrument (deed) legally sufficient to transfer title to real property.

Cooperative: An apartment house or similar property owned, usually in corporate form, by all the tenants. Each has stock in the corporation which owns the building.

Cost Recovery: Formerly known as depreciation. A provision of the tax law that allows the owner of real and personal property to recover the cost of that property over a period of time specified by law. Cost recovery may be straight line or accelerated.

Counter Offer: A change in price or terms of an unacceptable offer.

Credit Bureau: An agency that compiles data on an individual's credit history and, upon request, distributes a report to potential creditors.

Credit Bureau Report: The compilation of an individual's credit history. Potential creditors may request a copy from a credit bureau.

Credit Limit: Generally found when dealing with credit cards, this is the maximum amount the cardholder may charge to that account.

Creditor: The lender. The one to whom the debt is owed.

Cure Date: The last day given for bringing mortgage payments current at the beginning of the foreclosure process.

Dead Asset: An asset that an investor does not want; in the investor's eyes, it has no value.

Debt Service: The sum of the annual principal and interest payments expressed as a percentage of the amount owed.

Deed: An instrument conveying title to real property. It usually must be signed by the grantor (seller), witnessed by two persons, and recorded.

Default: Failure to discharge a duty or obligation.

Deficiency Judgment: A judgment rendered in court for the difference in the amount realized at a foreclosure sale and the amount owed by the mortgagor, if the foreclosure sale fails to completely liquidate or satisfy the debt.

Depreciation: (See *Cost Recovery*)

Devise: Disposition of land or real property by will.

Discount: The percentage of the original balance of the loan that is charged to the borrower; sometimes referred to as points. Also, the difference between the selling price of a mortgage and the amount due.

Discounting a Note: The process of offering a promissory note for less than its face value to enhance marketability.

Distressed Property: A bargain property that is substantially below its present or projected renovated value.

Dower: The legal rights of a widow in her husband's estate. These rights have been abolished in many states.

Due on Sale Acceleration Clause: (See *Acceleration Clause*)

Duplex: A two-family home where the units share a common wall and are situated side by side.

Earnest Money: A deposit of money given by a party to bind the contract, usually credited toward the sales price.

Easement: An interest held by one party in the real property of another, giving that person the legal rights to trespass on the other's property.

Effective Gross Income: The difference between the total gross income and the vacancy allowance.

Effective Interest: The interest rate the borrower actually pays as opposed to the nominal interest rate. The effective interest rate is made higher than the nominal rate by addition of points or discounting a loan.

Eminent Domain: The power of the government to take private property for public use in return for fair compensation. This power is exercised through condemnation.

Encroachment: An infringement, usually an improvement such as a building or fence, constructed on a property contiguous to the one infringing. An encroachment is usually revealed by a survey.

Encumbrance: A limitation on the title to real property. A mortgage or easements are examples of encumbrances.

Equity: In real estate, the value of an interest a person holds over and above any mortgages or liens on the property.

Equity of Redemption: The rights of a mortgagor (borrower) to buy back a property after a foreclosure sale. While equity of redemption does not exist in some states, in other it extends up to two years.

Escape Clause: A clause added to the contract that allows either party the option of exiting the contract; thus, both parties are no longer bound by any contractual obligations.

Escheat: The reversion of property to the state when an owner dies with no Will and no known heirs.

Escrow: Money or documents held in trust by a neutral third party.

Estate: Ownership interest in real property.

Estate by the Entireties: Ownership by husband and wife with right of survivorship.

Estimated Annual Gross Income: An estimate of the total amount of income one will receive in a period of one year.

Estoppel Letter: A letter certifying the exact balance of a mortgage or other loan at a given time.

Et Al: And others.

Et Ux: And wife.

Exchange: The exchange or trade of business property you own for another trade or business property that is like-kind. No taxes are due in such an exchange under a given set of circumstances.

Exculpatory Clause: A clause in a contract relieving one of the parties of personal responsibility of liability. In a lease, the landlord is relieved of any responsibility for injury to tenants leasing his or her property. In a mortgage, the mortgagor (borrower) is relieved of any personal liability or deficiency judgment if a deficit occurs at a foreclosure sale.

Expenses: The costs of maintenance, repairs, and rental costs that are deducted from a property's gross income.

Executor: The administrator of an estate; one who is specified in the Will.

Extension Clause: A clause contained within some lease option contracts that provides for the terms under which the contract may be extended.

Face Value: In reference to a note, the face value is the full amount for which the note has been written.

Fair Market Value: The appraised value of a property as compared with other property values on the market.

Flipping: The turnover of property. An investor buys a property to immediately sell it for a profit.

Fee Simple: The highest estate in real property; the ownership of real property without reservation or restriction.

Fiduciary: An agent in the position of confidence to his principal. Also, a relationship of trust and confidence imposed by law.

Financial Analysis: An investor's determination of the value of a property according to his or her specific needs.

Financial Leverage: The use of other people's money for investment purposes.

Financing: The way in which an investor obtains the capital with which to purchase a property.

First Deed of Trust: A deed of trust recorded first. Equivalent to a first mortgage.

Fixture: Personal property attached permanently to Real Estate and thus becoming part of it. A built-in oven is an example.

Flexible Seller: A seller who is willing to sell property in a non-traditional manner. This person may be flexible in terms, price, or both.

Forced Sale: The sale of a property used as a security for a loan in order to repay creditor(s) in the event of a default on the loan.

Foreclosure: The process whereby property pledged as security on a note is sold under court order because of default on the note.

Front Foot: The width of a lot at the front, usually given as the first measurement. (A lot 225' x 175' would have 225 front feet.)

General Partnership: A form of business where two or more persons enter into an agreement to conduct business. Profits and losses are shared in a predetermined fashion and all partners are jointly and severally liable for debts of the general partnership.

Grandfather Clause: Properties that do not conform to current ordinances, codes, or regulations, but are allowed to continue to be occupied because the properties predate the institution of the ordinances, codes, and regulations.

Grantee: A person obtaining title to real property by deed. The purchaser to whom the grant is made.

Grantor: One who conveys title to property by deed.

Gross Income: The total income from a property before the deduction of expenses.

Gross Income Multiplier: That number which, when multiplied times the gross income, would give an indication of property value. It is strictly a guide and frequently abused.

Homestead Exemption: Protection extended by law preventing the forced sale of an owner-occupied dwelling by certain creditors.

Homestead Tax Exemption: The credit against taxes, given in some states, to a person who owns and occupies a dwelling and to certain other individuals including disables Veterans, those over age 65, widowed, or handicapped.

Improvement: Buildings or other structures which become part of the land are known as improvements.

Indenture: A contract.

Installment Loan: A loan that must be repaid in no less than two payments. A loan of six months or greater is preferable when establishing credit.

Installment Note: A note which specifies how mortgage payments will be made, when they will be due, and for what amount.

Installment Sale: A sale which, for income and tax purposes, is not taxed totally in the first year of the sale. To be valid, there must a minimum of two installment payments over two tax years.

Interest Rate: An amount a borrower must repay in addition to the full amount of the loan. This is the premium the lender receives for the use of the money, plus compensation for the risk the lender takes in lending money.

Intestate: A person who has died without leaving a valid will.

Involuntary Lien: A lien, like real property tax liens, which are recorded against a property without consent of the owner.

Instant Equity: The difference between the property's value and what you paid for it.

Joint Tenancy: A joint estate whereby upon the death of one joint tenant, his or her interest will go to the surviving joint tenant(s).

Joint Venture: An arrangement where two or more individuals or corporations join together on a single project as partners.

Jointly and Severally: A legal term indicating that a contract has been entered into by two parties and the two parties are not only liable together but individually as well.

Leverage: The borrowing of money in connection with a real estate investment.

Judgment: The verdict of a court on a matter presented to it. A money judgment dictates that a party must make payment to another to settle a claim.

Junior Lien: A mortgage or other encumbrance with a secondary interest. A lien junior to another mortgage or lien.

Land Contract: (See *Contract for Deed*)

Land Trust: A form of ownership whereby property is conveyed to a person or an institution, called a trustee, to be held and administered on behalf or another person called the beneficiary.

Lease: A contractual agreement between the owner (lessor) and the tenant (lessee), which allows the tenant use and occupancy of the property for a specified period of time. A lease is an encumbrance against a title and gives the tenant an actual interest in the property, known as an estate, for years.

Lease Option: An agreement between two parties where the party who owns the property extends, to the second party, the right to purchase the property at a future date. The second party lives in the property until the lease option expires.

Leasehold: The estate of interest held by the lessee in the property of another.

Legal Description: The means to identify the exact boundaries of a property. A surveyor will use the recorded plats method, metes and bounds method, or the government survey method to describe the real property.

Lessee: One who contracts to hold occupancy rights in the real property of another.

Letter of Credit: A letter, usually from a financial institution, guaranteeing (collateralizing) a debt incurred by a third party.

Letter of Intent: A letter stating a buyer's intent to make an offer to acquire a certain property. It is not a binding contract.

Lien: The right of a creditor to take and/or sell a property in the event of a default to satisfy the obligation of a debt.

Lien Theory States: States that allow the lender to collect the debt owed by selling the property in the event of default.

Limited Partnership: A partnership composed of a limited partner(s) and a general partner(s). The limited partner(s) contributes capital but is not liable for any debts of the partnership, nor can he or she manage or control the partnership.

Liquidated Damages: Damages, usually monetary, spelled out in a contract which would be available in the event of a default, to the party not in default.

Listing Broker: A broker from the office which created the MLS listing on a property.

Marketable Title: A title free and clear of liens and encumbrances that might be objectionable. (Also known as merchantable title.)

Mechanics Lien: A lien right existing in favor of mechanics, suppliers, or other persons who have supplied materials or performed work in connection with the construction or repair of a building or other improvement.

Metes: Measures such as inches, feet, yards, or miles.

Metes and Bounds: A measure of land which describes the boundaries using metes and bounds. For example, "Then going north 223 feet to the right-of-way of Oak Street."

Moratorium of Interest: A time during the term of a loan wherein no payment of interest due is made.

Mortgage: A temporary transfer of property to a creditor as collateral for a loan.

Mortgagee: A lender of money under the terms of a mortgage.

Mortgagor: The borrower, usually the owner, who pledges his or her property to assure performance in repaying the loan.

Multiple Listing Service: A multi-realty service whereby members of the local Board of Realtors exchange their listings.

Negative Cashflow: When rental and other income is insufficient to cover all the costs of ownership.

Net Income Approach: A technique used to evaluate larger properties and determine their values by calculating the net income they produce.

Net Net Net: An agreement which specifies that the tenant pays real estate taxes, insurance, and all maintenance costs of the property.

Net Operating Income: Gross income minus any operating expenses. Debt service (principal and interest) is not deducted as an expense.

Net Spendable Income: Amount remaining after expenses and debt service and any taxes due have been deducted from gross income. (Also known as After Tax Cashflow.)

No-Doc Loan: A loan where the borrower is not required to present any documentation to secure a loan.

Nominal Interest Rate: The interest rate, usually below market stated on the note.

Note: Legal evidence of debt.

Notarize: To have a document signed by a notary public.

One Time Mortgage Insurance Premium: A refund of a portion of the insurance premiums that have been paid over the years with a 1984 or later mortgage where the mortgage insurance premiums were paid up front.

Option: An instrument giving the right of a party to lease or purchase the property over a specified time period for a specified consideration. It is binding for the optionor (seller) but not the optionee (buyer).

Optionee: The person who has the legal right to purchase or not to purchase (through a contract) a specific property in the future.

Optionor: The seller of a property who extends an option to someone else. If the optionee exercises the option, this person is legally bound by the contractual obligations. However, if the option is not exercised, then the optionor is released from any responsibilities.

Owners of Record: All owners that are listed on a deed that is recorded in the county courthouse.

Overdraft Protection: An extra service that most financial institutions offer their checking account clients. The client has a credit limit, much like that of a credit card. If the client writes a check for an amount greater than what is in the checking account, the bank automatically writes the client a "loan." Interest is charged on this, as is an annual fee in some cases.

Package Mortgage: A mortgage which, in addition to encumbering real property, also includes personal property such as a refrigerator, dishwasher, or oven unit.

Partnership: Two or more people associated for the purposes of carrying on business activities.

Pay Down: The amount of principal on a loan retired through payments at a given time.

Personal Property: All property other than real property. (It is also known as personality.)

Points: See discount.

Positive Cashflow: When rental and other income exceed all of the costs of ownership.

Power of Attorney: A written authorization to an agent to perform specified acts on behalf of his or her principal. Beyond these acts, the agent has no power.

Preliminary Title Search: The first review of all previously recorded documents regarding a specific property, to make sure that the property may be sold.

Premium: An additional sum of money paid as an incentive for someone to do something.

Principal: The sum of money used as funds for the investment.

Promissory Note: Usually a note if given to the seller by the buyer, which promises to pay back principal to the seller. It states the interest rate (if any) and the period of the note.

Pro Forma Statement: A financial statement based on anticipated, not actual, income and expenses.

Promulgated Rate: A formally and publicly stated rate.

Pro Rata: Buyer's and seller's portion of prepaid or unpaid expenses such as real estate taxes.

Purchases Money Mortgage: A mortgage given to the seller as part or all of the consideration for the purchase of property. In effect, it is money loaned by the seller to the purchaser.

Quit Claim Deed: A deed transferring whatever interest in the property, if any, that the grantor may have. They are usually used to clear title.

R.E.O. (Real Estate Owned): Properties that financial institutions have repossessed as a result of a default on a mortgage and which these institutions are willing to sell.

Real Estate Agent: A salesperson associated with a broker, who acts on behalf of a broker.

Realtor: A broker who is a member of the National Association of Realtors as well as state and local Real Estate boards.

Recording: The act of entering, in the public record, any instrument affecting title to real property.

Redemption: The buying back of one's own property after a forced court sale. (See *Equity of Redemption*)

Release Clause: A statement in a blanket mortgage that allows a specific described parcel to be released from under the blanket lien after a sum of money is paid.

Reproduction Cost Analysis: A technique used to evaluate a property by estimating the cost of building the same or similar structure, adding the cost of land and subtracting an allowance for wear and tear.

Restrictive Covenant: A clause in a deed in which there is an agreement between buyer and seller stating certain restraints as to the use of the property.

Right-of-Way: An easement on land whereby an owner grants or gives to another the right of passage over his or her land.

Riparian Rights: The rights of a land owner to the body of water adjacent to his or her land. In some cases these rights include the land under this water.

Sales Contract: (See *Contract for Purchase and Sale*)

Sandwich Lease: While having the option to buy a property, the investor subleases it to gain a positive cashflow.

Satisfaction of Mortgage: An instrument filed in the public records which acknowledges payment of an indebtedness secured by a mortgage.

Security Deposit: An amount of money paid by a tenant before moving into the premises to cover any damage incurred while living there, or to protect the landlord in the event that the tenant leaves without being current on rent payments. If the tenant is current and the unit only has a normal amount of wear and tear, then the deposit is generally refunded.

Servicing a Debt: The act of paying the periodic principal and interest payments on an outstanding debt obligation.

Specific Performance: A court order requiring a person to act or do a specific thing that he or she had agreed to do.

Tax Certifications: Bond sold to recoup unpaid property taxes by the county in which the property is located. When the property is auctioned, the certificate holders may either use the certificates as money to bid on the property or redeem them for face value plus interest.

Tax Deductible: An item that is not taxed.

Tax Liability: The amount of money one owes to the government for taxation purposes.

Tax Shelter: An income property that generates artificial papers losses, due to depreciation or cost recovery, that are in excess of the income produced by that property. These artificial losses can be used to offset other taxable income earned by the owners. In general, a tax shelter is any deferral, reduction, or elimination of a tax due.

Tenancy in Common: The ownership of an interest in property by two or more persons. Their ownership interest may be equal or unequal and there is no right of survivorship as with joint tenancy. The interest of any joint owner passes to his or her heirs or assigns after death.

Tenant: A person having the temporary use and occupancy of real property owned by another.

Tender: An offer to pay or perform.

Terms: The exact way a property will be purchased.

Testate: One who dies leaving a Will.

Timeshare: A piece of property purchased by two or more parties who have set specific times when each may use or occupy the property.

Title Insurance: Insurance issued by a title company guaranteeing the title to be good and marketable. Title insurance policies can be issued to protect the mortgagee only, the full interest of the buyers, or both.

Title Insurance Company: A business that reports on the status for the title on a specific property and whether or not it has any liens against it. After this title search has been completed, the company will issue a deed to be signed by all the owners of the property which should be notarized and recorded in the public records.

Title Theory States: States that allow the lender to become the legal owner at the time of making the loan. The borrower only has possession.

Township: A unit of measure used in the government survey method of land description equal to 36 sections (36 square miles).

Unilateral Contract: A contract in which one party is bound by another to do something. If the second party chooses to exercise the contract, the first party must perform any contractual obligations that party may have. However, if the second party chooses not to exercise the contract, the first party is released from any contractual obligations.

Unsecured Line of Credit: A credit history developed by an individual who borrows small amounts of money which do not require collateral.

Usury: The lending of money at a rate of interest about the legal rate.

Vacancy Rate: An estimate of the amount of time the rental property will be vacant (between tenants) multiplied by the rental rate of the unit(s). The amount is used in estimating the investor's value of an income.

Value, Assessed: The value as determined by the local tax assessor's office for the purpose of levying local taxes.

Value, Book: The value of a property carried on a company's books. It is usually the cost less depreciation or cost recovery plus capital additions.

Vendee: A buyer.

Vendor: A seller.

Warrant: To guarantee something to be as represented.

Wrap-around Mortgage: A mortgage held by the seller-mortgagee. The buyer-mortgagor pays the seller-mortgagee the debt service on the wrap-around mortgage and the seller-mortgagee continues to pay the debt service on the underlying or original mortgage.

Zoning: The laws which regulate and control for what the property may be used.

About the Author

Gary Wilson has been a Scout Master in Troop 194 of the Greater Pittsburgh Region and involved in scouting for more than a dozen years as an adult and was a scout as a boy.

He started investing in Real Estate at the age of 23, less than one month after graduating from Old Dominion University, and accumulated a 250-unit portfolio while teaching others to do the same.

Gary ranked in the top 5% of all Realtors in the Western Pennsylvania Market (according to annual Five-Star surveys).

He is a licensed broker in Pennsylvania and Virginia. He achieved the Platinum level of service while launching and growing Win Realty Advisors, LLC; Win Rental Management, LLC; and Win Settlement Services, LLC.

Gary has taught in classrooms across the U.S. and Canada to tens of thousands of students and has personally trained thousands of investors and agents who want to realize the pleasure of rental profits without the pain, flipping without the risk, and wholesale for profit so everybody wins.

For more information visit:
RealEstateWithGaryWilson.com